Chicken Soup
for the Soul.

The Magic of
Christmas

D1009295

Chicken Soup for the Soul: The Magic of Christmas
101 Tales of Holiday Joy, Love and Gratitude
Amy Newmark

Published by Chicken Soup for the Soul, LLC www.chickensoup.com
Copyright ©2022 by Chicken Soup for the Soul, LLC. All Rights Reserved.

The publisher gratefully acknowledges the many publishers and individuals who
granted Chicken Soup for the Soul permission to reprint the cited material.

Front cover illustration of house courtesy of iStockphoto.com/Rustic (©Rustic), illustration
of Santa courtesy of iStockphoto.com/juliaart (©juliaart), illustration of snowy sky courtesy
of iStockphoto.com/maroznc (©maroznc), illustration of small cardinal courtesy of
iStockphoto.com/Bastinda18 (©Bastinda18)
Back cover and interior illustration of cardinal courtesy of iStockphoto.com/Evgeniya
Ivanova (©Evgeniya Ivanova) interior photo of Santa hat courtesy of iStockphoto.com/
ZaharovEvgeniy (©ZaharovEvgeniy)
Photo of Amy Newmark courtesy of Susan Morrow at SwickPix

Cover and Interior by Daniel Zaccari

Publisher's Cataloging-In-Publication Data

Names: Newmark, Amy, editor.
Title: Chicken soup for the soul : the magic of Christmas, 101 tales of holiday joy,
    love and gratitude / Amy Newmark.
Description: Cos Cob, CT: Chicken Soup for the Soul, LLC, 2022.
Identifiers: LCCN: 2022940262 | ISBN: 978-1-61159-095-1 (paperback) |
    978-1-61159-333-4 (ebook)
Subjects: LCSH Christmas--Literary collections. | Christmas--Anecdotes. | Miracles--Literary
    collections. | Miracles--Anecdotes. | Gifts--Literary collections. | Gifts--Anecdotes.
    | BISAC SELF-HELP / Motivational & Inspirational | SELF-HELP / Personal Growth /
    Happiness | SELF-HELP / Personal Growth / General
Classification: LCC GT4985 .C378 2022 | DDC 394.2663/02--dc23

Library of Congress Control Number: 2022940324

PRINTED IN THE UNITED STATES OF AMERICA
on acid∞free paper

27 26 25 24 23 22   01 02 03 04 05 06 07 08 09 10 11

The Magic of Christmas

101 Tales of Holiday Joy, Love and Gratitude

Amy Newmark

Chicken Soup for the Soul, LLC
Cos Cob, CT

Changing your world one story at a time®
www.chickensoup.com

Table of Contents

❶
~Giving Thanks~

❷
~Tales of the Tree~

❸
~Making New Traditions~

❹
~Around the Table~

❺
~Getting Creative~

❻

~The Joy of Giving~

❼

~Family Fun~

8

~Through the Eyes of a Child~

9

~The Perfect Gift~

10

~The Spirit of the Season~

⓫

~After a Loss~

Chapter 1

Giving Thanks

Just Right Thanksgiving

Concentrate on counting your blessings, and
you'll have little time to count anything else.
~Woodrow Kroll

I rummaged in the silverware drawer for forks. Did we even have twenty-four forks? I was used to my mom inviting people to our house for Thanksgiving. But twenty-four? Things were getting out of hand.

After my family moved across the country away from all our relatives, my mom started filling the house with a random assortment of guests. She usually invited people who didn't have anywhere else to go for Thanksgiving — foreign-exchange students, bachelors, and families like ours who lived far from relatives. I missed the days of big family gatherings, but I admired my mom's generous heart and tried to have a good attitude about it.

This year, though, I was looking forward to spending the holiday with my family. I had a long weekend break from college, and my youngest brother had a stack of games ready to play with me. Plus, my grandparents were coming, a treat since we usually only got to see them in the summertime.

But then Mom showed me her guest list, which was half the size of our town's population, and my mood tanked. I didn't want to share my family with a houseful of random people. I yanked a fistful of knives and spoons from the drawer and started counting — twenty-four of each.

Our first guests arrived: three guys in boot camp at the naval base in the next town over. Mom's original plan was to host one recruit. She came back from the base with three. Someone told her the recruits who don't go home with a family sometimes break down in tears. Mom said she wished she could bring all of them home.

The recruits ambled into the kitchen, where I was pulling every glass we owned from the cupboard. Their glossy shoes reflected the fluorescent kitchen lights.

"We'd like to help, Ma'am," the tallest one said to Mom and stepped forward, leaving the other two standing rigid, hands clasped in front of them, uniforms starched to resist even hurricane winds. Mom made a joke about not being a drill sergeant and told them to please relax.

"We're not quite sure how to relax," said one of them. "We're used to people yelling orders in our faces."

"We can yell at you if that'll make you feel better," I said and handed an ice-cube tray to the recruit who'd stepped forward.

"Thank you, Ma'am," he said.

Ma'am?! I thought. *Are you kidding me? I'm the same age as you are!*

I wandered into the living room to help Dad set up chairs. Ding dong! *The warning bell,* I thought. The next installment of guests burst through the door: Mom's friend and her two sons. Right on their heels came a couple from town with their six young kids that Mom knew somehow. The volume — and the temperature — in the house instantly rose.

Luckily, dinner was ready before the house — or I — exploded. My construction-paper-turkey name card placed me at the end of the table between the father of the six little kids and the mom of two boys. I ate slowly, trying to keep my elbow from knocking into my neighbors. The dad juggled his fork and a fussy baby. A pudgy fist smacked my shoulder. *How'd I get such a lucky seat?* I thought, tucking in my elbows. My PopPop sat at the other end of the table near one of the recruits, chatting about military stuff. Bursts of laughter came from the kids' table in the living room. *Glad I'm getting in all this quality time with my family,* I thought.

Part of me felt embarrassed by my attitude. Another part of me was enjoying the prolonged sulk.

After dinner, my younger brothers tromped downstairs with the rest of the kids to practice the puppet show. The youngest kids have always been in charge of reenacting the first Thanksgiving using the cardboard figures glued onto paint-stirring sticks—the same ones Mom helped my older brother and me color when we were little.

We finished clearing the last of the dishes just as the puppeteers tromped upstairs. They rigged a stage with the coffee table and sofa cushions, and the show began. Native Americans boarded the *Mayflower*. King James made a cameo appearance in the New World. And cardboard fish and corn flew through the air.

When the play ended, Mom suggested that while everyone was together in one room, we each share something we were thankful for—another annual tradition at our house. The mom with all the kids spoke up. "I'm so grateful to this wonderful family for opening up their home to us." Then she thanked God for a bunch of stuff, and her eyes got watery. I'd forgotten until then that the family had seven kids until the prior week when their baby girl died after months in and out of the hospital. My sulkiness suddenly seemed incredibly petty. Would I be that grateful if someone in my family had just died?

Now Mom's single-mom friend was thanking my family for sharing our day with her and her sons. I remembered the shock we all had a few months ago when her husband abruptly left them. He had seemed like such a nice guy. My little brothers used to go to their house for chess tournaments with him and his boys. Now they were in the middle of a nasty divorce. I glanced at the older of the two boys, who was staring at his empty plate. Jeez, this was probably their first holiday without their dad around.

Then one of the Navy guys said something about how much it meant to be able to be with a family on Thanksgiving. A family. *My* family.

Then it was my turn.

"I'm thankful for a full house—that all of you could come share this day with us."

Wait... what did I just say?

I didn't hear what the rest of the people said. As I looked around the table, I gave myself a mental scolding: *What's the point in saying you're thankful if you're not willing to share your blessings—including your family?*

The day turned out to be one of my all-time best Thanksgivings ever. I held the baby, who stopped fussing once he got some food in his belly, and remembered that I actually really like babies. My brother and his friend wore crazy wigs and performed Weird Al Yankovic songs. The Navy guys told stories about life in boot camp, which gave me something else to be thankful for—that I wasn't in boot camp. Later in the afternoon, a bunch of us headed outside to play football.

One of the recruits, the one with glasses, hesitated. "We're gonna get reamed for messing up our uniforms."

"Who cares?" said the tall recruit. "It's Thanksgiving—it wouldn't be right not to play football!" He launched the ball at his buddy, who caught it and glanced down at his spotless shoes, then shrugged and tossed the ball to me. The recruit was right. It wouldn't be right not to play football on Thanksgiving. And everything about this day was just right.

—Karen Langley Martin—

A Covid Holiday Season

On November 19, 2020, my husband Tom and I tested positive for Covid-19. We had already made it safely through nine months of the outbreak by wearing our masks and social distancing. We thought we had done all we could to avoid becoming statistics of the pandemic.

Since we were both in excellent physical health for our ages, we assumed that would help us deal with the virus. Perhaps, we thought, we would be lucky enough to have mild cases and not become very ill.

Unfortunately, the weeks following our positive tests proved to be devastating. We both ended up in the hospital with pneumonia, and Tom developed two pulmonary embolisms that required him to be on oxygen for a month and medication for two additional months after that.

After four days in the hospital and significant weight loss, I had to spend another nine days in a nursing home before I was strong enough to return home. With physical therapy, I slowly began to regain my strength and eventually walk again without a walker.

I had never felt that awful in my seventy-two years of life. Not only did I feel bad physically, but I experienced emotional turmoil when I had to depend on others for my most basic needs. I couldn't see outside so a nurse wrote each new date on a dry-erase board. I would often ask if it was day or night, and for some reason I wanted to know if it was rainy or sunny beyond my claustrophobic hospital room.

It made me realize how terrible it must be for patients confined to an intensive-care unit for weeks or months on end. That isolated world revolves around noisy machines, flashing lights and constant activity.

Because of the Covid-19 restrictions, the only human interaction I had was with healthcare professionals who drew blood, administered IVs, checked my vitals and lifted my head so I could swallow mountains of pills.

I was grateful for the wonderful care I received. Every hospital employee — from the woman who was constantly sanitizing my room to the aide who brought me ginger ale and crackers when I couldn't keep anything else down — was kind and caring.

It was particularly comforting that each person who entered my room asked me how I was feeling. Sometimes, I didn't have the energy to answer. Even though my husband was in the same hospital, I could not see him. It was certainly understandable, but it made me more frightened and lonely. Kind words helped encourage me as I battled the vicious illness.

One day, I was at my lowest point and asked the nurse if I was dying. She replied, "No, but you are very sick, so you need to fight this with everything you have." Perhaps that was a standard answer, but I took it to heart, and those words helped me see a glimmer of light at the end of what seemed like a long, dark tunnel.

My husband was hospitalized a few days before me, so I spent Thanksgiving Day alone on the couch, barely able to function. Two days after Thanksgiving, I was struggling to breathe and called an ambulance. I was very concerned about what would happen to my dog. As they were taking me out of my house on a stretcher, two of my neighbors came, got my pet and took him to a boarder. I had peace of mind knowing that he was being well cared for while we were away.

Tom remained in the hospital for several weeks and was released the day before his seventy-fifth birthday. He spent what should have been a special day all alone, and hooked up to a big oxygen machine at home — while I remained in a nursing facility. When we were finally reunited, we were overjoyed to be together.

Good things often emerge from the most terrible situations. We both have a deeper appreciation for life and find pleasure in little, everyday things that we used to take for granted. We also discovered just how invaluable caring friends and family are during times of great need.

As I recuperated in the rehabilitation center, friends delivered everything from new pajamas and books to fresh clothing and personal items to me. One even brought a little Christmas tree.

During our convalescence at home, we had a steady stream of food and supplies placed on our porch. Other friends helped with things like picking up important medications.

In addition to many acts of kindness, we got constant phone calls from friends and family members who wished us well and asked if there was anything we needed. We were showered with everything from prayers for our complete recoveries to cheerful cards of encouragement.

All of that enabled us to concentrate on recovering. As we gained strength, we were able to relax knowing that there were loving people in our lives who helped us with chores we couldn't yet accomplish and gave us emotional support to make it through such an awful ordeal.

Although the journey was very difficult, we made it. We were grateful but also saddened by the fact that when we were struggling to survive, many others did not, including a very dear friend of ours who lost his battle with Covid-19.

Christmas was, of course, different for everyone in 2020. By December twenty-fifth, we were both home, enjoying the company of our little dog. We were still quite weak and obviously had not done anything to prepare for the holiday season.

We had no decorations up and, like many others, no family members with whom to share the season. The little tree my friend had given me and a pretty Christmas cactus a girlfriend had put on our porch a few days earlier were our only reminders of the holiday.

My husband looked around and said, "It sure is different this year.

No decorations, gifts, stockings or a tree." I agreed and responded that at least we could heat up a frozen casserole prepared by one of our neighbors for Christmas dinner.

"I'm glad that we are back in our own home," I said. "We may not have gifts for each other, but we got the best Christmas presents ever this year. We both lived through having serious cases of the coronavirus. And we are blessed to be surrounded by wonderful people who helped us so much on this terrible journey."

Tom nodded in agreement. Even though 2020 was a life-changing and horrific year for many, the two of us had much to celebrate.

Our future had not been stolen by the lethal virus. Thankfully, we had more days to enjoy life with each other, family, friends and our little dog. We have cherished every minute since our recovery from the coronavirus. We are thankful for countless special gifts, like being able to once again hold and kiss our grandchildren.

— Melinda Richarz Lyons —

A Recipe for Perspective

Gratitude is the fairest blossom
which springs from the soul.
~Henry Ward Beecher

There are times when I become so engrossed and emotionally invested in a task that I momentarily forget to focus on the larger reality. Such was the case on Christmas a few years ago.

Because it was the first Christmas since one of my sons had moved into his own place, I became even more ambitious than usual. In addition to the two kinds of yams, the green-chile-and-cheese zucchini, the homemade cranberry sauce that cooked on the stove for ten hours, quickie stuffing, baked potatoes, an elaborate green salad tossed with all kinds of chopped vegetables, hot biscuits, gravy, and two kinds of pie for dessert, I baked three different kinds of meat: a small leg of lamb, a roasted turkey breast, and a small prime rib. I was elated when the instructions in my forty-year-old cookbook (opened only for such occasions) informed me that the temperature and cooking time were exactly the same for each. Based on the arrival time my older son had given me, I wedged all three meat pans into the oven at the precisely timed moment.

My movement in the kitchen that day was a sort of dance. I flowed from task to task, peeling and chopping, mixing and stirring, encircling the meat pans with rows of potatoes and yams, and rolling them piping hot out of the oven. At exactly three o'clock, his planned arrival time, the table was set with brightly colored dishes, handmade wooden Santa placeholders, and ceramic and woven hot pads waiting for their steaming dishes. And then the phone rang.

Matter-of-factly, my son informed me that he and his girlfriend were about to leave. Depending upon holiday traffic, it would take forty-five minutes to one-and-a-half hours to arrive. In my mind's eye, I pictured the succulent prime rib as a wrinkled, high-top boot. The leg of lamb? Jerky on a stick. And the moist turkey breast became straw wrapped in a golden-brown skin.

Feeling the storm welling to the surface, I said nothing until I hung up the phone. And then it burst. I paced across the floor and poured out to my husband and younger son all my angst over the hours of precise preparation that had been foiled in an instant. My younger son joined in the rant, having changed his plans to meet his brother's schedule. Sudden, unexpected reversals that bring seeming chaos to painstakingly planned order tend to bring out this momentary overreaction. However, seeing my emotions reflected in my younger son, and not wanting this to be his experience of Christmas with his older brother, brought things back into perspective.

I suddenly remembered the first time I ever cooked an elaborate holiday dinner. It was a roast turkey with all the trimmings to celebrate Thanksgiving and Christmas — in October. It was 1966, and my nineteen-year-old, younger brother had just received orders to ship out to Vietnam. Feeling desperate and impotent, my mother decided to at least have the family holidays together before he left. Since she was working, she left me instructions and took my panicked phone calls as I worked to make as perfect a meal as possible. The turkey, moist and tender, stuck in my throat as I swallowed, there with my family in the charade we needed to assure ourselves that there would be more holidays together. And then I thought of the families this Christmas Day who would have been overjoyed to wait an extra hour and a half for their sons to arrive at their door — sons of thousands of families eating elbow-to-elbow on tin plates in tents and halls in the chaos of

Christmas in Iraq or Afghanistan.

Gratitude replaced the frustration I felt. In quiet tones, reflecting my new sense of calm, I shared my thoughts with my younger son and watched the rancor he had felt also fade. I returned to the kitchen and took the steps that somehow rescued the meal. None of us said a word to my older son about the delay; we did not need to speak about consideration or inconvenience or remind him that this had also happened on Thanksgiving. We were just grateful when we opened the door that they did not have to brave mortars and landmines to be with us. They had survived the tangle of the 405 freeway, and there were no longer miles between us.

—Diane de Anda—

The Thanksgiving Mystery

If you really are thankful, what do you do? You share.
~W. Clement Stone

Only eight days until Thanksgiving and there wasn't going to be enough money to grocery shop for the holiday. I promised my three sons that I would try to get all the fixings, and we'd have a nice family dinner — in our new home — unlike the prior year when we canceled Thanksgiving to deal with the loss of their father.

It was hard to put everyday food on the table for three growing 'tween and teen boys with the little I earned from work, but I promised a meal where I wouldn't ration each child's portion. We looked forward to a day of good eating! It would be a well-deserved break that we all needed.

But there was only enough bread in the house for a little stuffing, a few small sweet potatoes, one can of green beans, and two chicken breasts. It would have to do.

The next day, I met my friend and neighbor, Aleta, at her home. Her four boys and my kids were good friends. Her husband had recently lost his job due to illness, and financial difficulties hovered over their household as well.

"Were you able to get a turkey for Thanksgiving?" I asked.

"No, it will just be an ordinary meal for us."

"Hey, I have an idea how we can put together a meal where everyone will have enough." I stood up to get my big roasting pan and added the bread, potatoes, and can of beans. "Why don't we each put in the pot what we have in groceries to make a Thanksgiving feast? What do you have?"

"I have a few cans of green beans, about three pounds of chicken legs, and three apples. Oh, and a half-loaf of bread," she added.

"Great. I'll make the stuffing and a sweet-potato-apple casserole. You can cook the chicken and green beans. Let's meet at my house at 2:00 in the afternoon. If you have some peanut butter, I have enough flour and ingredients to make cookies."

My friend's fourteen-year-old asked, "What about the turkey and cranberry sauce, and mashed potatoes—and pie?"

I explained that unless they wanted to get out in the neighborhood and earn some money, the menu stood as planned. He grabbed the lawnmower and various gardening tools, along with two of my sons, and headed out to entice neighbors to hire them for yard work. Although it was late in the afternoon when they began their mission, they found a few neighbors who helped them earn enough to purchase most of the items they set out for, except the turkey.

Four days before Thanksgiving, I had finished baking the cookies. My friend called with news about a family living in our community who needed help with food and bills. The father had been in an accident and unable to work for the last few months. We didn't know the family well, but my friend and I went to visit them with the batch of our holiday cookies, hoping to help in some way. Maybe we could babysit their young children. Or, since they had never had to struggle, and we were near experts on how to survive on almost nothing, we could offer suggestions. We gathered in their living room. In no time, everyone devoured the cookies.

While everyone chatted, I snuck into the kitchen to see about the food situation. The cupboards were almost bare. No exaggeration. A single can of soup, a box of cereal, and a box of pasta sat alone in the cupboard. I was shocked. Just last year, we had attended their four-year-old's birthday party, and the cupboards were full. Fruit was on the counter, and the freezer was stocked. I know because I helped set up the food table.

Aleta and I knew the harshness of life during hard times, when a few cans of soup and a half-loaf of bread were the only nutrition available. We left the house, desperately wanting to help. But what could we do? Our own finances and food situation left nothing to spare. Simultaneously, our thoughts connected. Without a word, we looked at each other, asking ourselves the same question. Could we sacrifice a little more and give the family our holiday meal?

"What do you think?" I asked the kids.

"I can't believe you gave away almost all our cookies!" mumbled my youngest son.

My eight-year-old summed up perfectly the reason we needed to share our meal. "We're used to crappy Thanksgivings—and they're not." That didn't make me feel wonderful, but he was right. Our boys were survivors—adaptable and strong. They learned to make the best of situations and appreciate the times when the dinner table was covered with enough food to fill their bellies.

Early the next morning, we were able to deliver two full bags of groceries to our neighbors. Their young children jumped with excitement as they pulled groceries out of the bags. Their parents cried as they thanked us.

There were three days left until Turkey Day, although I refrained from calling it Turkey Day since there would not be any turkey. We once again looked forward to our compilation of foods that would create a fine enough feast with our friends.

Two mornings before the holiday, my oldest son opened the front door to take out the trash. He hollered, "Mom, there's something at the door."

"Shoo it away if it's an animal. Or salesperson!" I continued my busyness in the kitchen.

"I think you should come to the door, Mom."

To my amazement, four full paper bags of groceries waited outside the door. Now it was our turn to pull out plenty of holiday foods, including a turkey and apple pie! I called my friend to tell her the exciting news.

"Hey, open your front door," I suggested. "Maybe the heavens came down for you, too!" I soon heard the rejoicing on the other end of the phone from her family.

My sons and I happily put away the groceries and chatted about the revamped holiday menu. We wondered who would make such a considerate gesture. Even though our sons did not recall mentioning anything to neighbors, it is possible they leaked some information.

Weeks later, after we delicately tried to interrogate neighbors about the four bags of groceries, we were still clueless. But it didn't matter how they discovered that our families needed help. It was obvious that whoever did the good deed wanted to remain anonymous.

We got an unexpected BOGO deal when we gave away two bags and received four! None of us will ever underestimate the power of giving. The mystery of the Thanksgiving groceries remains unsolved but never forgotten.

— Nina Ward —

The Turkey That Got Away

*Abundance is a form of gratitude, a generosity, a
modesty, a bow toward others — what we can give,
what we can share, rather than what we can take.*
~Terry Tempest Williams

The day before Thanksgiving, I finished setting the table in our farm's community room for the next day's feast. On the way back to the house, I stopped in the barn to check on the thirty-pound turkey in the barn fridge, the only cold place large enough to hold it. Truthfully, we didn't need a thirty-pound turkey, but somehow my order had ended up in the "extra-large" category. I wasn't even sure it would fit in our oven, not to mention having to get up earlier to give those extra pounds time to roast.

As I opened the barn fridge door, I expected the top shelf to be full of turkey, but I found an empty space instead. I stared at the shelf long enough to confirm it really was gone. Unwilling to concede the absence, I checked the second and third shelves, which were much too small for the turkey, but they were empty, too. I even looked in all the fridge drawers and door shelves where a thirty-pound turkey obviously could not hide.

Next, I looked all over the barn, thinking John had left the turkey out accidentally, but there wasn't a turkey in sight. I even looked in the fridge again to be sure I wasn't overlooking a big bird. Nothing, not even a drumstick, did I find. By then, I was pretty sure I wasn't going to find the thing in the barn. I might have laughed at my antics if fifteen people weren't coming for Thanksgiving the very next day.

What to do but go ask John if he had brought the turkey into the house without my having seen it. Of course, he hadn't. So, where could that turkey be?

Then I remembered it was Wednesday, the day the food-pantry people come for the vegetables we donate to community families each week. Every Tuesday, I send an e-mail to the friend who picks up our veggies to tell her what we have. I looked back at that week's e-mail and saw that I had mentioned the turkey on the top shelf because I needed to let her know the veggies would be on the second shelf that week. Re-reading the note, I realized that she must have sent someone else for the pick-up. Even though the turkey part of the message was vague, I knew she would never have interpreted it to mean "take the turkey." On the other hand, someone less familiar with our arrangement certainly could think a turkey donation accompanied the vegetables so close to Thanksgiving.

Since the pantry was closed by that time of the day, I tried to contact my friend. She must have left town already for the holiday; she wasn't answering e-mail or picking up her phone. Now the need for logistics took hold. It wasn't that we minded the turkey having gone to the pantry, but we still needed a turkey — and it was 4:00 P.M. the day before Thanksgiving. Would we really be able to find an organic turkey at this late hour?

John jumped in the truck while I called a local store to try to reserve a bird. Lucky for us, they still had an organic turkey — twenty-one pounds, which was plenty — and they would hold it for him. When John got home, he said everyone in the meat department had a good laugh about our "donation."

In fact, I was glad not to have to cook that thirty-pound turkey. We had plenty at our Thanksgiving meal, with most of it — potatoes, leeks, squash, onions, carrots, parsnips, beets, herbs, and even wine — grown on our own farm. Seated by the wood stove as the snow fell gently outside, we thought about all the Thanksgiving dinners that would include something from our land.

Later, we would learn that our turkey fed not just one family but took the place of honor at a special dinner for the entire senior center in our little town. At our own table, we laughed at the gift of a good story with which to remember this Thanksgiving — a reminder to be grateful for all we have and all we can share. For that, and so much more, we are thankful.

—Kayann Short—

Her Highness

Oh, what marvels fill me with thanksgiving!
~Author Unknown

It was a cool, crisp fall day. Thanksgiving was only a few weeks away. The chickens were still in the barn with the door open to allow sunshine to find its way inside.

My timing was perfect. I saw her through the large picture window in the kitchen. We might have seen her a time or two far out in the field scratching up any last bit of seed that was left after a combine had gleaned the farm fields. But she had never come right to the house before. Today, she was strolling through the yard like she owned the place. She had a beauty all her own. I saw a slight sway as she gracefully moved and her magnificent, folded tail swung in the opposite direction with each step.

She walked between two barns and into the open area and then kept moving toward the chicken barn. It is an old horse barn turned into a shop and chicken house. The old, wood double doors hung there, welcoming her to stop for a bit. This magnificent wild turkey decided to grace our presence. She walked along the front side of the barn and stopped right in front of the door. The only thing standing between her highness and the flock was a wire panel insert, a few steps and a ramp. Both were loaded with chickens all vying for any space to investigate this odd bird unlike themselves. She stood there staring at the chickens, and they eyed her back.

The windows were closed tight. It would have been wonderful

to hear the chatting back and forth between her highness and my feathered flock. Her visit with the chickens didn't last long, and she walked calmly down the remainder of the barn as peacefully as she had arrived.

Then, she vanished into the barren field. She is always welcome back for a visit. Needless to say, we did not have turkey that year for Thanksgiving.

— Darci Werner —

The State of Virginia

*Some people arrive and make such a beautiful impact
on your life, you can barely remember
what life was like without them.*
~Anna Taylor

Quietly, I slipped my phone out of my back pocket to take a picture. At the kitchen counter, my daughter Audrey and our friend Virginia both leaned conspiratorially over the pie crust, their fingers pinching the edges, their words barely audible. Inches apart, both wore masks, but from my standpoint, with their backs to me, I couldn't tell. Their giggles filled the kitchen with warmth, and if I half-shut my eyes, they were simply two girls whipping up dessert together in the waning afternoon light.

Audrey had turned twelve a couple of weeks earlier and marked her birthday with a Covid-19 vaccine. Virginia turned twelve a month after Japan bombed Pearl Harbor, and the United States entered World War II. Since then, Virginia has witnessed a multitude of world events that I have only read about in books.

She grew up in a small Missouri town, married an Army man-turned-professor, and traveled the world with him while raising their two children. She has funny stories about finding a restroom in Thailand and poignant ones about buying handmade blankets from poor women in Guatemala.

I had no idea when I met her seven years ago that she'd be such a blessing in my life.

When we moved to the neighborhood, Virginia, with her cloud of white-gray hair and tall, trim figure, was the first to welcome us. "Here's my phone number. If you need anything, I'm just two doors down," she said, standing on my doorstep and handing me an index card. Her brown eyes sparkled.

"The lady who lived here before you," she continued, "was my friend. So, I have lots of good memories of this house."

She meant to be my friend, too. I could tell.

When the door to my bedroom swelled from the August heat a few weeks later and trapped me inside, I called her. "I can't get out," I said, perched on the edge of my bed. My two young children had tried to free me but with no luck. "Can you help?"

Footsteps sounded on the stairs not long after. "Mary Jo?" Virginia called. "I brought Ron with me. We're here to rescue you!" The two octogenarians stood outside my door. Her husband pulled the knob and, within seconds, the door popped open.

"Thank you," I said, my face flushed with embarrassment. "I don't know what I would've done without you." I would've been stuck for hours until my husband came home. That I knew.

Rescuing me in my own home was the first of many occasions over the next few years that solidified our friendship.

At Christmastime, Virginia invited us over for the afternoon. "I thought Audrey and Aidan might like to unwrap my nativity set and arrange it on the top of the piano," she said, eyes twinkling like the lights decorating the pine in the corner. My kids sat on her pale-blue sofa and carefully unwrapped each sheep and shepherd from the cotton batting until every figure had a place in the barn.

"Now it's time for Baby Jesus," Virginia said, handing my daughter the last wrapped piece of porcelain. "Audrey, would you like to put Him in the manger?"

My daughter carefully unwrapped Baby Jesus and gently set Him on the piano between Mary and Joseph.

Virginia smiled at her. "Well done!" she said. The tradition continued the next year and the year after.

How fortunate we were to have Virginia living two doors down!

"Too bad there's a house between us," she has said, chuckling, on more than one occasion. I've always agreed. The trip across lawns for a cup of sugar or an extra egg would be shorter indeed.

Or to give a dress.

"I have this beautiful yellow dress I thought might fit you," she told me one afternoon as we chatted on the phone. "Tags still on. Are you interested?"

She came over a few minutes later, and I tried it on in the bathroom. I stepped out and twirled around. It was a classic, fitted dress that I wore to Easter mass.

"Thank you," I said, and gave her a hug.

Though we had a forty-plus-years age gap, Virginia didn't feel grandmotherly. Rather, she felt like what she was: a friend.

We talked on the phone every few days, took walks together to the end of the street, and compared tulips and daffodils in the spring. We both loved gardening, politics, and my children. I found myself confiding more in Virginia than any woman my age. Because neither of us had extended family in the area, we, along with our husbands and my children, celebrated many holidays and birthdays together.

When her husband Ron's health deteriorated in 2019, I could see the sadness in Virginia's eyes. But I also saw strength and resolve. He didn't have long, and they'd said their goodbyes. Days after he passed away in March 2020, my children's school closed, and people started to panic.

But Virginia stayed calm, handling everything that comes with death and a pandemic as she usually did: with grace.

I wanted to hug my friend. But because of the virus, we kept our distance, and I had to read her expressions in her eyes because mask-wearing had begun.

The months that followed in many ways brought us closer, even though we couldn't touch. We took turns ordering groceries and shared news on the phone.

When the Michigan snow receded and warmer weather emerged, my friend and I resumed walks down the street and through our back yards — with a few cautionary feet between us.

The months during the pandemic ticked past one by one. We continued birthday celebrations under shady trees in my back yard and had a Christmas gift-exchange in her snow-covered driveway.

How can I possibly put into words the value of a deep friendship? Despite the many years between us, Virginia has the spritely energy of someone much younger but the wisdom of a woman who has lived through, and seen, so much more. We've both remained healthy and happy during this pandemic, and her friendship has helped make that possible.

I've read a lot during this time about how many of us have naturally edited our friendship circles—making them smaller and tighter because of the virus, and keeping only those in our lives who matter most.

Virginia doesn't text or e-mail. She picks up her landline and calls me. She writes handwritten cards with thoughtful messages. And she stops by my back door to say "Hi" on her way down the street to look at the lake.

Virginia has been my friend who matters.

Back in the kitchen, she and Audrey finished the apple pie and put it in the oven. It was the first time we'd been inside Virginia's house for more than a few minutes since the pandemic started. Aside from the masks, it felt normal.

Before we left, I said, "Can I give you a hug yet?"

Virginia's eyes creased, and I knew she was smiling. "I've made it this far," she said, taking a step back. "I'm going to wait until the numbers go down a little more."

I nodded, understanding.

I'm looking forward to that day, too.

— Mary Jo Wyse —

Tiny Stitches

Memories of childhood were the dreams
that stayed with you after you woke.
~Julian Barnes, England, England

I only see him during the Christmas season when he can be easily overlooked amidst all the merrymaking. He is so small that he fits snugly in the palm of my hand.

He was a Christmas gift to my mother many years ago, half a world away in a World War II prison camp. She was a young girl then. Her parents, one from Kansas, the other from Indiana, were teachers who had each traveled to the Philippine Islands. There, they met and married, and my mother was born. They taught school in the capital city of Manila, which by the late 1930s had swelled with refugees from war-torn Europe, Russia, and China. Many of them hoped to gain passage on a ship to Australia.

In December 1941, Japanese bombers attacked the Philippine Islands eight hours after Pearl Harbor, and life changed for all who lived there. Within weeks, my mother, fourteen years old, and her parents — along with three thousand other Americans and Europeans — were herded inside the walls of Manila's centuries-old University of Santo Tomas. They would remain imprisoned there for three years, nearly half of my mother's teenage years.

By December 1944, conditions had deteriorated within the barbed-wire and cement confines of the crowded prison camp. Food rations had been severely reduced, prisoners were dying from starvation or disease, and security measures had been tightened as the bayonet-armed Japanese guards reacted to an impending defeat. Yet, the prisoners were determined to celebrate the Christmas holiday. They decorated corner posts with remnants of ribbon and string, joined in singing carols, and exchanged simple gifts and hand-sketched cards.

My mother told me of the young couple who shared a thatched hut near that of her own family on the crowded grounds. They had arrived carrying a baby with them. They didn't speak English and my mother never learned where they were from or how they came to be in Santo Tomas. Had they fled their homeland with urgency and left loved ones behind? Had others who joined them perished in the flight? The little family had somehow reached Manila, only to be imprisoned there by the Japanese forces.

The young mother had likely lost everything except her husband and child. Perhaps during that Christmas season of 1944, she yearned for the home she had left behind. I try to picture her gathering needle and thread, and then, perched alongside her napping child, passing the hours stitching tiny folds of salvaged fabric. When the stitching was done, she offered a little St. Nick to a young girl, who maybe reminded her of someone she had known, one who would later become my mother.

He's only four inches tall and is sewn from pale blue homespun that snugly wraps his little body around and around like a mummy, with no need of buttons or clasps. Atop his head he wears a pointed stocking cap that tips whimsically to one side, low across his forehead. It is made from some type of ribbing fabric — perhaps the ankle sleeve of a worn-out sock — just a shade darker than his clothing. His little legs are angled to one side as if he's blowing in the breeze. One arm rests close at his side; the other lifts up in a perpetual wave. He has no particular feet or hands. The fabric merely wraps around his arms and legs, tucking in at the ends. His little white face shows wide-set eyes, carefully drawn in black, but there is no nose nor any hint of a mouth that could ever smile. From under the back of his cap floats an airy web of wispy white. Across his chin, strands of the same wispy white drift onto his little chest.

As a child, I was intrigued by this elfish figure that appeared every year when the Christmas decorations were unpacked from their storage boxes. I saw the gentle smile on my mother's face as she lifted him from crinkled tissue paper and placed him on the tree, way up high and safe from our rowdiness and jostling. To me, he was plain and ordinary; he seemed so homely alongside the glitzy tinsel and glass balls of red and green and silver and gold. I occasionally asked about him — where had he come from? — but I was usually on hands and knees, pawing through presents piled under the tree. I don't recall at what age I finally listened and came to understand his story.

My mother saved the childhood Christmas projects of my brother, my sisters and me, so little St. Nick is not the only handmade decoration we saw during the holiday season. But I think she treasured him more than any of those we had made. He wasn't created, as were many of ours, with messy piles of glitter and glue in a school classroom just before lunch when a steamy bowl of tomato soup and a grilled-cheese sandwich awaited us. Instead, he was fashioned from what little could be gathered in a place where an anticipated meal was just a bowl of watery rice. I've not experienced the deprivation and hunger that the young mother endured, nor the oppressive confinement of prison walls. Nor can I even begin to imagine the anguish she likely suffered as she fled her homeland.

My mother never learned the fate of that young couple and their child. During the excitement and chaos after the camp's liberation by American forces in February 1945, survivors celebrated and eventually burst forth to seek loved ones and carry on with their lives. Fierce fighting continued in Manila; more than 100,000 Filipino civilians and Allied and Japanese soldiers were killed in just a few weeks. By the time the war ended in September 1945, much of once beautiful Manila was rubble and smoldering ash. There was nothing left of my mother's house except the front concrete steps. She and her parents moved to the United States to begin life anew, with little St. Nick tucked among the few belongings they brought from across the sea. They settled in Washington State, where my mother earned a college degree, married my father, and raised four children.

My mother is no longer alive, and little St. Nick lives with me these days. Each December, I lift him from his tissue-paper wrappings gently, as did she, and place him way up high, safe from any rowdiness and jostling, as did she. When I walk into my living room where my tree stands, decked with the trimmings of my life, I meet his eyes and am blessed by the presence of that little man in blue.

— Cyndy Irvine —

Ragged, Forlorn... It's Perfect

> *The smell of pine needles, spruce and the smell*
> *of a Christmas tree, those to me,*
> *are the scents of the holidays.*
> *~Blake Lively*

"Mom, I can't believe you haven't put this tree away. It's been months since Christmas," Laura said, looking at the eighteen-inch Charlie Brown Christmas tree on the mantel. There it stood — eleven sparse, misshapen branches. And it only had one ornament. "It didn't look good at Christmas, and it doesn't look good now," she continued.

I remember when I purchased that tree. It was my first Christmas since divorcing, and I didn't feel like putting up a large Christmas tree or holiday decorations. Then I found the Charlie Brown Christmas tree, which was dropped inadvertently among some toys at the drugstore. The artificial tree seemed perfect — humble with just a hint of a holiday.

The next year, the Charlie Brown Christmas tree took its place once again on our mantel. The magnificent, six-foot family Christmas tree stood beside it, decorated with ornaments accumulated through the years, including handmade ornaments from my daughters. These custom-made masterpieces included Christmas trees fashioned from Popsicle sticks, snow people made from felt, beaded snowflakes, construction-paper ornaments that framed my daughters' photos, baby's first Christmas ornaments, and gingerbread people crafted from salt dough. The tree topper was a gold, papier-mâché angel that was made by my mother. Our family's history was generously represented on the large, perfectly shaped tree, and it triggered a lot of good memories.

But the scrawny Charlie Brown Christmas tree brought new meaning to our festive Christmas decorations. It represented the kid who was picked last to be on a team — or maybe not at all; the kid who wasn't invited to a birthday party; the woman who wasn't invited to join a yoga class with her colleagues; and the man who was overlooked for promotions.

After finding her baby's first Christmas ornament on the tree, Laura fixed her gaze on the Charlie Brown Christmas tree. Originally, the tree only had one ornament, which was red. Then, she noticed that a lavender-colored ornament had replaced the red one.

"Nice try," she said. "But I stand by my first opinion of that tree. Maybe you could add a few more ornaments. I saw some tiny ornaments at Michaels. They also have tiny garlands with colored balls, beads, or lights. That tree definitely needs something. I know — Miracle-Gro," Laura said and laughed.

"Very funny," I said. "The tree is fine as it is."

In the TV show, *A Charlie Brown Christmas*, Charlie Brown faced the same opposition when he picked out a scrawny tree. His friend Linus reminded him of Lucy's opinion of the tree, "This doesn't seem to fit the modern spirit."

Obviously, my daughter agreed. Or maybe Laura wants the comfort of our family's Christmases past. To make everyone happy, I continued the tradition of putting up both trees during the Christmas holidays.

Ten years later, I remarried. The Charlie Brown Christmas tree still made its annual appearance on the mantel, looking a little more worn with each passing year. After the holidays, my husband Larry said I should leave the Charlie Brown tree up all year.

"It's simple and reminds us of what's important," he said. "Life doesn't have to be filled with glitz and glamour for us to be happy."

So, the Charlie Brown tree made its permanent residence in our living room — with just one ornament.

That tree also triggered memories of a story my therapist told me a few years ago. He talked about a Christmas tree farm known for its beautiful, magnificent, and seemingly perfect trees. As life would have it, one small tree was overshadowed by the perfect-looking trees. A branch was broken, the tree leaned to the side, and a lot of dried needles blanketed its feet. My therapist asked me if that tree ruined the Christmas tree farm because of its lack of perfection. The answer, "Obviously not."

That comparison was about life. Every one of us has weaknesses and things we wish were different about us. Most of us have probably been overlooked sometime during our lives. That doesn't mean we're inadequate or bad people. There is beauty and strength in us and all around us.

My husband and I look at the Charlie Brown tree and think about how rich we are. We're lucky to be Americans and born into this country, where we can vote for our leaders, speak our minds and enjoy freedom. We're lucky we found each other, got a second chance at love, and enjoy wonderful relationships with our children. We're thankful that all of us are healthy and content with our lives, and blessed with good friends and jobs. We're lucky we have the opportunity to grow from our mistakes and misfortunes. This simple, little Charlie Brown tree reminds us to enjoy the little things, which are often beautiful.

— Michele Sprague —

Chapter
2

Tales of the Tree

10

Finding Christmas Behind a Door

The perfect Christmas tree?
All Christmas trees are perfect.
~Charles N. Barnard

S even-year-old Robin stared in awe at the glittering Southern California beach and ocean before him. "Wow!" he cried. "It's just like in the movies! I never saw so much water in my whole life!"

His four-year-old brother Jay held up his sand bucket and shovel. "And I never saw so much sand! Yay!"

Six-year-old Chat frowned. "But I don't see any snow, Mommy! We've got to have snow! It's almost Christmas. How can Santa's sled come without snow to ride on?"

His father and I chuckled.

Snow, indeed! We had just driven over 2,000 miles from our landlocked suburb in northern Illinois — all five of us plus our suitcases crammed together in an ancient VW Bug, fleeing blizzards all along the way. How thankful we were to reach this blissfully snowless paradise — not to enjoy a relaxing vacation but to save our three sons' lives.

Sadly, they had been in and out of hospitals for the past two years with pneumonia and other illnesses. We dreaded having them face another long winter of thirty-degree-below-zero nights and constant six-foot snowdrifts at our front door. So did our family physician.

Since he'd been stationed in San Diego while in the Navy, he suggested Southern California as a good place to help them regain their health.

So here we were, reaching our destination at last, just a couple of weeks before Christmas. We'd rented a room in a small, well-worn motel near the beach while we looked for a permanent place to live. Yes, a house or apartment where we could unpack, set up a Christmas tree, adorn it with all the trimmings, and surround it with joy and gifts. A real tree for a real Christmas to start our brand-new life in a brand-new state!

But San Diego was full of Navy families also looking for homes to rent. So we still hadn't found a place to live. And it was now December twenty-fourth.

"Couldn't we just get a small Christmas tree and set it up in this room somewhere?" asked Chat. "That way, Santa Claus will know where to put our presents.

"Yes, a Christmas tree!" echoed his younger brother. "I want a Christmas tree!"

I sighed, looking around at our squeezed-in beds and cots. "But, honey, the five of us can barely move around in here with all our suitcases and everything. I'm sorry, but we just don't have the room for something extra like a Christmas tree."

Our oldest son had been listening quietly. Suddenly, he grinned. "Yes, we do."

I stared. "Where?"

He pointed to our motel room's door. "Right there — on the back of that door. Please, Mommy, if we can't get a real tree, can't we make a pretend tree and put it up there? Then Santa will know we love Christmas just as much as he does."

"And leave us some presents, too!" Chat added.

Make a tree? Impossible — at least the three-dimensional kind. But I looked at the newspaper that I had spread out on our little motel-room table when I was searching for places to rent. If I taped some of those pages together, cut them out into a tree shape, and bought some poster paint and brushes at the drugstore next door...

Now, I was grinning, too. "Okay, boys! Ready to make the very best Christmas tree in the whole wide world?"

"Yes!"

So we taped and cut and painted — first green all over, and then, when that was dry, we painted and cut out colorful "ornaments" to paste on its "branches." We even placed a rather crooked but bravely shining star on top. Then we taped our creation onto the back of the motel-room door. Magnificent!

No, it didn't smell like pine or fir. But it glowed with love — the same love that surrounded a very special baby long ago on the very first Christmas night. To a family that couldn't even find a crowded motel room to stay in like we had but slept in a barn instead.

So, that night, we shared that awesome story and sang some carols there in our little motel room. Then, after the boys fell asleep, my husband made another quick trip to that drugstore next door — fortunately, still open late that holiday night. He tiptoed back inside with his arms full of bags from Santa, maneuvered around the boys' cots, and handed the presents to me to wrap in the tiny bathroom on Santa's behalf.

The next morning when our sons awoke, we heard, "Mommy! Daddy! Look! Santa did find us after all — even without snow!"

They tumbled off their cots to wonder at the gaily wrapped presents under their beautiful "tree."

No, Santa didn't need snow for Christmas to come. All he needed was love — in the shape of a Christmas tree.

— Bonnie Compton Hanson —

11

A Creature Was Stirring

Next to a circus there ain't nothing that packs up and
tears out faster than the Christmas spirit.
~Frank McKinney Hubbard

My wife and I dragged in the final section of our seven-foot artificial Christmas tree from the garage. It was heavy, so we plopped it down and took a deep breath or two prior to opening it up.

Before setting the tree in its stand, we slid our couch over so we would have the room needed for our large tree to fit in the living room. In a moment, we would form the branches that would hold our ornaments.

Everything was going smoothly, and my daughter announced the stand was ready. I lifted the bottom section of the tree and was about to place it into the stand when I heard the shriek.

It was so loud that I assumed someone had broken into our home.

"A mouse! A mouse!" screamed my daughter. My wife screamed just as loud, and pointed.

My wife and daughter jumped up on the couch as the baby mouse ran to one side of our living room and then the other. Because of the piercing screams, the mouse was frightened and disoriented. The little rodent had obviously found a home in our Christmas tree.

Once we brought the tree inside and opened the branches, the baby mouse fell out of its temporary home and smack dab into the middle of our living room.

"Get the mouse!" my wife and daughter screamed.

It was so tiny and quick that I wasn't sure what to do. I tried grabbing its long gray tail, but it scurried away and up the fireplace brick.

I had an idea. "Get a shoebox," I said. But my wife and daughter simultaneously shook their heads. They had no intention of moving from the couch.

I ran to our bedroom and came back with an empty box. Then I grabbed a fly swatter. My plan was to stun the little mouse and put it in the box.

I was about to smack it with the swatter when my wife yelled out, "Don't kill it! It's a baby and kind of cute." My daughter agreed with her, and I could tell by its frightened eyes that the little mouse did, too.

The tiny mouse twitched its mouth. It seemed to be saying, "Listen to them. I don't want to be killed. This is my first Christmas!"

As I saw the fear in the mouse's eyes, I gained some Christmas compassion.

I slowly inched toward it with a small towel. It climbed a little higher and fell from the fireplace brick. Then it raced under a coffee table and then to a corner of the room. The mouse was disoriented again and froze in the corner of our living room. I jumped into action. I put the box over the mouse and slid a lid underneath it.

Our surprise Christmas guest was safely captured.

I asked my wife and daughter if they wanted to say goodbye. They both declined and requested that I take it outside. I took the baby mouse for a short walk and let him go near a little open field nearby. I wished him a merry Christmas and then made my way back to our house. Once I was home, my wife asked me to shake each section of our tree to make sure there were no more mice. Thankfully, we didn't have any others.

Things settled down, and the tree went up without any further ado.

Now each year before putting up the tree, I'm required to shake it out vigorously and double check for mice.

People may say, "Not a creature was stirring, not even a mouse," but we learned the hard way that it's always good to double check!

— David Warren —

All in the Family

*A Christmas tree teaches us that we can create magic
with happiness and unity of the loved ones.*
~Author Unknown

My husband Larry and I had decided our artificial Christmas tree was too large. It was six and a half feet tall and had beautiful, filled-out branches. Some of the branches had different needles, some short and some long. It was just a wonderfully designed artificial tree.

But when it came to decorating for Christmas and putting up this tree, our living room became overcrowded. We had to move a chair from the living room to the spare bedroom to make room for the tree. Basically, we had to rearrange the whole living room. Then, in the spare bedroom, we had to move the bed over for the living room chair to fit. It took almost a whole day just to do the rearranging.

So, we decided to get a smaller tree and get rid of this one. It would make decorating for Christmas easier on us.

I tried to think of someone in the family who could use this tree. I knew that none of my brothers needed it. Some of them lived far away anyway. So I decided to call my sister Janet and her husband Buck. We live about ten miles from each other.

I told my sister how large the artificial tree was and assured her it was still in excellent condition. But, politely, she refused it. She said their tree was still in good shape, and they wouldn't need another tree.

I was a little disappointed, but I decided the next best place would be the local hospice store. They could sell it, which would bring in money to help them. Plus, it would go to a good home. My husband went out and got two large boxes to put it in. We wanted to keep the tote it was in for our next tree. I had to wait for the hospice store to start taking Christmas items for the holiday season. When they did, we drove to the store and donated the tree.

Time passed, and the Christmas season was upon us. We always take a drive around different areas this time of year to look at all the festive and beautiful Christmas decorations. I called my sister and told her that we would be in her neighborhood. I asked her if we could stop by. She said, "Yes, come on down."

I am always excited to see her Christmas tree and decorations. She is so creative with decorating, and she makes everything look so joyful and merry. She makes a lot of her decorations by hand.

We arrived at their place and got out of the car. We proceeded to go inside and visit with her and Buck. Their Christmas tree was so elegantly decorated with many different ornaments. Some were old-fashioned. I had to get a closer look.

I looked at the branches. Different types of needles were on a lot of them. Some were darker green than others. It was so full and such a beautiful tree. I told Janet, "What a beautiful tree! Is this the same tree?" Janet then proceeded to tell me that they had gotten their old, artificial tree out of the box. The needles were shedding badly. She and Buck decided they needed to purchase another Christmas tree. They heard that the hospice store had several really nice artificial trees.

So off to the hospice store they went. The artificial trees were all on display. Janet told Buck, "This tree is beautiful! I want this one." They paid for it and took it home.

As I examined it more closely, I noticed the branches were designed identically to the one we had donated. I asked Janet about any markings for the branch placements because Larry had to take some paint and remark some of the branches. The original paint had worn off. Janet told me, "Yes."

After asking her a few other details, I said, "Janet, this was our tree that we were going to give to you guys!" Janet and I both laughed.

We couldn't believe it! Our tree had ended up in their home after all!

The Christmas tree looked so beautiful in their home. I was glad my sister had ended up with it. It did end up in a good home. In a roundabout way, the Christmas tree did stay in the family.

— Candy Thompson —

13

Oma's Ornaments

*Some Christmas tree ornaments do more than glitter
and glow, they represent a gift of love
given a long time ago.*
~Tom Baker

Blame it on the shopping district full of people. Blame it on my indecisive nature. Blame it on our long shopping list. Whatever the reason, by the time the big-box store turned out not to have the Christmas tree we wanted, both my husband and I were exhausted.

"We can check at the one by us," Ben said. Our apartment was only a short drive from another branch of the store.

I agreed, reasoning that the car ride would rest my aching feet. Normally, we would've gone home. We'd already spent most of an afternoon buying gifts; any other shopping could wait.

But not the Christmas tree.

When we arrived, I made a beeline for the former garden section, now Christmas Central. We found the trees in boxes. I pulled up the item number so we could find the tree we'd chosen as the first Christmas tree of our married life.

This store didn't have it either.

I walked away, suddenly so angry I couldn't risk speaking or I'd explode. Ben followed silently at my heels. All the way back through the store, I tried to talk myself out of my surging disappointment. It was just a Christmas tree.

Once we got to the parking lot, my throat constricted, and my eyes stung. By the time we reached our car, my vision was blurring. *You're a grown woman,* I told myself. *You are not going to cry over a Christmas tree.*

But my next thought caught me off guard. *It's not the tree. It's Oma's ornaments.*

The realization sent tears slipping silently down my cheeks. After my grandmother's funeral, during the last, agonizing walk through her empty house, all the cousins had gone through her things that no one had claimed.

I'd been shocked that no one wanted them: the pearly pink teardrops and deep purple globes with a tasteful dusting of glitter; the silver corkscrew icicles; the vibrantly colored bird which, despite being the most interesting thing on the tree and clearly deserving a place of honor, always perched on a random branch as though taking momentary shelter. All of them, mine?

Not sure whether I was committing sacrilege or a sacred rite, I took the ornaments. Since my family's tree was already overloaded with decorations, I left Oma's in a box for my future Very Own Tree.

My borderline obsession with getting a tree made more sense now. Still, when Ben and I got home — laden with gifts but still treeless — I plunked down on the couch and wept.

Eventually, I tried to explain, blubbering that it wasn't the tree; it was Oma's ornaments. Ben understood. He fetched me tissues and waited patiently for me to calm down.

I didn't calm down, and I didn't wait patiently for it to happen.

My thoughts ran in infuriating circles — feeling ridiculous for my attachment to the ornaments, trying to talk myself out of it, guilt over not using them yet, right back to feeling ridiculous for caring.

Finally, I sobbed, "But it doesn't really matter!"

Ben looked me in the eyes. "If it matters to you, it matters."

When I finally finished crying, Ben made me ramen noodles and got himself a sandwich. We watched TV.

But I couldn't let it go. I found myself perusing the box store's website, just in case. I finally found the tree — and the words: Out of Stock. This time, I was prepared for the flood of disappointment and tried to accept the inevitable. I would not have a tree that night.

Ben pulled up a search of a different store and found the tree. Also out of stock. "Popular choice." He started browsing the store's selection. "Hey, how about this one?"

I leaned over to examine the image. Thick, close-set branches. Six feet high — a good size. Only five dollars more. "Yeah." I shrugged. "Worth a try. We could go see it." I bit my lip, thinking through our schedules. We wouldn't have many chances to shop after tonight.

Ben selected the store closest to us. "They have one left."

I swallowed a wave of panic. "Aren't they already closed, though?" I'd shopped there enough to know they were open until 9:00, and it was now 9:30.

Ben found the store's hours. "Open till 10:00. Holiday hours."

"Really?" I couldn't stop hope from creeping into my voice.

Ben raised his eyebrows. "Want me to go get it?"

"I…" Get it without seeing a display version first? And yet, I was beginning to realize, I didn't care what it looked or felt like. "Do you want to?"

My husband smiled. "I do." He poked me gently. "And I don't want you to go out in the cold, so you just stay here."

Part of me wanted to object, but my feet still really hurt.

"Give me ten minutes." Ben hurried to get his shoes and coat and dashed off in a whirl of heroism.

I sat on the couch and tried not to feel like a jerk. What kind of person sends her husband to get a tree so late at night? I distracted myself with TV, but my gaze kept moving to the clock. Ten minutes turned to fifteen. Fifteen to twenty.

How far was it to that store, anyway? Maybe Ben couldn't find the tree. Perhaps they'd already sold it. But he would call then, right?

At long last, the doorknob rattled, and my heart jumped with relief. Ben came back — dragging a massive cardboard box and sporting a huge grin.

First, we opened the box to feel the branches, and then we got out the individual pieces. Before we knew what was happening, we'd assembled the whole tree and started the lengthy process of straightening the branches.

"We were gonna vacuum first," I objected weakly.

Ben pointed out the plastic needles already littering the carpet. "We'll vacuum after anyway."

We kept going.

I was giddy. Every branch was a wonder. Neither of us could stop saying how nice it looked.

Ben had never had an artificial tree before. "You can literally bend the branches any way you want!"

I laughed at his amazement.

When we finally finished, the tree stood like a sentinel in front of the French doors, guarding the apartment. As I decorated my Very Own Tree, I could feel Oma's gnarled hands handing me each globe and icicle. I could hear her lilting, musical voice pointing out the bare spots where they might fit best.

And in a burst of assertiveness, on the very top of the tree where a star or angel might go, I perched the most interesting, vibrantly colored bird.

—K. R. Powers—

14

A Tree of Memories

Those who we have loved never really leave us.
They live on forever in our hearts, and cast their
radiant light onto every shadow.
~Sylvana Rossetti

I shove the last of the decorative pumpkins into an orange container and shut the lid on fall. It's December first and, like clockwork, I'm ready for Christmas.

My six-foot-tall, artificial Christmas tree sits ready and waiting under a film of plastic wrap. Its top layer is flattened by the ceiling. I give the tree a pat, bypassing it and heading for the big red containers with the green lids on the far wall. They contain my ornaments as well as all the ornaments I've inherited from my mother and grandmother's large collections. Each container weighs about twenty pounds, and every inch is packed carefully and lovingly by me every year in anticipation of my favorite holiday tradition: decorating the tree.

I tell Alexa to play holiday music as I struggle up and down the basement steps three times, carefully depositing each container in the living room, warning my cats not to play on them. They ignore me. I can hear them bouncing on and off those precious boxes as I begin the strenuous process of bringing the tree upstairs. I could wait for someone to help me but I feel the need to get this done today. I like to be alone while I unpack my ornaments, a little me-time moment I look forward to every year.

Two snacks and a nap later, I've got the whole tree upstairs. I lock the top portion, now unflattened, into place. I wrinkle my nose at it because it's off-center, but I know no matter how hard I try it fix it, it will lean slightly forward. Oh, well. It's an old tree after all.

I open the first box and unravel strings of white Christmas lights. It takes me about fifteen minutes to get those up. I take in the moment, watching the lights as they twinkle. Listening to Crosby crooning from the other room, I step back to admire this slightly lopsided, most precious tree. It was my mother's. She bought it for thirty dollars at a July Fourth sale, and she was so proud of it. This tree has been there for every one of our family's Christmases for almost thirty years. It's even pictured in the background of one of my favorite photos of my mother on the night of her last Christmas, showing off her favorite ornament in her palm: a little basket of kittens. That was ten years ago.

Although it's sagging in places and branches are missing, I wouldn't trade it for anything. I love this old tree. I give it and myself a little shake. The Christmas blues aren't going to get me this year, I think to myself as I heave one of the boxes onto a side table, roll over my three-tier craft cart, and begin the long process of carefully unwrapping and sorting all my ornaments.

For hours, I sift through hundreds of ornaments, unpacking generations of memories. Each ornament has a tale of its own. A marker of our family's history, of milestones met. Of graduations, marriages, baby's first Christmases, vacations, hobbies, pets, and so much more. A wooden clown, a gift from my aunt to my grandmother, both long gone from this Earth goes toward the right. A little old lady with a broom — once my great-grandmother's, brought with her from Italy — is placed toward the middle. A glass photo ornament of a wedding party, our smiles wide, our joy eternalized, hangs from the top of the tree. Here's the silver bell my mother would ring every New Year's Eve at midnight. And there's the spaceship my father won at a charity auction. Here is my sister's gift to me last year: a resin Christmas cookie just like the ones our grandmother made when we were kids. Pictures of lost loved ones encased behind silver frames, hung with red ribbons. My favorite: a ballerina, spinning on tiptoes, her purple tutu catching the light as she twirls.

So many Santas and too many snowmen to count. The angels I set aside for a smaller tree. The handmade ornaments I place in a special section off to the side. Any ornaments of yarn I leave on the bottom boughs for the cats. The fragile ornaments, like my grandmother's antique glass balls, I carefully place at the very top of the tree next to the big Santa tree topper. The shabbier ornaments go in the back. The larger ornaments I use as filler to hide bald spots in the branches. I can almost hear my late grandmother telling me, "You've got a space there" and "More on the top" as I decorate. Lastly, I place my mother's miniature ornament collection at eye level on the front of the tree. Her *Wizard of Oz* ornaments, a famous mouse, a china teacup — all gifts from her children.

Finished, I stand back and admire my hard work. Wait a minute. I squint at the tree. Where are the miniature kittens? This happens every year without fail! My mother's favorite ornament is missing. I groan as I turn over all the packing material on the floor, careful where I place my feet in case I step on it like last year. I riffle through mounds of tissue paper but still no kittens.

My own cats are crying for their dinner now. It's dark out, and the lights from my neighbors' newly installed Christmas lights are dancing in my peripheral vision as I stand between the window and the tree, scanning each ornament for the missing kittens. Maybe I put the ornament in another part of the tree without realizing it. I know I unpacked it! I turn the lights of the tree up higher, practically blinding myself.

Every year, I lose this ornament, and every year it turns up where I least expect it. Two years ago, it was found under an end table. The year before, the dog pawed it out from behind the coat rack. My mother once left this ornament on the Christmas tree the day it was thrown out. She had to chase down the garbage truck to get it back. It has made its escape every year since. Not this year, though! I feed the cats and then get the flashlight out and search every inch of that tree, every nook and cranny of that living room. I even search under the couch cushions, but it's nowhere to be found.

I must look just like my mother, I think. Hands on my hips, lips pressed together, hair in a messy bun. Looking for those darn kittens again. Oh, how she would laugh if she were here.... Then again, it wouldn't really feel like Christmas without the annual hunt for her favorite ornament.

I feel one of my cats, Sami, rubbing up against my leg. I look down and there, in the cuff of my jeans, is the miniature basket of kittens! Like a gift from heaven. Oh, I can almost hear my mother's laughter. I pick up the ornament, with the hook still attached, and place the kittens front and center on the Christmas tree.

"Merry Christmas, Mom," I whisper.

For once, my Christmas tree is up and fully decorated on the first of December. My family and I will have the whole month and then some to enjoy it. Heart full, I can't help but peek my head into the living room every now and again that night to glimpse my tree fully adorned, shining bright. What a perfect start to the holidays.

— Melanie R. McBride —

15

The Gingerbread Mistake

Bake the world a better place.
~Author Unknown

Christmas is a hectic time. As moms often do, I stretched myself thin last Christmas. But I had a schedule, and if I stuck to it every task would be complete on time.

One of the most time-consuming traditions I practice every year is baking cookies. I go all out — at least ten different recipes and growing each year, totaling about 750 cookies. Last year, I made all the quicker recipes in late October and early November, storing them in my extra freezer in the garage that had been purchased solely for this reason.

However, with my extra social events and duties, I had to postpone the more time-consuming recipes until mid-December. That meant delaying gingerbread cookies, my four-year-old daughter Avery's favorite. She had been talking up gingerbread baking all year. At random times in the summer, she'd say, "I love gingerbread." By October, she had made a game plan. "First, I'm going to eat one of the boy ones with blue icing. Remember those, Mommy?"

I promised I'd get to them in due time and would save her a blue boy.

One night in December, while my husband Matt and I were doing dinner dishes, Avery ran into the kitchen.

"Where have you been?" I asked.

She grimaced in discomfort. "Dirt fell in my mouth."

"How did dirt fall in your mouth?"

"I was outside, and some fell off from up top and fell in my mouth."

Matt and I looked at each other. For one thing, we knew she hadn't been outside. It was below freezing that evening, and she wore no coat or shoes. Secondly, why would dirt fall from the sky and magically land in her mouth? We didn't buy it.

"Avery, you weren't outside," I said. "Tell me what happened."

"Um, okay, um…" She guided me out of the kitchen, looking around as if finding reminders of what had happened. She was acting like the criminal in a movie who had to make up a name and use objects nearby to aid in the fib. Had she eaten something bad?

"Avery, tell me."

"Come on." She led me upstairs into her room. Her books spilled over from the shelf to the floor, and Barbies lay in disarray in various states of undress. Nothing unusual I could see.

She gave me an I-don't-know shrug. I asked her to open her mouth, and dark crumbs speckled her tongue. As my oldest son liked to drink tea in his room, I thought maybe she had consumed the tea leftovers at the bottom of the mug. Gross, but not worrisome.

"Did you get it from Luke's room?"

She nodded and took me to her brother's room.

"Where is it?" I asked. No mugs sat on his desk or dresser.

She walked from wall to wall, moaning to herself. "Um… uh…" Looking for anything to blame.

Having ruled out tea, worry set in. "Did you spit out what was in your mouth?"

She led me to the bathroom sink and pointed to the basin. A streak of deep brown bits dribbled to the drain.

I toughened my tone. There was an unknown substance in the sink, my daughter had it on her tongue, and she was clearly covering up the truth. I crouched to her eye level. "Avery, you're lying to me. Show me where you got this stuff. I need to know if it is poison or bad for you. I don't want you to get sick."

Her shoulders dropped, defeated. "Fine. It was the cookie."

"The cookie?" I straightened, racking my brain. What was she referring to? I didn't serve cookies for dessert.

"Downstairs," she said, as if the answer was obvious to everyone in the room. "I didn't know."

And then it hit me. I held in my smile as reality sank in. My childhood urge had manifested in my daughter. But, unlike me, she had the guts to go for it. "I see." I took her little hand in mine, and we walked back down the stairs into the family room.

To the Christmas tree.

There, just within Avery's grasp at the center of the tree, hung a deliciously decorated gingerbread ornament. With an arm missing.

I bit my lip, the smile impossible to hold at bay. I slipped the ornament off the tree as my husband inquired about the truth from the kitchen.

I said nothing. I simply held the cookie ornament out to him. What joy it brought me to see his expression go from confusion to understanding.

"Avery!" His reprimand came out with a big grin.

I lost it and laughed, too. Every year, I had helped my mom decorate our tree, and every year I had picked up the preserved gingerbread ornament, compelled to take a bite. I never knew anyone else had the urge — until my daughter's crime.

We explained to her that it wasn't a real cookie, which she learned the hard way. More importantly, it wasn't good to lie. Matt and I were not genuinely upset — just relieved to know the truth.

Avery went off to her room, and Matt and I continued with the dishes, laughing together about the incident. Five minutes later, Avery returned.

Her eyes watered, and she fidgeted with her hands. She managed to get out the words in sorrowful sobs. "I'm really sorry about the ornament." She wiped her eyes with her sleeve. "I won't do it again."

We comforted and consoled her, assuring her that everyone made mistakes now and then. It warmed our hearts to see how regretful she was. We also joked to one another that we didn't have to worry about her lying since her cover-up story was so far-fetched.

But desperate times had called for desperate measures. I took Avery's blatant hint and rearranged my holiday schedule. The gingerbread cookies were baked and decorated soon after.

Avery was given the first one to taste: a boy with blue icing, of course.

— Mary Shotwell —

16

Christmas Sparrow

Rich or poor, we will keep together
and be happy in one another.
~Louisa May Alcott, *Little Women*

The year my house burned down (which followed a flood eight months earlier) was my first experience with Christmastime failure. Unfortunately, it was not the last.

The fire took everything but love from us just weeks before the holidays. We were in such a state that I couldn't afford gifts for my children. I didn't even have a tree.

Before I lost my job (right before my house burned down), my employer gave me a gift card for a local restaurant. Not being able to give the children a traditional Christmas, I took them to a Christmas breakfast at this place before depositing them with my ex-mother-in-law so they could actually have Christmas.

As we waited for the waitress, the boys chatted excitedly about going to Grandma's house, and I started crying. One minute, I found myself overflowing with joy at how happy they were. A moment later, I was devastated by the thought that someone else would be providing all the wonderful things about Christmas that children look forward to.

I couldn't even afford a tree, and I think that's what got me crying. It's such a small thing to have a tree, but I didn't even have a living room to put one in.

My children were stunned by the sudden burst of emotion and were naturally concerned. When I finally said, "I can't even afford a

Christmas tree," my youngest son decided he could fix that at least. He had a dollar in his pocket and asked if he and his brother could go and play the "Crane Game."

Seeing an opportunity to get myself under control, I allowed it and began pulling myself together. Soon, Steven stood next to me, patting my shoulder. I looked up at my beautiful boy, who was smiling.

He said, "Here, Mommy. Now you'll never have to go without a Christmas tree again."

With fifty cents, he had managed to snag a "stuffed" Christmas tree. It stood no more than sixteen inches tall. It had a droll face on it and an adorable, cartoon-type smile.

My heart melted.

It took three years to recover from the flood and fire, so that little tree served as my Christmas tree each year. Even after I managed to purchase a tree, I kept that one and put it out every year as a reminder of how blessed we are to have each other.

Little did I know that twelve years later I would be in a position to use that tree again.

My new husband worked in a fast-food setting with a young mother named Sparrow. She had four children and was a hard worker. She rode the bus everywhere she went because she couldn't afford a car.

Feeling sorry for her, my husband took her home one night after they closed. Less than two hours later, we got a call that the apartment complex where she lived had burned down.

She'd gotten out with her four children (all under the age of seven) and nothing else.

We, along with a lot of other people, managed to help Sparrow get things they needed. Being the hard worker she was, she quickly secured a place to live for her and her children.

Still, her situation nagged at me. She had basic necessities, but no one had checked to see if she had fun things for the children, and Christmas would soon arrive. I had little difficulty remembering how it felt having nothing right before Christmas.

As I put up my artificial tree that year and got my family ready for Christmas, I couldn't help thinking that I wished I could afford to help Sparrow.

Her children didn't even have stockings. As I brought out the new stockings that I'd bought the year before, I lost my enthusiasm for the task and dropped them back into the box with tags still on them.

As I talked to my son Steven that afternoon about how I felt, he decided to help. He rallied his church to provide Christmas gifts for the children. They even managed to get together a hundred dollars for Sparrow to buy a Christmas meal for her and her children. I provided the new stockings since my children were grown, and their old ones worked just fine.

Still, the tree is the symbol of Christmas for me, something we almost never had growing up. Mom's family didn't observe Christmas. And even when we could've afforded one, she often forgot to get one.

I had paid almost two hundred dollars for my tree after Christmas the year before, and I wasn't ready to part with it. But every time I came home, I looked at that tree all decked out for the holidays, and the image of Sparrow's children having so little smacked me in the face.

One afternoon in early December, I passed by my bed while heading to the bathroom. Steven's tree sat on the bed looking at me. I decided then and there to give my big Christmas tree to Sparrow. Steven's tree was more than enough.

I put the stuffed tree into a chair surrounded by the few gifts we had and then dismantled my tree.

Though small by most standards at five feet tall, it quickly filled up Sparrow's small, cinder-block apartment. The children could scarcely contain their excitement. The only ornaments I didn't bring were the ones that had personal meaning for me.

When her girls saw the snowman on the new tree skirt, they squealed with excitement. Still, I wanted to do more for them. So, I invited them over to my house to bake some cookies that they could take home.

The girls and I baked cookies, colored, and played with my Christmas village. I gave each of them an apron for baking that I made just for them. Afterward, I drove them out to a neighborhood that has a light show between houses and their own radio program that the lights move to. The children squealed with magical excitement, and I almost hated taking them home!

That weekend at a coffee shop with our friend Steve, we talked about Sparrow and her girls, and I could see Steve's wheels spinning. I half-expected him to come up with something special for them, too.

After coffee, my husband and I followed him home and cleared room for his Christmas tree. Afterward, we went to the tree lot so he could pick one out. He did that quickly and, to my surprise, he asked us to pick one, too.

Every time I looked at the "real" tree that Christmas, my heart leapt. It served as a reminder of thinner years when a little, stuffed tree meant the world to me.

—Veronica I. Coldiron—

17

The "Ditch Willow" Christmas Tree

I never thought it was such a bad little tree. It's not bad
at all, really. Maybe it just needs a little love.
~Linus van Pelt

Amongst all the hustle and bustle of raising four kids and running two businesses, my parents procrastinated until the very last minute one Christmas and did the unthinkable: They waited so long to get a Christmas tree that stores all over town were completely sold out.

I think my mother had procrastinated on purpose because she thought the cedar made the baby's allergies act up, so she figured it would be good if we only had the tree a couple of days. But then there were none left. We had fought the idea of getting a fake tree, feeling that it couldn't bring the real Christmas spirit.

In any case, it was a disaster to me, a child who loved Christmas with all my heart. Not gathering around the Christmas tree with my family under its brightly colored lights while Mom rocked the baby and sang "Silent Night" on Christmas Eve — I just couldn't stand the thought of it. Decorating the Christmas tree and gathering around it with my family were magical things that I looked forward to all year long. My eyes filled with tears as we pulled back in the driveway, feeling totally defeated.

That's when my dad got a brilliant idea. He said, "Let's go cut down our own tree," and he led us kids outside to search the fields. At first, we were a little confused because Christmas trees don't grow in the wild in South Texas. But we quickly got into the excitement of picking out a tree, forgetting what shape or type of tree it was. Who needed an evergreen anyway? We just wanted a real, special tree. We lived out in the country on a little piece of land with about two acres, so we hunted around with flashlights in the dark.

There were not many trees growing on our property, but there was a lot of scrub bush and weeds growing around the banks of our little fishing pond. We eventually found the "perfect tree." Dad chopped down the tree/giant weed, commonly called a "Ditch Willow," and brought it inside. My mom was no doubt shaking her head the entire time. Ditch willows were normally considered a nuisance in our area, as they commonly grow along the drainage ditches of old county roads. I will admit it looked pretty ridiculous in our living room, but it felt like an old-fashioned Christmas, going out in search of a tree that Daddy cut down for us.

It was so crooked and flimsy that we had to lean it against the two walls in the corner of our living room to make it stand up. The trunk was far too skinny to fit into the base of our tree stand snugly. Its branches were pretty bare, too. But by the time we got through with it, it was the most Christmassy Christmas tree we had ever seen (at least to me). It was wacky and certainly eccentric, but to us it encapsulated all the same love and joy of the tallest, prettiest Christmas tree in the world.

My brother, sisters and I filled it with all the colorful Christmas lights that its little branches could hold, and we found a place for most of our handmade Christmas decorations to hang, although it couldn't hold the heaviest ones. To make the thin branches more festive, my sister and I lovingly made red and green paper chains out of construction paper. We still have a few links of those chains some twenty years later.

My mother remembers that we liked how bare the branches were because we could clearly see all the ornaments dangling around. Decorating the wobbly, wacky Christmas tree was sort of a balancing act, but we loved it.

I doubt my mother thought that tree was as beautiful as we kids did, but I think she loved the smiles it brought us (and there was no cedar allergy). Despite its off-the-wall appearance, it was a magical tree, a Christmas Eve miracle to my siblings and me, who were so close to not having a Christmas tree that year.

Before bedtime, we all sat around the glowing lights of the Christmas tree and sang carols while Mom rocked the baby to sleep.

A few years later, my little sister married a boy whose family opened a Christmas tree farm in town. They sell hypoallergenic trees, so we never had to worry about finding a wacky Christmas tree again. However, even our more traditional trees would never have looked "perfect" in the eyes of an interior designer. Mom always let us kids have fun, putting our love and creativity into every branch of the Christmas tree. Nothing matched, nothing was even, but its branches were filled with love and Christmas joy.

I'll never forget the wackiest one of all, though — a big, beautiful Christmas "ditch willow."

That night, I learned that any old tree can be a Christmas tree. Adorned with lights, ornaments and an angel, surrounded by family — that's what makes a tree a Christmas tree.

—Kayleen Kitty Holder—

18

A 1967 Christmas Story

Christmas is a tonic for our souls. It moves us
to think of others rather than of ourselves.
It directs our thoughts to giving.
~B.C. Forbes

Christmastime brought magic to our rural Indiana town. Citizens visited the brick post office to mail Christmas cards and visit Postmaster Clarence Pook. Across the street at the library, Edna, the Story-Hour Lady, dressed in pioneer clothes and read holiday stories to children.

The day after Thanksgiving, the volunteer firefighters hung giant red-and-white plastic candy canes from the lamps on State Street and displayed a life-size manger scene near the three-way intersection at the south end of town. Snow came early and blanketed the ground until after the state boys' basketball tournament in early spring.

My father bought our real Christmas tree from a local farm every year. Our ranch-style home lacked a fireplace, so my brother and I hung our red-and-white flannel stockings on the windowsills. Mom used Elmer's glue and green glitter to paint our names on the furry white part of the Christmas stockings.

My father taught high-school science and agriculture and advised the Future Farmers of America chapter. The FFA chapter raised money, bought the high school a real Christmas tree, and decorated it with blue, green, and red bulbs and fragile, sparkling glass ornaments. The school community enjoyed the tree until the semester ended.

Tradition dictated that the FFA boys and my father take the tree and decorations to a needy family chosen by the other teachers. Our 1965 Chevy Biscayne station wagon was inadequate to cart the nearly nine-foot tree to this family. Dad borrowed the school's World War II-era Army truck from Willie Sims, the maintenance man and let the chosen family know they would be receiving a large, fully decorated Christmas tree. Dad and several FFA boys would bring the tree to their home.

Dad had his students put the decorated tree in the back of the old truck. The three of them — the thirty-something schoolteacher and the two teenage boys in blue corduroy Future Farmer jackets — were in a festive mood, congratulating themselves on the good deed they were about to do for a family of twelve children with a father who was out of work.

They traveled east on the state highway past the well-manicured farms, bright, freshly painted red barns, and white fences. As the old truck turned onto a county road, pieces of packed ice and gravel spit up from the truck's worn tires.

Nearing the family's home, Dad turned around and looked in the truck bed to check on the gift.

No tree.

No lights.

No decorations.

No green and red metal tree stand.

Nothing but an empty and scratched truck bed.

Dad turned the truck around. He and the students retraced their steps to the town where the shops had closed for the night. The twinkle of holiday bulbs and the Evangelical United Brethren Church lights signaled evening.

Nothing could be found.

Dad thought about it. "What should I do? Should I go home and get our tree?"

He did not believe that was a good choice, with his two small children enjoying the tree, but he steeled himself for that option. If need be, he thought, his children could learn about sharing.

As darkness fell, the gray truck and three not-so-wise men arrived in town. A tree lot at the used-car place was closing for the night. Dad reached in his wallet and bought the most excellent tree on the lot. Then, off to Huffman and Deaton's Hardware for lights, ornaments and a new metal tree stand. Joe Huffman was closing his register for the day but recognized my father and let him in.

With a new tree in the bed of the beat-up gray truck, the group headed east again. As they tentatively approached the family's large farmhouse, they could spy children watching them from each window. The family's older children greeted the group and set up the tree in their living room. Dad noticed a stack of presents and bags of candy and fruit donated by the Lions Club and other community groups.

The scent of anticipation and cinnamon apples hung in the air. The teacher and the teenagers left the family in happiness and wonder. Dad and those high-school students received a huge blessing when they saw the lights in the eyes of those children.

Several weeks after that Christmas, Dad went into the brick post office to pick up the mail and chat with Clarence, the postmaster. A man whom Dad did not know came in and began talking to Clarence loudly.

"Clarence," the stranger said. "It's the oddest thing. I was driving out east of town a few nights before Christmas, and you would not believe it. I found a completely decorated, beautiful, nine-foot Christmas tree that someone had thrown in a ditch!"

— Amy McVay Abbott —

Chapter
3

Making New Traditions

19

Our New Christmas Tradition

For it is in giving that we receive.
~Saint Francis

As Christmas vacation was quickly approaching, I began to feel the butterflies in my stomach once again. It had started five years earlier, when I agreed that my two boys could spend ten days, almost all of their Christmas vacation, with their father and his relatives. Since my ex-husband's people were more traditional when it came to Christmas and had a larger family gathering, I put my needs aside so that my children wouldn't miss this celebration.

The usual weekend away with their dad was sometimes a welcome respite from motherhood. But a week and a half was far too long for me to be without my children. My new husband and I would be visiting his parents, sister and nephew for Christmas dinner, and I looked forward to my stepdaughters visiting, too, but I still had to make a conscious effort to be positive when my ex pulled his car into our driveway.

"I love you. Have a great time," I said to my boys as convincingly as possible.

I hugged them tightly, each in turn, bundled up in their winter wear, before I released them to their father's care. Their stepdad moved toward them and hugged them both.

"Have a good time," he said. "See you next year."

"Love you," my boys chanted and headed off.

I closed the door and looked at my husband sadly, already missing my children.

I turned on the kettle to make tea, and while waiting for the water to boil, the phone rang.

"Hi, Shaina," I answered, excited to receive a call from an old friend.

Just hearing her voice lifted my spirits. We talked about our families, as usual, but I could tell by her tone that she had an ulterior motive.

"We have a really big favour to ask you two," Shaina said.

"Go for it," I said.

"Well, Morrie and I were wondering if you and Dave wouldn't mind taking our kids for a couple of days so we can have a little getaway," she asked tentatively.

"Of course," I answered without hesitation. "I don't even have to ask Dave. I know he won't mind."

My husband — a big, burly, fun-loving man — seemed to naturally attract children of any age. Dave looked over at me questioningly. I stared back at him enthusiastically while listening to my friend.

"This will be the first time they'll be away from us," Shaina admitted.

The two well-behaved children that my friend was referring to were a girl of nine and a boy of four. No parent would refuse to host these two cuties.

"We'll be honored," I answered.

"We really appreciate it."

"No problem. Throw them at us; we'll be here."

After we arranged the particulars, I hung up the phone. I walked over to my husband with a big grin on my face and said, "That's so sweet that they thought of us."

"We must be doing something right," Dave said and smiled.

Keila and Gabe arrived two days after Christmas, during a blizzard, complete with their belongings and a small box of food to cater to their fussy diets. Keila, who was an incredibly picky eater, oddly enjoyed tomato soup. Her parents, not knowing what our pantry consisted of, included a couple of cans. Neither her mom nor dad could get her to eat any fresh vegetables and told me that I would receive an award if I did. When heating up the soup for lunch, I assured Keila, "Of course, tomato soup is a vegetable."

"Oh, good," she said contentedly.

During the three days and two nights when we opened our home to these two beautiful children, we tried to keep them entertained. We had a kid-friendly bedroom for them to stay in, with lots of age-appropriate toys. But, of course, we strived to make their stay more special. The first afternoon, once the snow stopped falling and the ground was covered in puffy, glistening white flakes, I asked the kids, "Hey, do you two want to go tobogganing?"

"Okay," they answered eagerly.

We supervised dressing the children from head-to-toe, literally, from hats to snow pants and boots. Dave packed the toboggan, and the four of us drove to a local hill. We took turns walking up the snowy incline with the sled in tow. Dave, the big adult child, sat on the back of the toboggan for many of the rides, with one of the siblings in front as his legs reached around them. I watched them slide down the hill beaming, emitting gleeful cries even when they tumbled off.

In the midst of all this fun, I began to yearn for my boys. I could easily imagine them going down the hill like maniacs. I found myself fussing over Keila and Gabe like a mother hen, retying hats, exchanging wet mittens for dry ones, and hugging them with fervor. Unbeknownst to them, these two children helped fill the empty space in my heart. After numerous runs and rosy cheeks, we returned for hot chocolate and cookies and settled in to watch a movie.

The next day, we took the two youngsters to visit our good friends, Jeannie and Phil, who had four children in the same age range as my boys and our guests. We were glad to provide other kids for Keila and Gabe to play with while we enjoyed a visit with the adults. By witnessing them having a great time with the other brood, it was obvious that the feeling was mutual.

"I know you miss your kids, so is that why you decided to have surrogates?" Jeannie asked me and laughed.

"Is it that obvious?" I said.

Jeannie knew me well enough to recognize that taking care of these children fulfilled my needs as much as it aided their parents.

Three days with our young visitors went by quickly and without incident. We had a great time playing with Legos, making up games, and reading books together. When Shaina and Morrie returned to retrieve their children, they were clearly more relaxed and rejuvenated from their time alone.

"We're so grateful," Morrie said.

"They were perfect," I said and smiled at the children. "Same time next year?" I asked, probably sounding very desperate.

Not only was the time with these two little ones the best gift that year, but it was the start of our new Christmas tradition.

—Dalia Gesser—

20

The New Elf on the Shelf

You will do foolish things,
but do them with enthusiasm.
~Colette

Dwight on a Sprite became our family tradition a few years after the explosion in popularity of The Elf on the Shelf. We had been inundated with social media posts from our friends of their Elf on the Shelf dolls. It was cute — at first. Elfie most often was cleverly posed, complete with props, custom scenes and every other thing imaginable. One day, maybe Elfie was lifting weights. The next, he might be eating cookies, and the next day perhaps he was watching a movie.

Three years ago, we decided that we wanted to start our own family tradition, similar to Elfie. However, I promised myself that our tradition would never involve the actual Elf on the Shelf.

I had gone shopping one late October day, and I happened across a Dwight Schrute action figure. Dwight was on the television show, *The Office*. I can't remember what inspired me, but "Dwight on a Sprite" just popped into my head. I immediately purchased the action figure and a 16-ounce bottle of Sprite. I took him home and tied him to the bottle with a piece of ribbon. Just like that, Dwight on a Sprite was born. His catchphrase was based upon the character in the show: "Find me… if you dare!"

Here are our rules for Dwight on a Sprite: Each night, a different person hides him. He must remain inside the house and not in the attic or basement. The person finding Dwight gets a piece of candy from the family Advent calendar, and then that person becomes the next hider. If Dwight is not found by 6:00 P.M. the following day, all family members who were searching must pay a one-dollar penalty. As a reward for such a good hiding job, the person hiding Dwight gets to eat that day's Advent calendar candy. Any "penalties" from not finding Dwight are collected, set aside and later given as a donation to our local animal shelter.

The first year, Dwight wasn't found for four consecutive days, and he accumulated a twelve-dollar fine. In December 2020, during the worst of the Covid outbreak, Dwight remained hidden from December fourth to the seventeenth. During that time, he collected a whopping forty-two-dollar fine and a total of seventy-eight dollars for the season. It turned out that he had been hiding under a pile of decorative bathroom towels. It is safe to say, it has become harder and harder to find Dwight when he is hidden.

On December twenty-fourth, Dwight packs up his Sprite and heads back to the North Pole until the following December first.

So, Dwight on a Sprite has become our silly tradition. It's fun and for a good cause. And, of course, I make sure that I post his location on social media each and every time he is found. Take that, Elfie.

— Brian Michael —

21

The Little Tree of Life

The darkness of the whole world cannot swallow
the glowing of a candle.
~Robert Altinger

Just a few weeks ago, on a warm Sunday afternoon, my husband and I embarked on an adventure. As parents suffering from a fresh case of "empty-nest syndrome," we went in search of an interesting way to spend the day together.

As we drove the streets of Los Angeles, my husband suggested we visit the Simon Wiesenthal Museum of Tolerance. I had often thought of taking a tour, but like most residents of Southern California, I got distracted and forgot. We agreed that it would be an educational experience to share.

As we approached the museum, I felt an inner tension building within me. For just a moment, I became anxious and afraid, and almost suggested we turn the car around and go someplace else. My husband could sense my uneasiness, and he gently took my hand to comfort me. By now, we were turning into the dark, cavernous underground parking structure. As we descended into the parking lot, I felt a sense of foreboding.

Our tour began with an experience that truly caught me off guard. As we stood in line with our tickets in hand, a security guard asked me to step through an archway metal detector, which had just been set off by my large silver earrings. I felt very vulnerable, humbled and almost naked. Then the security guard asked me to relinquish my purse for an inspection.

He matter-of-factly emptied all personal contents of my purse onto a large table to examine. We were told this procedure was done routinely to prevent any acts of violence to the Holocaust exhibition. As the guard returned my purse to me, I found myself slinking away from the crowd to hide near a water fountain. I felt stripped and humiliated, and I realized later that day what a powerful impact those first few minutes had on my heart and soul.

We were then given instructions to wander about the designated areas of the museum and to return to the lobby area at 4:00 P.M. for admission into the private areas and displays. As my husband and I wandered the halls of the building, I continued to feel anxious. To distract myself, I went into one of the museum's gift shops. I was instantly attracted to a case full of exotic earrings. Then, suddenly, I spotted a small table filled with an assortment of menorahs. Some were ceramic and painted with bright colors. Others were more traditional and made of metals. What really caught my eye was a little menorah that looked like a small silver tree. It was appropriately called "The Tree of Life."

As I stood there holding the menorah in my hands, I traveled back to a long-forgotten time in my childhood. I was born to Jewish parents and raised in a rather non-religious Reform Jewish home. We did not attend a temple but we did celebrate certain Jewish holidays. That memory carried me back to our celebration of Hanukah and the small, tarnished menorah filled with tiny, colorful candles that we burned each night for eight nights. It was a happy and joyful time for our family.

Suddenly, my mind returned to the present. I found I was holding the little silver "Tree of Life" closely to my chest and felt warm tears trickling down my cheeks. I had somehow bonded with the little menorah, and I decided to purchase it.

It was an extremely emotional event for me because it would be the very first symbolic possession of my birth as a Jew.

It was an amazing act on my part because, twenty-eight years earlier, I had attempted to run from my family, my past and my Judaic heritage. As a young girl of eighteen, I ran away as fast as I could to save myself, not realizing until now that I also ran away from my roots, my heritage, my genesis....

I dated Gentile men exclusively, and at the age of twenty-one, I married a handsome, soft-spoken Episcopalian man with an English last name. I hid behind that name and ignorantly tried to build a new life and identity.

Our next stop on the museum tour brought us to a large Plexiglas display case filled with the personal possessions of an exterminated Jewish family from Poland. There were baby pictures, tiny infant shoes, a man's antique pocket watch, and a large china serving plate with a lovely little girl's photographed face in the center.

I felt like an intruder sifting through the delicate remains of this Polish family who were long gone. What I then realized was that those Polish Jews were not strangers at all. In some poignant and historical way, we were very much connected because I, too, was born a Jew. Once again, I found myself wiping away more tears from my cheeks. Suddenly, I recognized that the little girl's face on the china platter was not an anonymous stranger. She strongly resembled our own beautiful, older daughter, Sasha. At that moment, as I gazed into the face of that innocent Jewish child, two opposing points within me finally met in the middle.

For the first time in my life, I felt balanced and complete. It was as if the past and the present were truly face-to-face, desiring peace and oneness, no longer needing to hide!

As we continued on the tour, we saw walls covered with photos of many non-Jewish people who came forward and risked their own lives and their families to help hide Jews from the Nazis. I learned a powerful lesson about heroism that day.

The museum was filled with many multiracial and multiethnic visitors. At times, I would catch an uncomfortable glance from someone standing near me who was Black or Hispanic. I felt I was being silently judged for living in a white woman's skin. Did they know I was a victim of prejudice? That, as a small child living in a predominantly Gentile neighborhood, I was made fun of for being the only Jewish child, and

I became the target of taunts and stones being thrown?

What I learned that day at the Museum of Tolerance will live within my heart forever. I will never again casually dismiss all the events of the Holocaust or the many people, both Jewish and Gentile, who perished in vain. I will also never be ashamed to call myself a Jew… a member of a strong, surviving people.

Tonight, my husband and I lit the third tiny, colorful candle in my precious "Tree of Life" menorah. This is the first Hanukkah as an adult woman that I have felt free to celebrate my rich heritage. It is my way of saying to all those who perished in the Holocaust, "I promise, you will all live on in my heart and never be forgotten."

—Judith Hayes—

22

Chipotle Christmas

It is Christmas in the heart that puts
Christmas in the air.
~W.T. Ellis

The candles had melted to half their height by the time the children arrived for Christmas dinner. I scurried around the kitchen trying to reheat food in the microwave, salvage soggy salads, and get dessert on the table before everyone was too tired to enjoy pie, but the stress of the day was palpable.

Splitting time equally between Mom's house and Dad's house on Christmas Day had always been challenging for the children — an unfortunate consequence of living with divorced parents. And now that they were both married, with new family obligations of their own, there simply wasn't enough time in the day to please everyone.

Christmas had become a burden. So, late that evening, after everyone left the house, when not a creature was stirring (not even a mouse), I made a promise to myself: Next year, I would simplify Christmas!

The following year, when the holiday season arrived, I remembered the intention I had set to simplify Christmas. But where was I to begin? Sitting in front of the fire, sipping on coffee and planning the holiday schedule, I suddenly had a revelation. Divorced families didn't have traditions because everything they had experienced before, as a family unit, was gone. This was the reason why Christmas had gotten so complicated.

I set my half-empty cup of coffee on the table and began to weep.

Making New Traditions |

How much time had I wasted trying to force old habits into new rhythms that simply didn't work? What my family needed was a respite from the angst of trying to manage unrealistic expectations, like sharing equal time on Christmas Day between four families. Healing for everyone would come when obligation was replaced with anticipation, creating new rhythms that would allow our family to celebrate Christmas at a time and place where joy was possible and gratitude was plentiful.

Sniffling, I leaned over and tended to the fire with an iron poker. With each gentle prod, the logs shifted back and forth, forcing air between the spaces and allowing new flames to burst forward. That's when it hit me. Moving was the answer to my dilemma!

Although we had always celebrated Christmas on December twenty-fifth, I was pretty sure God would be happy to honor Jesus any day of the year, so I opened the calendar app on my phone and swiped forward to December sixteenth. Nine days before Christmas would be plenty of time to avoid the chaos of managing overburdened schedules, so I sent an e-mail to the family explaining my desire to simplify Christmas and asked them to save the date for a holiday celebration. To my surprise and delight, the response was overwhelmingly positive. Everyone could make it — even Santa agreed to send his elves with presents — and my holiday spirit began to soar.

The next hurdle to jump was how to handle all the cooking! Preparing and serving a holiday meal was a lot of work — especially for a single mom like me — and most of Christmas Day had traditionally been spent preparing food. Truthfully, I didn't want to cook anymore! What I yearned to do was spend time together laughing, eating, watching movies, and eating pie! I was tired of shopping, cooking, and baking for days, only to be disappointed by having to cram all our holiday fun into ninety minutes of frustration. It was like waiting in line for hours, on the hottest day of the year, for a roller-coaster ride that lasted thirty seconds. What I needed was a pass to the express lane.

In order to spend less time cooking and more time having fun, I needed to get out of the kitchen. I had always served a traditional Midwestern meal for Christmas dinner: turkey, "real" mashed potatoes, vegetables, Jell-O salad, and pie. The new tradition, however, would be simpler. I made a radical decision to order our Christmas meal online from Chipotle.

I downloaded the app to my mobile phone and waited for it to load. Ordering food online was truly a maverick moment for me, and I was worried I wouldn't know how to do it. But the menu was easy to navigate, and I quickly chose the perfect meal: two types of meat, rice, beans, toppings, and chips. It was everything we needed at the click of a button. There was one last thing to do before completing the order. Paying a fee to deliver the entire meal to my front door was a small price for the convenience of not having to leave the house, so I checked the box and placed the order.

If I was being true to my new tradition, no cooking also meant no baking. Scanning the Internet, I found a local bakery that made fresh pumpkin pies daily, and I made a note on my calendar to call three weeks before Christmas to place my order.

I had never experienced such ease preparing for a holiday meal.

I waited for December 16, 2017, with anticipation, wondering how the new tradition would feel for my family. My eyes sparkled with delight when the family arrived, and I watched the events of the day begin to unfold. Instead of greeting each other with an apology for being late like we had done for so many years in the past, we turned our frowns upside down and welcomed each other with warm smiles and grizzly-bear hugs. It was the most meaningful exchange I had experienced with my adult children in several years, and I could feel my emotional tank filling with holiday cheer.

The food arrived from Chipotle thirty minutes later, hot and ready to serve. The children offered to transfer the food to some of my fancy china dishes to make the meal seem more "formal," but I declined, acknowledging that I would rather watch a movie after dinner than wash dishes, and they spontaneously applauded. It wasn't until that moment that I realized the burden my precious children had been carrying all those years. They had never had time to enjoy Christmas. Creating a new tradition by simplifying the way we "do" Christmas together restored what divorce had stolen so many years ago — Christmastime with Mom.

One year after our first Chipotle Christmas, nineteen years after my divorce, I married Mark, blending our new family of eight. Three weeks after getting married, Mark and I were sitting by the fire in our new family home planning the holiday schedule. Mark confessed that he was struggling with how to celebrate Christmas as a divorced father because it felt so… sad. I smiled warmly and gave him a big hug. "Chipotle Christmas," I whispered in his ear. And the rest, as they say, is history.

—Denise Fleissner Ralston—

23

Three Kings Day

Travel and change of place impart
new vigor to the mind.
~Lucius Annaeus Seneca

B linking back tears, I wrapped my red wool scarf more tightly around my neck. I'd been told that Spain almost never had snow like this, but the bitter cold didn't bother me nearly as much as being away from my friends at Christmas.

I appreciated the opportunity to see Europe, an experience of a lifetime many teens would never have. Even so, I longed to be attending Christmas parties and dances, not scouring the streets of Granada in freezing weather with my mother, looking for something that resembled the holidays back home in Pasadena.

My parents, who are teachers at the local community college, had both received sabbaticals after waiting years, and we were traveling to the places they'd dreamt of visiting all their lives. Their plans happened to come together my senior year of high school, so instead of the bustle of a high-school senior year, I was taking my classes by correspondence. In the days before online courses, I filled out worksheets that I mailed to instructors and then took exams at embassies in the different cities where we stayed.

I reminded myself how lucky I was to be seeing these foreign countries, and I did enjoy learning about the different cultures. I'd never seen anything like the lavish Spanish Catholic churches filled with gold leaf statues and stained-glass windows; the bustling open-air markets offering handicrafts; and the lively flamenco music with guitar players, singers and dancers in brightly colored shirts and swirling dresses. Still, the holidays were hard.

I made sure not to complain. I knew that my mother thought this trip was the best present she and my father could give each other and me. But it was Christmas Eve, and we couldn't find a single Christmas tree, bit of holly or even a plastic Santa to decorate our hotel room. Every shop window was filled with nativities and other religious memorabilia. Of course, that was as it should be for the sacred meaning of Christmas, a celebration of the birth of Jesus Christ. But I couldn't help missing the tinsel-wrapped lampposts of Pasadena, shop windows animated with Santa and his elves, and our family's traditional Christmas Eve with friends singing carols and exchanging presents.

"Don't worry," my mother said. "I have something for you to open tomorrow."

At least we weren't following the Spanish tradition of waiting until January 6, Three Kings Day, to exchange presents. Also called the Epiphany, this was the day when the Magi visited the Christ child with their gifts of gold, myrrh and frankincense.

We spent the night before Christmas on a train to Madrid and checked into the Hotel Nacional on Christmas Day. The next morning, my mother gave me a beautiful wool sweater that she'd knitted on the planes and trains we took that fall and winter, and I loved it.

Next, we took the train to Barcelona where people were shoveling snow off sidewalks with dustpans because they had never needed a snow shovel before. Even as I immersed myself in the sights of our guided city tour, I grieved for the warmth and sunshine of southern California in December.

On New Year's Eve, I wrote letters to my friends back home, picturing them camped out along Colorado Boulevard in Pasadena where we always awaited the fabled Rose Parade. How I wished I could be with them. Over the next few days, although my mood matched the bleak weather, I focused on reviewing my high-school French and hiding my sadness from my parents.

On January third, we flew to Nice, France, and checked into a pension. Each day, we had breakfast and dinner with several other guests and the owners of the pension — an amiable couple with a boy and girl in their early teens. My father had been on a mission to France and was comfortable chatting with them. I remembered a little French from high school, and so did my mother, so we enjoyed those meals and the developing camaraderie with the owners.

On the morning of January sixth, breakfast included something special along with the baguettes, jam, tea and hot chocolate. Our hostess had baked cakes called the "Galette des Rois," or "Cake of the Kings."

Evidently, Three Kings Day, the Epiphany that I'd learned about in Spain, was also an important holiday in France. One of the most beloved traditions of Three Kings Day was the King's Cake. The cakes looked somewhat like large, round, fruit-filled danishes. Our hostess's eyes twinkled as she explained in halting English that we had all been given a traditional Three Kings Cake, and she had baked a small, porcelain king into one of them. Whoever got the miniature would be king or queen for a day. She insisted that even she didn't know whose piece held the king.

"Check each bite," she advised.

"I want it, I want it," all the young people cried, their faces alight with excitement. "I want to be king."

"I never win anything," I muttered under my breath as I carefully carved out bites with my fork and ran my tongue over the morsels as I chewed. "Tink." My fork hit something hard. I cautiously scraped cake away from the small figurine. "I have it!" I gasped.

Our host and hostess, several other guests and my parents burst into applause. I giggled with delight as our hostess placed a cardboard crown on my head. "You are the queen," my mother said, her smile as broad as mine must be.

I walked with my parents along the shore of the Mediterranean that day in my cardboard crown, enjoying the swelling and breaking of gentle waves on white beaches. Everyone we passed smiled, nodded and pointed to my crown. Shopkeepers fussed over me as we searched for a Three Kings Day gift for the family at our pension. Taking part in one of their most important traditions, feeling so special, I couldn't stop smiling.

The more I thought about it, the more my appreciation grew for Three Kings Day, not just for my crown but for the idea of setting aside Christmas as the major religious holiday and Three Kings Day as the day more about gifting friends and family.

I will never know for sure, but I like to imagine our hostess recognized a young woman badly in need of cheer, and she created a holiday experience for me that I will remember forever. I now honor that experience by making January sixth Three Kings Day, a day to do something special for my family and friends.

— Samantha Ducloux Waltz —

24

Chicken Soup for the Soul

Keeping Cards, Keeping Memories

The bond that links your true family is not one of blood,
but of respect and joy in each other's life.
~Richard Bach

Because I worked retail for many years, my relationship with Christmas — especially decorating — is mostly one of convenience. Thanks to an article I read about ways to lower stress and streamline to-do lists for the busy holidays, I pack away all the Christmas cards we receive every year with the Christmas decorations.

When the next Christmas arrives and we break out the decorations, it is easy to remember who I need to send a card to because the cards from the previous year are in my hand.

But there's also something wonderful — if bittersweet — that came from the habit.

I didn't have grandparents until I was in my thirties. My mother's father passed weeks before she was born. My father's father died shortly after my parents were married. My father's mother died before I was born, and my mother's mother came to live with us for hospice when I was barely a toddler. My vague memories of her include aniseed candy and being asked to sit quietly while my mother tended to her.

Meeting the family of someone you love is always tricky, but when you're a gay couple, there's an extra level of nervousness. Both my then-boyfriend (now-husband) and I were born in England, and so when a trip to England was planned for his nan's ninetieth birthday, I found myself going with him.

I was terrified.

I'd never really interacted with grandparents, and my relationship with my parents had not survived coming out. That his family had been incredibly loving and welcoming was not lost on me, but it wasn't quite a panacea for the worries I felt about being introduced to his grandmother.

I'd prepared for dissembling, for potential downgrading to "a friend," and all the other possibilities that might come into play to keep things smooth.

Instead, my introduction was clearly stated by my boyfriend's father. "This is Nathan. He's Dan's boyfriend."

We shook hands and said hello, and then — since I truly was the stranger in the room — I let the families all greet each other and catch up. I sat with my boyfriend, and he smiled at me between catching up his grandmother on his life.

Little by little, I relaxed.

The following morning, I was one of the first to wake, despite the time change going in the other direction. I washed my face and sort of stumbled around, trying to decide if I should go back to bed or not, and walked into the small parlor.

Nan sat there, already up and about. She smiled at me.

"Good morning."

"Good morning," I said, not quite panicked at being alone with the ninety-year-old grandmother of my boyfriend, but pretty darn close.

"You're up early," she said.

"I don't sleep very well at the best of times," I said. "With the time change, I've no idea if I'm coming or going."

She laughed at that — and commiserated, saying she was a terrible sleeper, too. Then we sat in silence for a bit, and she asked me if I'd mind making us both tea, which I happily set to. When I came back into the room with the cups, she was looking at the dozens of cards on display.

"You know," she said. "I had three more birthday cards last year."

I handed her some tea and then considered. "If it makes you feel better, I probably only got three cards in total for my last birthday."

She smiled and then tilted her head, returning her focus to the array of birthday cards on the mantel. "Oh. Wait. No. It's fine. They died."

I'd been halfway through a swallow and did a little choke-laugh around my tea. She grinned at me, and I realized she'd timed her comment on purpose.

It was the first of many signs of Nan's lovely sense of humor.

From that morning on, my name was included on all the birthday and Christmas cards from Nan every year. Her handwriting was a perfect mix of shaky and beautiful penmanship, and I took delight in writing cards back in return with my own — far poorer — handwriting.

We visited her a few more times over the years when she trounced us at *Scrabble* on a regular basis, did the daily crossword every morning, and had a (very) generous glass of sherry each afternoon. We talked about the books we'd read and our love of English birds, and at one point she even confided in me that she always left a little bit of food on her plate at every meal because she knew it annoyed her caretaker.

As I said, she had a lovely sense of humor.

But to me? When I think of my husband's nan, I always think of those cards.

The year after Nan passed, when I opened the box and started going through the cards, I found the last Christmas card we'd received from Nan in the pile.

I hadn't considered how keeping the previous year's cards could be a memorial, too.

It was like finding a message from her again. I remembered the day I met her, and the morning we'd sat together in her parlor having tea, and talking about her upcoming birthday, along with the number of cards and the reason for their decline. My husband and I set that final Christmas card aside and hung it on a string.

We put up her final card every year.

— Nathan Burgoine —

Making New Traditions | 85

25

Chicken Soup for the Soul

My First Christmas

What one loves in childhood stays in the heart forever.
~Mary Jo Putney

W e didn't celebrate Christmas, and I couldn't have a Christmas tree even though I longed for one. Walking down the dark winter streets at night, I thought the Christmas trees lighting up my neighbors' windows were the most beautiful and magical things in the world. I tried asking for a tree. Begging, actually. My mother gently explained, "We are Jewish. Jews do not celebrate Christmas." On one level, I understood. On another, my heart was broken.

It wasn't easy being a little Jewish girl at Christmastime. The world suddenly became confusing. Was I allowed to sing Christmas songs with my class, or should I just mouth the words? Why did the teacher show a movie about "Christmas Around the World" and not one about "Hanukkah Around the World"? Was it all right for me to join in when the whole class made Christmas ornaments for their trees?

Then, one Christmas, my grandfather came over. He was a big, powerful man, an immigrant who helped organize the Chicago Ladies' Garment Workers' Union, fighting against sweatshops and twelve-hour workdays. He asked if I would like to go to a Christmas party with him.

"Jews don't believe in Christmas," I told him.

He laughed. "Well, I think we must believe there is a Christmas. And my union is putting on a big party for all the workers and their children. Would you like to come?"

I wore my velvet party dress, gripping my grandfather's hand as we entered the enormous Union Hall. The room was filled with people. Children raced around. Musicians dressed as elves played Christmas songs. Long tables were filled with trays of holiday cookies, cakes, punch, candy canes — everything to gladden a child's heart. Tall piles of wrapped presents filled the large stage, and a majestic chair sat in the center. Best of all, Christmas trees ringed the room. Under them were boxes of tinsel and decorations so everyone could help trim the trees. I joined a group of other little girls, laughing as we hung ornaments and threw on strands of tinsel as high as we could reach.

Suddenly, the band stopped. There was a drumroll as Santa Claus entered the hall. The children screamed, and I followed my new friends, falling in line behind the laughing giant as he made his way to the stage. One by one, he called us up. By the time it was my turn, my heart was pounding. I could hardly breathe. I glanced at my grandfather to be sure it was all right for me to go up. He smiled and nodded. Santa asked if I had been a good little girl all year. "Yes," I said quietly, too shy to look at him. Then he reached down and handed me one of the presents. Mrs. Claus gave me a little paper bag as I left the stage. Inside were wonders like large, jeweled rings, candy necklaces, and a little pin with two tiny pinecones and a sprig of fake holly. My grandfather pinned it on my dress. It looked beautiful.

On our way home, I asked him why I couldn't have a Christmas tree at home but could go with him to his union's party. After a moment's thought, he said, "There's a difference between celebrating something because you believe in it and helping friends celebrate something in which they believe. You invite friends to your home to help celebrate Passover and Hanukkah, but does that make them Jewish?"

"No," I said.

"And did helping my friends celebrate Christmas today make us Christian?"

I smiled. "No."

He squeezed my hand gently. "It is important to take pride in those things that are important to you and to share them with friends. It is equally important to honor those things important to your friends.

Does that make sense to you?"

It did. It made perfect sense. The next day, I invited my best friend over for Hanukkah to play dreidel, eat latkes and help light the Hanukkah candles. The next week, I went to her house to help her family celebrate Christmas. We sang songs, decorated the tree and baked Christmas cookies.

For many years, long after my grandfather passed away, I kept that little pin with the two pinecones and sprig of holly on my dresser. It was a daily reminder of my wonderful memories of him and the life-long lessons learned at my first Christmas.

—Sue Rissman-Sussman—

26

Giving Cards Their Due

*At the heart of every family tradition
is a meaningful experience.*
~Author Unknown

"Why do you have Christmas cards out? It's spring," asked my neighbor one sunny day.

We have this tradition in our family to read a Christmas card each night before dinner. Sometimes, it takes us into spring.

In December when these winter wishes come to our mailbox, life is hectic. The busyness of baking, cleaning, buying, and wrapping presents can make one's head spin. When those holiday cards come into our home, all I can do is glance at them or do a quick read.

The custom of placing all holiday cards in an assigned wicker basket helped us keep track of the influx.

At the dinner table, a card is picked from the basket and read out loud. Praying for the health of that person or family helps keep them in our memories. Conversations about people that we don't get to see very often help the children feel more connected to our extended families. Slowly relishing the cards and the stories helps make them very special.

This "treasure of wishes" that we keep in our card basket allows our celebration to continue through the next few months.

— Christy Piszkiewicz —

Hanukkah Goes On

*The future belongs to those who give
the next generation reason for hope.*
~Pierre Teilhard de Chardin

The growth of our family has given me pause to reflect on their diversity and individual choices in life. Each and every member of this very special clan has a different mindset in job choices, living locales and religion.

Our children were raised to analyze choices in life and think for themselves. My mother is Catholic and my father Jewish. We were raised celebrating all the holidays. We lit the menorah on Hanukkah and decorated the tree for Santa. I looked forward to every celebration and raised our own children with that in mind.

Our children married and our family became even more diverse. Only one married into the Jewish faith, the others into different forms of Christianity. We were blessed with five grandchildren. Two of those grandchildren are now married and are living in different states. And along came a great-granddaughter!

I have watched as attendance has dwindled for our family traditions, and I've worried that this new generation will not know of the special wonders of their great-grandmother's Jewish faith.

In an effort to make sure our great-granddaughter living in another state was exposed to all the wonders of the holiday season and was included in the traditions of her Jewish heritage I began a new tradition between the two of us.

I bought her a menorah and candles and printed the words to the prayer and the song to sing when lighting the candles. I bought a book for her mom to read to teach her the meaning of this beautiful holiday. I bought her a dreidel to spin and Hanukkah Gelt (chocolate coins). And I wrapped eight small gifts and numbered them for her to open each day of Hanukkah. Coloring books and crayons, small dolls, jewelry, puzzles, baking utensils, aprons for cooking with her grandma and so much more.

What fun it's been for me to pick up small gifts all year with her Hanukkah package in mind. How exciting it's been for the last three years to watch her on Zoom each morning for eight days open her packages with such enthusiasm. And most of all, what a warm and wonderful feeling I have inside knowing that my heritage will continue to live on in this very diverse and wonderful family.

— Kristine Byron —

Chapter
4

Around the Table

28

The Passing of the Table

In every conceivable manner, the family is link to our
past, bridge to our future.
~Alex Haley

My mother seemed fragile. She had lost her strength for the first time in my life, after losing both her parents in the past thirty days. I was driving her back to my grandmother's home to meet her six siblings, where they would divvy up their parents' possessions.

There was nothing much of monetary value there. The distribution should've taken only a few hours, but there were memories to re-live and feathers to be ruffled.

Not a single one of the seven siblings acknowledged the most oversized item in the tiny house. They walked around it like it wasn't there. The oval maple table with eight chairs — shabby and well worn but the heart and soul of that home. Mamaw had been the cook, the magician of the kitchen. Her food was medicine; it could cure anything.

"I'll take it," my mother murmured.

All eyes shifted to her and a silence fell over the room.

Finally, Uncle George asked, "You know what comes with it?"

Mom said, "I do."

She placed a cigarette between her scarlet lips and lit it with a match, steadying the flame. She had just accepted the position of matriarch of the Saylor clan.

Three months later, on a cold Thanksgiving morning, I drove myself to Mom's in the wee hours of the morning to help. We chopped more celery and onion than any family might imagine and peeled potatoes for hours. Thank God for the Cuisinart, a luxury my grandmother didn't need or want.

With the inheritance of the table, Mom took on the responsibility of hosting Thanksgiving and Christmas. Mamaw had managed it effortlessly, baking and prepping weeks before the dinner. My mother inherited the skill to cook for thirty-five or forty people with no RSVPs; she knew they would come. Ten months out of the year, seven siblings and their families lived separate lives, but holidays were sacred family times. On Thanksgiving and Christmas, nothing could keep them from being together.

My mother was not concerned about a tidy house. Nor did she fret about her attire. Like her mother, the focus was on the food. The anxiety of recreating the food as delicious as Mamaw's caused Mom to bite her long fingernails to the quick.

The kitchen on 317 Catalpa Street was twice the size of the one on Saylor Road, with two full-sized refrigerators, the Cuisinart, and a dishwasher. Attempting to reassure my mother, I pointed out that things would be easier than at Mamaw's. The cigarette smoke was thick in the kitchen, and one cigarette was lit off the last red ember of the previous one.

One family group at a time trickled in, tossing coats toward the coat rack. The rowdy conversations ensued as if nothing had changed. Typical Saylor giggling, gossiping — and critiquing each dish. "The macaroni salad needs more pickles," Linda said.

"Then, put 'em in it," Mom yelled.

The door slammed. A bellowing baritone tune rang through the rooms. "Over the river and through the woods... Where do you want these chocolate pies?" Uncle Doug asked.

The homemade stuffing was the main conversation piece of the day and the most troublesome for Mom. Deep inside, she knew the dressing, not her hospitality, would make or break her debut as matriarch.

The Saylor clan stood around the stainless-steel bowl dipping fingers into the raw stuffing.

"It's dry," Pauline said.

"Needs more sage," S.V. piped up.

"Oooh, too much onion," declared someone with tiny fingers.

"Don't taste like Mommy's, is what," mumbled Aunt Phyllis. Aunt Phyllis finished every sentence with "is what."

My brother Clinton was finishing up the deviled eggs when Mom roared, "Don't forget the pep-a-reek-a!" We all laughed at her pronunciation.

"It's 'paprika,'" Clinton responded.

Mom said, "Whatever. Just make them pretty."

It was time to mash the potatoes. I could see Mom's exhaustion as she wiped the sweat from her brow. Reluctantly, I reached for the mixer.

"NO LUMPS," Mom ordered. "You'll never hear the end of it if you make lumpy mashed potatoes."

I closed my eyes and channeled my inner Mamaw. I mashed over ten pounds of potatoes without a lump in the entire batch.

Strangers peering through the bay window might witness a jubilant family, a festive Thanksgiving gathering full of joy. But a palpable undercurrent hung heavier than the cigarette smoke in that room. This Thanksgiving was different.

We placed the food on the table via a chaotic assembly line. Salads, casseroles, broccoli, beans, mashed potatoes, sweet potatoes, peas, giblet gravy, and baskets of dinner rolls.

Many dishes were placed on the beloved table with platters of stuffing at each end. We all scrambled for seats, waiting for the turkey. It took two men to hoist it out of the oven and onto the platter. They set the oversized golden bird onto the table. Mom settled at the head. Everyone started filling their plates—chaotic, as always. No "Pass the potatoes, please." Everyone talked over everybody else. It was a free-for-all of reaching for this or that.

Then I heard a creak.

Without warning, the table started giving way from the middle, collapsing in slow motion.

The commotion came to a halt. There was utter silence. All the food began to slide to the center in a large heap. My heart skipped a beat. "Oh, God," someone whispered.

I can still see Uncle George's lanky body slithering out of his chair, sliding beneath the table and scuttling to upright the center. Dishes slid like pinballs, bouncing off each other. A bowl of cranberry sauce teetered toward the floor. The gravy bounced off my potato bowl. The turkey platter tried to stay centered. Mom's eyes grew wide, her hand covering her mouth. The collective energy, shock and disbelief kept us from uttering a sound until Aunt Pauline, trying to suppress her earsplitting cackle, let it loose.

Her burst of laughter was contagious. Laughter filled the room as food scooted this way and that.

The table was falling apart.

"Hurry up! I can't just sit here while y'all eat!" George yelled.

"Why not?" Pauline yelled back.

My dog Tinker frenetically cleaned up the food falling on the floor — causing more chaos.

At last, the serving bowls were relocated to the stove and kitchen counters. Some of us ate standing; others sat in chairs around the broken table with plates in laps; some carried food to the living room and den. The Saylor families were scattered throughout my childhood home, and it felt right. Just like Thanksgiving in Mamaw's tiny house.

Each holiday after that the family gathered around the reinforced table reminiscing about the first Thanksgiving without their mother, the irony of the table collapsing, and the possibility that Mamaw may have orchestrated the whole thing. She knew exactly how to use her food and that table to unite her brood.

— Charlotte Bowling-Roth —

Thanksgiving with Strangers

Thanksgiving is a time of togetherness and gratitude.
~Nigel Hamilton

I t was just three days from Thanksgiving, and my husband, Gerald, and I were very far from home. As a touring music duo, we'd gotten used to being away from our family for months on end. We'd missed countless birthdays, anniversaries, and family celebrations because of our unconventional work schedule.

But this was the first time we were going to be away from our families for Thanksgiving. We were currently on our first tour across the Canadian prairies. I'm not exaggerating when I say that we didn't know anyone for hundreds of miles!

Technically, I knew we would be away for Thanksgiving, but the reality of it didn't really dawn on me before we hit the road. Now, the date loomed on the calendar.

I could just see it: In three days, we would be alone in a hotel room, eating cheap take-out, watching reruns on hotel cable, and feeling very sorry for ourselves.

The thought of it was more than I could bear.

I decided to be proactive. I wrote a post on Facebook: "We're about to spend Thanksgiving alone in Winnipeg, Manitoba. Does anyone know of a church or community center hosting a public dinner?"

There, I thought. *With all the people we know, someone has to have*

Around the Table | 97

some idea!

A friend immediately wrote back. "My friends live outside the city. I'll connect you with them."

So, three days later, we found ourselves driving to the small town of Dauphin, Manitoba, to spend Thanksgiving with strangers.

Our hand-scrawled directions led us off the highway and down a gravel road. We pulled up in front of a small, lakeside house. A smiling couple waved at us from the front porch. Gerald and I stepped out of the car, a little tired, a little hungry, and mildly apprehensive. Thanksgiving is a time for family. Would it be okay to intrude on this private celebration?

As we stepped into Betty and Gary's home, we were immediately met with warmth. The wood stove took every bit of fall chill out of the air. The sun on the glittering lake was blindingly beautiful, and the smell of food enveloped us like a soft blanket. Turkey, stuffing, veggies, and piles of desserts — what a feast!

And the warmth didn't just come from the home or the food. It came from Betty, Gary, and their guests. We gathered around the table; introductions were made. We discovered that no one there was family by blood. Instead, we were all connected by something much greater.

Our apprehension melted away as we were drawn into this circle of friendship. We told stories, shared laughs, and, as the day called us to, gave thanks.

I was raised that you never go empty-handed to a dinner party, but making a dish is a bit of a challenge when you're on the road. Instead, we offered them something else. I quietly pulled Betty aside and said, "After the meal, if you like, we would love to perform a mini-concert for your guests as our contribution to the evening."

She replied, "You have no idea how much we would love that!"

So, as everyone licked up the final crumbs of pumpkin pie, Gerald pulled out his guitar, and we began to sing. We shared songs we had written, filled with a message of hope and joy. We sang favorite hymns, and got our new friends to sing along with us. We ended with a prayer of thanks and a roof-splitting version of "How Great Thou Art."

Since that time, Betty and Gary have become our true friends.

We've spent many nights in their sweet cabin by the lake and shared countless meals together. We've fallen in love with the glorious sunsets that blaze across the prairie sky. We've sung in their local church, joining friends and strangers together in song.

We thought we were going to spend Thanksgiving with strangers, but we really didn't. Something special happens when good food is generously shared around an open table. Conversations begin. Laughter starts to flow. Divisions disappear. Relationships are born. Memories are created.

Through the simple act of sharing a meal together, we discover we're connected by our desire to love, our need for understanding, and our common humanity.

What a perfect way to celebrate Thanksgiving!

—Allison Lynn—

Christmas Dinner

No matter our age, everyone in our household knows
that cooking and eating together is where the fun is.
~Corky Pollan

The house was full
with family and friends
gathered from near and far.
Full with sounds
of laughter and caroling
tinkling piano, hum of guitar.

Full with aromas of Christmas
cinnamon, vanilla
caramel, chocolate
sweet yams and baby peas.
But most savoured of all

meat.

Roasting for hours
sage and thyme.
The crowd raced to their places
when the dinner bell rang.

Mouths watering
heads bowed in solemn thanks
as the crowning centerpiece arrived.
But the delighted sighs
turned to a collective gasp
when the lid lifted to reveal

a tofurkey!

— Michele Rule —

Chicken Soup
for the Soul

Turkey Tales

*The most important thing in the world
is family and love.*
~John Wooden

Weeks before it arrived, my anxiety about Thanksgiving mounted. We had recently made a cross-country move with our three young children and were still rooting through boxes.

"We should start thinking about plans for Thanksgiving," I suggested.

"Don't worry about it," my husband shrugged. "Heat up some hot dogs, maybe some mac and cheese, and the kids will be happy."

That sounded great. I was off the hook! In holidays past, I had never been solely responsible for cooking a full Thanksgiving dinner. My job was always to bring beverages or a side dish to a large gathering (items that had the highest success rate) and help clean up after the meal.

But as the days crept on, the children began returning from school with their backpacks bulging. They gleefully brandished newly created turkey crafts made from brightly painted handprints, crooked Pilgrim hats, and carefully colored printouts of the *Mayflower*.

"Let's go on a walk and try to find a rock that looks like Plymouth Rock!" Jill shouted to them as they scrambled for their shoes. "Take us on a walk, Mommy!"

The excitement was building, and I had an unnerving feeling that greasy hot dogs and a box of Kraft were going to be woefully insufficient.

"I'm going to try and put on Thanksgiving, Leonard," I blurted late one night.

He eyed me cautiously. "You sure?" Then he sighed. "Okay, then, if you think you can handle it."

"Circumstances demand it," I said nonchalantly. "I've got two days to prepare. The grocery store is open twenty-four hours. I'm going to the store!"

Unfortunately, only a couple of scrappy turkeys remained, and the one I wanted was missing a tag. I found it at the bottom of the bin. "Got it! This is going to work out fine!" I stuck the damp tag on the turkey, so delighted to have it that I paid no attention to the weigh-in at the checkout.

Early Thanksgiving morning, I dragged and bumped the bagged turkey up the stairs to the bathroom scale. (It didn't cross my mind to bring the scale to the kitchen.) My breath was ragged from the effort. The scale read a whopping twenty-eight pounds! I quickly pawed through the kitchen trash to read the tag I'd just thrown out. In small print, it read, "12 lbs."

"What? A twenty-eight-pound turkey for a twelve-pound price? I just committed theft!" I moaned.

Realizing it would take hours longer to cook, I busied myself making an entire dinner, including hors d'oeuvres and three kinds of pies. As a special treat, I laid out a beautiful red tablecloth, candles, and our best china. I was exhausted but knew all the work was worth it for a Thanksgiving to remember in our new home.

Finally, the turkey was done, and we sat down. Everyone ate hungrily as the room grew quiet.

"How come the cheesy zucchini casserole is so crunchy?" Leonard asked.

The kids paused eating.

I froze. "I wondered that myself. It's, uh, kind of a weird recipe. Just smother it in butter."

"This green skin on here," he squinted, holding his fork aloft. "It looks like unpeeled cucumbers!"

"Ewww!" the kids squealed in unison.

In my haste (or ineptitude), I had chosen cucumbers instead of zucchini. "They weren't peeled because I, uh, thought they were zucchini! No one peels zucchini!"

At this point, everyone at the table (including myself) became suspicious of the rest of the menu. We shrugged and moved on to dessert. Fortunately, I am a much better baker than a cook. We sampled all the pies and brownies, and I wrapped up a mountain of leftovers.

After bedtime stories, I tucked the children into bed. It was the end of a good day. We were stuffed and content (I thought). As I dimmed the lights, a whimpering voice spoke. It was Jordan, age seven.

"Wait! What about Thanksgiving?"

"We already had it!" I smiled. "Remember all the food and desserts?"

His blue eyes filled with tears. "That was it? But where were all the people?"

I realized then that a twenty-eight-pound turkey and three kinds of pie can't take the place of the warmth of friends and family.

"Next year, we will invite all the neighbors and get Grandpa a plane ticket so he can come!" I assured him. (My elderly father has a voracious appetite. Combined with his excellent tolerance for less-than-delectable food, it makes him the perfect guest.)

So, for Thanksgiving next year, I have made some promises to myself. Our home will be filled with guests even if it means obtaining them by placing an ad in the local newspaper. I will shop early, maybe even the day after Halloween. I'll choose a turkey with a firmly attached tag. I'll keep warm cucumber dishes off the much smaller menu.

And, just in case, I'll make sure not to overlook the one guest who can help me when all else fails: Oscar Mayer.

— Connie L. Gunkel —

32

The Twenty-Pounder

You can't have Thanksgiving without turkey.
That's like Fourth of July without apple pie
or Friday with no two pizzas.
~Joey Tribbiani, Friends

I never expected to have so much trouble finding a turkey to my liking. Four days before Thanksgiving, I usually purchase my twenty-pound, frozen Butterball turkey so it has time to defrost before cooking.

On the Sunday before Thanksgiving, my ten-year-old granddaughter Olivia and I set out on our task. We went to ShopRite hoping to find a turkey big enough to feed a family of twelve. After fifteen minutes of searching in the freezer and handing frozen turkeys back and forth, trying to see how many pounds they were, we were told that Butterball turkeys that size were not delivered to their store this year. That meant I had to settle for two smaller birds or try elsewhere.

I called my son and told him of my dilemma. He said he would start looking in his area to find me a twenty-pounder. I told him I was still on the hunt and to hold off. I didn't want both of us coming up with two turkeys to cook.

The next store on my list was Aldi before going to Costco, both in my area. For a small store, Aldi seemed to have a better selection of larger Butterball turkeys. All I needed was one. Olivia did some serious freezer diving. I felt like an auctioneer when she read the weight of the turkeys to me, and I repeated them out loud.

"A sixteen-and-a-half-pounder... Can we try for seventeen? Do I hear seventeen? Seventeen, yes. Do I hear seventeen and a half or eighteen? Eighteen and a half, going for nineteen. Do I hear nineteen?"

When Olivia blurted out twenty-and-a-half pounds, I immediately yelled out, "Sold to the highest bidder!" A small group of people had gathered around us, probably confused as to what we were doing. A few caught on and started clapping when I found my turkey.

"Do you always have this much fun shopping together?" one lady asked.

"I always have fun with my granddaughter, shopping or not," I replied.

Olivia's hands were red and cold from the frozen tundra she had been diving in. I promised her a cup of hot chocolate when we got home.

In the process of shopping, we bought some pumpkin cookie-dough ice cream, which we both enjoyed while drinking hot chocolate. It was a delicious treat after our energetic turkey shopping spree.

I am thankful for Thanksgiving and being able to share it with my family. I am also thankful that I only have to shop for a twenty-pounder once a year.

— Irene Maran —

33

Christmas Pancakes

A good cook is like a sorceress
who dispenses happiness.
~Elsa Schiaparelli

"How long does it take to make pancakes?" my boyfriend Randy asked in exasperation as he sat at the kitchen table. It was early Christmas morning. The night before, we had eaten dinner, opened presents with my three boys, and gone to midnight mass.

It had been a perfect evening, but this morning Randy was more than ready to head back home. Randy had been divorced for many years, and his grown children spent Christmas with his ex-wife. He refused to make a big deal about it and wasn't excited about the holidays. I was determined to give him a perfect family Christmas.

Ben, my youngest, had insisted that we have homemade pancakes for breakfast Christmas morning, and he wanted to help. Here I was at 6:00 A.M. with sausages sizzling in the skillet, the electric griddle warming up, and Ben stirring pancake batter. His help did not speed up the process, and now I had a complaining boyfriend to contend with. I decided to ignore Randy's attitude and carefully broke eggs into the bowl.

"Seriously, who takes this much time to make pancakes?" he whined. "You buy a box of pancake mix from the store, mix in some water, and you're done. How hard is it?"

I said a small prayer for patience and continued to ignore him.

"Are we ready for the magic ingredient?" Ben asked.

I smiled and planted a kiss on his little, blond head.

"Yep," I answered, pulling a carton of buttermilk out of the fridge and measuring out the correct amount.

"Seriously, pancakes aren't even my favorite breakfast food," Randy complained. His brow furrowed into a frown.

I leaned my hip against the kitchen counter and spared him an exasperated look.

"You don't have to stay for breakfast," I said, a warning tone in my voice. I didn't want him to leave. What I really wanted was to recapture the lighthearted mood from Christmas Eve that seemed nowhere to be found this morning.

I turned the sausages so they would brown evenly.

"Does this look right?" Ben asked as he stirred the batter.

I looked at the batter, and after a brief discussion, we decided that a little more buttermilk would make for the perfect consistency.

"Okay, we are ready for the test pancake," I announced.

"Are you freaking kidding me?" Randy asked. "What is a test pancake?"

"It's where Mom tests one baby pancake on the griddle to see if everything is okay," Ben explained.

"You have to be kidding," Randy growled. "I've never heard of a test pancake."

"You also believe that pancakes come from a box," Gabe, my middle son, said as he poured himself a glass of orange juice and took a seat at the table. "You know, if you keep complaining, Mom might not even let you have one."

"I might starve to death before she even gets one cooked," Randy grumbled.

Randy's complaining was seriously dampening my holiday spirit.

"This is so stupid," he complained.

I shot him a warning look and helped Ben flip the small tester pancake.

"Come on, Gabe. You've got to admit this is a lot of fuss over pancakes," Randy said, trying to recruit Gabe to his way of thinking.

"You do realize that my mom makes the best pancakes in the world, right?" Gabe answered.

"I seriously doubt it," Randy countered.

Another minute passed, and Ben carefully scooped the pancake onto a waiting plate. As the cooks, Ben and I split the teeny, tiny pancake.

"Perfect," Ben declared.

I had to agree. It was a pretty good pancake.

I lightly greased the hot griddle and poured the pancake batter into perfectly round puddles.

Ben excitedly waited for the bubbles to appear and the edges to crisp before we flipped them over. We waited patiently for the other side to cook, and then Ben scooped them off the hot griddle onto the waiting platter.

I stacked several pancakes on each of my three sons' plates. Randy held out his plate expectantly.

"Sorry, sweetheart," I said. "The first pancakes go to the non-complainers." I tried to soften the words with a smile as I loaded the last pancakes onto the plates.

Randy scowled at me.

The boys ignored him and added pats of real butter and warm maple syrup to their stacks of pancakes. They sank their forks into the fluffy creations, and I waited for the griddle to heat back up. I carefully started the second batch of pancakes.

"I think this is the best batch ever," Nicholas, my oldest, declared as he added more syrup to his stack.

Randy watched my boys as they devoured the pancakes.

"They do look good," he said.

I carefully stacked three pancakes and added a couple of browned sausage links onto Randy's plate.

He added a couple of pats of butter and a lot of maple syrup to his stack and sank his fork into the most perfect batch of Christmas pancakes I had ever made.

He took one bite, chewing slowly. The boys watched him as he closed his eyes in a single moment of bliss.

"These are the best pancakes I've ever eaten," he declared. The boys erupted into a chorus of "I told you sos." Randy's grouchy mood seemed to lessen with each bite.

Too soon, it was time for the boys to leave for their dad's house. They gave each of us big hugs and reserved some kisses for me. They whispered "I love you" in my ear and yelled "Merry Christmas" as they headed out the door.

The door had barely closed behind them when Randy enveloped me in a big hug.

"Thank you, sweetheart," he whispered, his voice full of emotion.

"For what?" I asked quietly. I was sure this wasn't about the pancakes.

"For giving me a real Christmas," he said simply.

We stole a few hours that morning. We snuggled on the couch next to the twinkling lights of the Christmas tree. We both had a million things to do, but we stopped and savored the moment and the spirit of the day.

Randy didn't live to see another Christmas. He died of cancer the next summer. He changed me for the better and taught me to value what was important. We no longer save "Christmas Pancakes" for one day of the year. We find time to have them on a regular basis. No matter what day of the year it is, someone tells the story of Randy and that morning when we gave him a real Christmas.

— Theresa B. Brandt —

The Stuffing Dreams Are Made Of

When you look at your life, the greatest
happinesses are family happinesses.
~Dr. Joyce Brothers

My fiancé, Don, and I had just gotten engaged and were spending our first Christmas together with his family. I had met his parents, brother, and five sisters previously. The meeting was brief — not long enough to make a good impression — but they were lovely people, and I wanted them to like me.

Having never had sisters of my own, I was overwhelmed by his. Each one had a strong, independent, outgoing personality, while I was painfully shy at the time.

Don told me that his family made a huge to-do about Christmas with tons of presents and a huge dinner. Evidently, his mother began shopping for the next year on Boxing Day, Canada's equivalent to Black Friday.

My childhood Christmases, in comparison, were always sad and uneventful. We never exchanged gifts. We were dirt poor. As newly landed immigrants, my parents did their best, but they could barely afford food, let alone extravagant toys we'd outgrow quicker than our clothes. Christmas treats consisted of a handful of walnuts, figs, and a tangerine for myself and my three brothers. Apart from that, the holiday was just another grim, boring day.

At eighteen, I'd never even shopped for Christmas gifts. That year, I obsessed over the bargain presents our combined meager budget would allow. I set off to the stores, armed only with a sparse list of suggestions that my fiancé, like most disinterested men, had given me before focusing his attention back on the hockey game. I could barely get his siblings' names straight after only one encounter, let alone their ages, sizes, or preferences. I spent hours wrapping my selections after being assured in a bored tone, "Yeah, yeah, she or he will love it."

On Christmas morning, I was a nervous wreck. I hated eating in front of new people, worrying I'd have my mouth full or have food stuck in my teeth when asked a question. I wondered if I didn't mix up the baking soda with powder in the chocolate cake I was bringing, or if I used cayenne instead of paprika on the deviled eggs.

I tried on everything I owned. According to my jeans-and-T-shirt-clad fiancé, who was patiently flipping through a sports magazine while he waited for me, I looked "beautiful" no matter what I wore.

Finally, I couldn't stall any longer. While Don drove, I chewed my way through six fingernails and checked my hair in the rearview mirror so often that it became too fogged up in the heater-less car to serve its purpose.

"Don't you have a mirror on that powder stuff you women pack on your faces?" Don asked, and I tore through my purse to whip out the compact I forgot I had.

When we arrived, we were greeted warmly. The food was torn out of my hands, and my future brother-in-law immediately helped himself to three deviled eggs. His head didn't explode, and he gave me thumbs-up, so I assumed I got the paprika right.

We stepped into the living room gingerly. Don wasn't exaggerating when he said "tons of gifts." Only the top half of the tree was visible, peeking out from a pile of presents that surrounded it and spilled onto the floor, almost reaching the hallway where I stood gaping.

"Just put your stuff in with the rest," someone bellowed from the kitchen and disappeared again. I couldn't tell who. All I saw was a flash of dark hair. They all had dark hair then.

Don immediately sat down on the couch next to his father after moving a bunch of presents to yet another precarious stack. I shyly poked my head into the kitchen where I saw the women in a frenzy of activity preparing food.

"Can I help?" I offered quietly. Of course, no one heard me over six females laughing and babbling to one another in loud voices while my mother-in-law-to-be barked instructions. Even the youngest, Sharron, who was only eight, was carefully arranging sliced cucumbers on a plate.

"Can I help?" I asked louder. Don's sister, Lorraine, pointed to the sink.

"Can you wash some of that?" she asked, indicating a mountain of dishes, pots, pans, and cutlery that outnumbered the gifts in the other room.

I immediately got to work. The more I scrubbed and washed, the more I was handed from six different directions. I had no idea where anything went after drying, so I placed things on a clean space. That pile disappeared almost immediately, returned for rewashing several minutes later.

My mother-in-law finally announced it was time to open gifts while the turkey finished roasting. Everyone congregated in the living room, scrambling for spaces to sit. I found a tiny spot on the floor near the tree after pushing aside a few parcels. Luckily, I was thin and small then, but I still had to hunch over each time Don's father reached over me to grab and distribute gifts or to pick up discarded wrapping paper to stuff into an industrial-sized garbage bag. I learned quickly that this family did not recycle wrapping paper or ribbons, prompting me to stop carefully peeling off tape from the generous collection of presents plunked into my lap.

Amid the joyous cries of delight, giggling at gag gifts, and tears of happiness over much wanted but inexpensive and thoughtful items, everyone was thrilled with even the smallest gift they received, including mine.

Two hours later, we gathered at the table for the meal. During the melee of food being passed back and forth over my head, no one cared how I ate. When we were halfway through the meal, Don's oldest sister, Heather, fixed her penetrating gaze on me.

"Which stuffing do you like better—mine or my mother's?" she asked. Of course, my mouth was full.

"I—er..."

"Mine is the one on the left—the darker one."

"Mine is much better, don't you think?" my future mother-in-law, Annie, challenged.

I chewed quickly and swallowed before responding diplomatically, "They're both delicious."

"That doesn't cut it! Choose!" Heather demanded.

"Leave her be. She doesn't want to admit that you use too much sage!" Don's mother argued.

"You put in way too much salt!" Heather countered.

"Yours is always too dry!" Annie retorted.

"Yours is mushy!" Heather retaliated.

"Yours stuck to the foil like a stubborn booger!"

"Yours slipped off like a greased pig on a metal slide..."

"You have lettuce stuck between your teeth," Marlene, another sister who would later go on to become a dental hygienist, interjected, pointing to me. "Do you want some floss?"

"Floss won't do it. It's probably Heather's stuffing," Annie taunted. "She'll need sandpaper."

I was speechless until both women burst out laughing, and I realized they were actually teasing each other.

"They do this every year," Don whispered in my ear. "You'll get used to it."

And I did, gladly, because that Christmas, complete with the stuffing competition, was exactly what I had always dreamed the holiday should be like—full of laughter, warmth, friendly teasing, and a loving family. And I would finally become part of one.

—Marya Morin—

35

Thanksgiving Half-Time

Thanksgiving dinners take eighteen hours to prepare.
They are consumed in twelve minutes. Half-times
take twelve minutes. This is not a coincidence.
~Erma Bombeck

Dinner's ready!
voices shout
no one moves a muscle
glued to the game

Dinner's ready!!
breaths held
no sound made
field goal kicked

Dinner's ready!!!
feet stomp
not on the stairs
interception at five-yard line

Dinner's ready!!!!
hands slap high-five
no one listens
touchdown

Dinner's ready…
gravy's cold
turkey's dried out
half-time feast

— Christy L. Schwan —

36

Bingo!

Not what we say about our blessings, but how we use them,
is the true measure of our thanksgiving.
~W.T. Purkiser

The week before Thanksgiving, my parents found them-selves enjoying a leisurely evening at the Elks Lodge with my grandparents, courtesy of my grandfather who had invited them there for dinner and a wild night of Bingo. Mom and Dad had never been to the Elks Lodge before, and while they had enjoyed the delicious meal, Mom couldn't wait to try her hand at Bingo.

After dinner, they made their way to the Bingo hall, where they strolled around and examined the prizes on display. "Look at this," Mom said, stopping in front of a beautiful, mosaic table decked out in shiny, ceramic tiles of the brightest colors imaginable. It was love at first sight. With a twinkle in her eye, she said, "You watch. I'm going to win this table and take it home with me."

Once they'd finished eyeballing the prizes, the four of them found their seats. While they waited for the fun to begin, they chatted about their upcoming traditional Thanksgiving dinner, which my parents hosted each year. My grandparents wanted to know who was coming and what they could bring in the way of food.

Before they knew it, Bingo started and, with it, the fun. Game after game went by, and none of them won, but they had a blast try-ing. Near the end of the evening, it finally came time to play for the table. "This is my game," Mom announced. "Watch me. That table will soon be mine."

It was a game of Blackout, and as Mom's card quickly filled up, her hands started shaking from the excitement. She knew, beyond a doubt, that within minutes the table would belong to her.

"Bingo!" rang through the air, but it wasn't Mom who yelled it. It was an older gentleman sitting next to her who had won the game... and Mom's coveted table.

"That's my table," Mom teased. "It was supposed to go home with me."

Everyone introduced themselves, and then Mom put out her hand and congratulated the gentleman on his win.

"It's a beautiful table, isn't it?" he said.

"It is beautiful. I hope you'll enjoy *my* table."

"You didn't really want that table, did you?"

"You know I did."

"Well, then, I have a proposition for you. I'll give you your table if you'll invite me to your family's Thanksgiving dinner. I overheard you talking about Thanksgiving, and your gathering sounds like so much fun. I don't have friends or family, and I hate spending it by myself every year. Do we have a deal?"

My parents answered at the same time. "Deal!"

"We'd love to have you over for Thanksgiving dinner," my mother said, "but keep your table. You won it fair and square."

"Never," he said. "A deal's a deal."

My sister and I were preschoolers at that time, but we still remember that Thanksgiving well. While we greeted our new guest with open arms, we couldn't pronounce his name.

"Call me Mr. Cider, like the apple cider you drink," he said, pointing to a large glass jug of golden cider sitting on the kitchen counter. And so we called him Mr. Cider for the rest of our lives. We didn't know if he was a grandpa, uncle, or cousin, and we didn't care. From that minute on, he would always be family.

Our guest of honor took his place at the large dining room table along with the rest of the gang, which included two sets of grandparents, aunts and uncles, and a few people who were related somewhere along the line. That's how Thanksgiving usually went in our home, for we never knew who might show up for the meal. With his charm and humor, Mr. Cider fit right in and had a grand time with everyone. It especially warmed my parents' hearts to know that this kind gentleman had not spent Thanksgiving alone.

Thanks to a fun night of Bingo and a little serendipity, Mr. Cider would grace our lives for many years, spending the rest of his living days enjoying Thanksgiving, Christmas, and other special occasions in our home as a cherished and much-loved member of our family.

—Jill Burns—

Chapter 5

Getting Creative

Tacky and Wacky

It's always consoling to know that today's
Christmas gifts are tomorrow's garage sales.
~Milton Berle

There are many men in my family: fathers, brothers, cousins, brothers-in-law, and nephews. The men outnumber the women. And they all have one thing in common: They are fashion-challenged. All the women share stories about the men in our lives wearing too-tight pants from high school that, according to the men, "Still fit perfectly," or the extra-baggy skateboard jeans that went out of style in the '80s. The stories (as well as the fashion faux pas) are amusing and never-ending.

One summer, on our family vacation in Big Bear, my husband Mike and I readied ourselves for a day of shopping, lunch and a walk around the lake. I had already showered and dressed, and I was applying make-up at the mirror. Out of the corner of my eye, I noticed my husband wearing an extremely peculiar outfit. We had only been married a few months, so, being the ever-so-accepting new wife, I said nothing about his outfit.

I headed downstairs and joined my sister, her husband and my brother at the breakfast table, where we had a perfect view of the staircase. As my husband came into view, we could see the outfit unfold... construction boots, white socks, and black shorts with red, orange and yellow flames, topped off with a blue Hawaiian shirt! Everyone stopped eating, including the men, and became very silent. Mike stopped and looked at all of us, wondering what the problem was. The silence was broken moments later when my brother exclaimed, "Oh, heck no! No way! Get back upstairs and change!" Even my brother realized how ridiculous my husband looked. Mike sheepishly went back upstairs. I followed and helped him pick a more suitable outfit. Crisis averted.

Ever since I can remember, the men in my family have exchanged T-shirts for Christmas. The tackier the T-shirt, the better. Currently in our closet hang several of these T-shirts. Some of the less tacky ones read, "10 reasons why beer is better than women," "It's a beautiful day to leave me alone," and, my current favorite, "I never dreamed that I would be this old and grumpy, but here I am killing it."

Suffice it to say, now that Mike has been in the family for over thirty years, he has amassed a ridiculous number of these "gifts." This is verified by the fact that one quiet evening, we had just fallen asleep when a thunderous crash jarred us awake. It had come from the direction of our closet. Mike crept in expecting an intruder or maybe a wayward car that had crashed through the wall. Nope. The wardrobe bar was so weighted down with T-shirts that it tore out of the wall and crashed to the floor.

That was enough with the T-shirt giving.

At our next family gathering, I relayed the story of that fateful night to all the women in my family. We laughed and reminisced about the many T-shirts our husbands had given and received over the years. We made a pact. This year would be different. The women would shop for the husbands instead of letting the men do it for each other. We agreed this would be a great way to get them to start dressing better.

While doing my shopping that year for Christmas, I carefully chose exactly the right sweater for each of the men in my family and just the right colors for each man to bring out his eyes or compliment his hair color. I was thrilled with my choices. I lovingly wrapped each one, attached the name tags, and set them under the tree. This was going to be the Christmas that changed the long-standing T-shirt tradition. The women and I compared notes and agreed that we were excited to see our men dressed appropriately in their new clothes. Christmas couldn't come fast enough.

On Christmas Day, I was so excited that I handed the men their presents first. Tony was the first to open his. There was the sweater I had chosen—a soft, burgundy sweater that had been folded carefully and nestled in tissue paper. He picked it up and… tossed it behind him! At the same time, underneath the sweater, much to my surprise, was a, yep, you guessed it, tacky T-SHIRT! No sooner had I blinked than he took off his current shirt and put on his new one. He smiled as if this was the best gift he'd ever received. I turned and shot my husband the evil eye. He was grinning from ear to ear. Somehow, he must have heard my plan and opened and then re-wrapped Tony's sweater, adding his own special gift inside. I felt deflated.

One by one, each of the men opened their boxes, and the same thing happened: a beautiful sweater tossed aside to reveal a hideous, tacky T-shirt. All the men were in on it!

The women in my family learned two valuable lessons that day. One, we love our crazy men more than we care about what they wear. And two, sometimes it's not the thought that counts; it's the gift.

— Crescent LoMonaco —

38

Chicken Soup for the Soul

Never Know What You're Gonna Get

You can't use up creativity. The more you use,
the more you have.
~Maya Angelou

A couple of Christmases ago, I kept drawing a blank as I was shopping for gifts. Sure, it's easy to buy gifts for the kids; they are always head over heels for the latest toys. But I could not think of anything meaningful to give some of the other most important people in my life — my mom and dad.

On a lunch date with my mom a few days later, we ate at a Chinese buffet restaurant, and we both got fortune cookies with our plates. We got some especially funny fortunes and had so much fun reading and laughing about them. I am a writer, so that sparked a little idea. What if I got a box of fortune cookies and replaced all the notes with fifty special memories or things I love and appreciate about the blessings I call Mom and Dad? Then I took it a step further and reached out to lots of their friends, family, nieces and nephews to get a personalized message from each of them for Mom and Dad's big Christmas surprise.

It was a big project, but it was almost just as much fun for me reading everyone's special memories about Mom and Dad. I collected most of the messages on Facebook and by text. Then I printed them out and stuffed them inside fortune cookies.

My parents loved it so much. I instructed them to only open one each day, but I think Dad went through his like wildfire. My mom, on the other hand, would read one of her "family fortune cookies" every morning with her coffee (as instructed). Then she would spread the fun by sending a picture of the message to the writer with a message for them, too. The fortune cookies got a little stale despite my attempt at resealing the individual packages with tape, but a new tradition was born.

I have found these gifts are more meaningful to people than anything I could ever buy them. And the process of searching my heart for all the reasons I truly love and appreciate them is good for me, and a lot of fun, too — especially knowing how much joy this gift will bring my favorite people.

The first ten notes pop out of my brain fairly fast and easy. But, after the first few, I find that I need to take some time to contemplate and think about what my favorite people truly mean to me. I've found that digging down deep also gives me a chance to express my sincerest thoughts, which I might not otherwise find a chance to express without feeling totally corny. You can say a lot of things with a pen that you can't easily say with your mouth.

Since then, I have done spinoffs of this gift idea for various people, such as a box of chocolates with a note underneath each one. It's a little less time-consuming than taking apart and reconstructing fortune cookies, and it tastes better, too! Sometimes, I do notes written just from me, sometimes pictures and notes from the grandkids, and sometimes I gather other notes from friends and siblings and put them together. I try to do a box or two of special chocolates for at least one family member or friend each year. As Forrest Gump might say, in a box of Kayleen's Christmas chocolates, you never know what you're gonna get!

This Christmas, imagine my surprise when I opened a gift from my sister Brittany and found a box of chocolates with notes underneath each chocolate. It's even more fun than I imagined to be on the receiving end, and I promise that I only read one each day (most of the time).

— Kayleen Kitty Holder —

39

Through the Years

Trapped by reality, freed by imagination.
~Nicolas Manetta

While straining to sing the chorus of "Hard Candy Christmas" in tune with Dolly, I lit the cookie-scented candle on the mantle and allowed the smells of vanilla, cinnamon, and nutmeg to envelop me. The angels and stable animals from our nativity set nestled into the original packaging with ease, but I had to wrestle Mary and the manger to fit them in the box. Despite my gentle touch, beads of Styrofoam swirled across the hardwood like a dusting of snow. My irritation dissipated as my husband wheeled the vacuum toward the circle of pine needles marking the floor where our tree once stood.

Grateful for his help, I headed for the stairs and unclipped the collection of our family's Christmas card photos from the strands of twine strung along the banisters. As I tucked the pictures into an envelope for safekeeping, I paused to reflect on our annual visits to a popular conservatory located on one of the seven hills of our hometown. Taking a picture in front of their impressive poinsettia display has been a tradition of ours for the past eighteen years.

I spread the photos across our dining room table in chronological order for one last look. The faces of our children matured before my eyes. My laugh lines deepened with each passing year. My husband wore the same shirt two years in a row — an important detail missed when I selected our outfits, which no longer seemed important.

Throughout his childhood, my husband had wandered alongside his mom and grandma through the humid houses of this conservatory, admiring spiky cacti, delicate orchids, and twisted bonsai trees. The December after we married, he took me to see the conservatory's annual holiday show. A large tree created from over two hundred poinsettias caught my attention. We posed beside this display and asked a volunteer to take our picture, which we would send with our holiday cards.

My husband whispered that we should start a tradition and have a family photo taken by the poinsettia tree every Christmas.

When our two daughters were tiny, we dressed them in coordinating holiday outfits. Those early pictures show happy, little girls with goofy expressions. My husband and I wore slightly strained smiles, reminding me of how they squirmed in our arms as we struggled to get them to face the camera and say, "Cheese!"

Our girls soon outgrew the holiday plaids, velvet dresses, and tights. With two busy teenagers, we have had to squeeze in the traditional trip between swim practices and winter percussion rehearsals. In 2019, we couldn't find time for all four of us to visit the conservatory until after Christmas. We included a different recent photo in our cards, later learning through phone calls and e-mails that our disappointed loved ones looked forward to finding the poinsettia picture in their mailboxes each year. We discovered our family tradition had, in a way, become a tradition for others. During the week between Christmas and New Year's Eve, we made the conservatory visit a priority. Anyone who told us they missed our annual family photo received two cards from us that year.

The conservatory closed its doors for the 2020 holiday season due to the pandemic. Like many families, we modified our holiday celebrations. Unwilling to disappoint our loved ones again, especially not during these trying times, we brainstormed various ways to continue the Christmas card photo tradition.

Following our daughters' directions, we positioned a tripod on the kitchen island, set the timer on my iPhone, and snapped about twenty pictures until we got a decent shot. The girls digitally manipulated the image to show us standing in front of a poinsettia tree they copied and pasted from a previous card photo, one of the many technological skills they acquired during months of remote learning. The resultant image may have been grainy thanks to wonky lighting, but we were all smiling and healthy.

The show returned to the conservatory for the 2021 holiday season. I studied our most recent picture before sliding the stack of images into the envelope. I closed my eyes and considered how our Christmas card photos might look over the next eighteen years. Would our daughters wear sweatshirts bearing the names of their chosen universities? How would we pose once their spouses joined the family? Would we one day be surrounded by grandchildren? In each image I envisioned, our smiles were bright, our faces full of joy.

I returned to the family room and extinguished the candle. A sense of peace swelled within me. Traditions help us remember what is important in life. This long-standing tradition of ours promises to keep us connected with our loved ones for years to come, no matter what might be going on in the world around us.

—Laurie Stroup Smith—

40

Chicken Soup
for the Soul

Back to the Future

Our hearts grow tender with childhood memories and
love of kindred, and we are better throughout
the year for having, in spirit, become a child
again at Christmas-time.
~Laura Ingalls Wilder

I have four sons, and while the two youngest were still easy to buy for, the two older ones left me in a quandary when Christmas was approaching. To make matters even more challenging, my oldest son had recently been in a car accident that left him paralyzed. A new life in a wheelchair just added to the nightmare of finding the "perfect" gift. Santa Claus had to get creative.

I lay in bed, tossing and turning, but nothing came to mind.

One day, I heard Jason and Brian laughing and acting like idiots in the other room (nothing new there). Jason was now twenty years old, and Brian, two years younger, but the sound of that laughter took me back to a time that was more carefree and simple. It was a time before spinal-cord injuries, college courses and big, smelly feet. Those two young "men" sounded like two rambunctious little boys.

That night as I got ready for bed, the sound of their laughter replayed in my head, and it made me smile. I fell asleep with visions of them many years before — two little boys playing together, fighting over this toy or that toy — a time that I wished would have lasted longer.

Suddenly, like a bolt of lightning, I got an awesome idea. I would take them back. I would recreate Christmas past.

I got on the Internet and began my search for "toys of the '80s." As the images popped up on the screen, memories flooded my head. I couldn't believe how quickly I was transported back to those two little boys sitting on the living room floor.

I scoured eBay and Craigslist. I was on a mission to recreate the Christmases of their childhood. As each package arrived in the mail, I gave the toys a good scrubbing. One by one, they came back to life. I could not wait for December twenty-fifth. Since Jason's car accident, I struggled to find joy in the everyday things. This project gave me a purpose.

Christmas morning, the boys waited while we dressed Jason and got him out of bed. We decided not to sit on the floor as in years past because Jason could not join us. We all took a seat on the sofa instead, all of us at the same level.

One by one, our two younger boys opened their gifts. They were still in the "gimme" stage of life.

Jason and Brian were patient as they watched their younger brothers tear open boxes. Then I handed each of them a box. Since Jason no longer had use of his hands, Brian was in charge. My heart was pounding fast as the "magic" unfolded. Their faces were priceless as they opened a Cabbage Patch Kid. In unison, they screamed, "Warren Bernard!" Oh, my God, they remembered his name! That doll took a beating back then as they would fling him across the room, and then fly around in their Superman pajamas trying to save him. In the '80s, everyone "adopted" a Cabbage Patch Kid, and Warren Bernard was our "baby."

The next box contained Pogs, those little, round cardboard discs that I still don't quite understand, but they examined each one just as they did so many years before. Then there was Kup, one of Jason's favorite Transformers. If only he could use his hands to transform him. I was trying to hold back tears as Brian did the work for him — two brothers working as a team to turn Kup from a car into an Autobot. I can't tell you how many times I tripped over Megatron or one of the other Transformers that took up residency on our family-room floor.

Brian tore into a box that contained a stegosaurus from Playskool's

"Definitely Dinosaurs" collection. These prehistoric creatures came complete with little plastic cavemen that rode on the backs of these giant reptiles. We laughed as the verbal "fight" began of who had the Stegosaurus and who had the Triceratops, an ongoing battle between siblings. To this day, we never have figured out who is right in that argument, but it was fun to listen as they picked up where they left off some fifteen years earlier.

As they unwrapped each box and pulled out a used (sometimes worn and tattered) toy, they would stop long enough to tell a story, laugh, and remember. I sat and enjoyed the memories with them. It was not a Christmas filled with shiny and new, at least not for these two brothers. This was a Christmas morning of toys long forgotten but revived thanks to some savvy shopping by Mrs. Claus.

There are times when I wish we could go back and do it all again — relive all the moments that went by too fast. I would sit with them and play a little longer, hug them a little tighter and try my best to stop the clock from forcing them from toddler to teen to adulthood. Time stands still for no one. This is true. But on that Christmas morning, we got to hit the rewind button and go back just one more time, and I am thankful for the memories.

— Trish Bonsall —

41

A Fort Benning Christmas

You are my home. Wherever you are,
that's where I'm meant to be.
~S.I. Naeole

While my husband centered the Christmas tree in front of the living room window, our teenage daughters pulled decorations from a stack of boxes. The sound of holiday music and the smell of hot chocolate filled the air.

"Oh, look," said Rachel. "The angel Grandma made for the top of the tree."

"And here is the wooden nativity scene you made, Daddy," called Rebecca.

The ornaments, figurines, and other decorations conjured up sweet memories from past Christmases.

As I wrapped garland around the stair railing leading down to the front door, I clung to the hope that my G.I. Joe son might get a few days off for the holidays. He was stationed at Fort Benning, three and a half hours away. A phone call later that day dashed those hopes. Joseph told me he would get Christmas Day off but had to report for duty the day before and after. My soldier boy sounded as miserable as I felt.

Our family would not be together for Christmas.

Suddenly, my husband suggested the most wonderful thing. "Let's take Christmas to Joseph. We'll take all the presents and get a hotel room close to his base."

I know folks who enjoy a destination Christmas at the beach or in the mountains, but I'd never considered celebrating Christmas anywhere but home. The thought of being away from our tree, special decorations, and traditions made me sad, but the thought of being away from Joseph was worse.

Five bulging stockings had been hung by the chimney with care, but I tossed them in a box with our gaily wrapped gifts. I baked a batch of Joseph's favorite chocolate-chip cookies while my husband and girls loaded the car.

What was it like celebrating Christmas away from home? Away from everything familiar? In another town? In a hotel? That Christmas turned out to be one of the best ever!

After depositing our suitcases and packages in the hotel room, we hurried down to wait for Joseph in a visiting area adjacent to the lobby. Twinkling lights, a massive Christmas tree, and a crackling fire in a stone fireplace provided a lovely, festive setting. Soft Christmas music played in the background. I couldn't have been more delighted and looked forward to Joseph's reaction.

When my son's muscular, six-foot frame appeared on the other side of the glass double doors, his hazel eyes lit up. He wasn't smiling at the fireplace, tree, or lights. He wasn't looking around for gifts or stockings. All that mattered to him — all that mattered to any of us — was being together at Christmas.

The hotel staff kindly arranged five metal chairs and a card table in front of the fireplace. For most of the next twenty-four hours, our family told stories, laughed, hugged, played games, munched on cookies, and took pictures. One of my favorite moments was captured in one of the photos — Rachel and Rebecca piled on top of Joseph, with big smiles on every face.

We eventually got around to opening presents, but they were almost an afterthought.

When I think back on the Fort Benning Christmas, my eyes burn with tears of joy. Christmas, I realized, isn't about red and green packages, gold and silver bows, decorations, lights, or music. The holiday isn't even about being at home. Christmas is enjoying the season of giving with the people I dearly love. They are my home.

—Arlene Lassiter Ledbetter—

42

The Gift of Time

Love is not about how many days, weeks or months
you've been together. It's all about how much
you love each other every day.
~Author Unknown

One Christmas many years ago, I asked my husband for a special gift, even though I knew the chances of receiving it were slim. Larry was always thoughtful when buying gifts for me, but on this particular Christmas, I didn't want something that was purchased — I wanted his time! More specifically, I wanted him to share his time with me enthusiastically and without making me feel guilty for keeping him from doing things he'd rather be doing. It was a rare occurrence when he was lucky enough to take a two-week break from driving his eighteen-wheeler back and forth across the country. Hopefully, he would give in to my request.

I was asking for Larry's help with a video I wanted to make for my dear friend LaDonna, whom I had never met in person. We were introduced by our sons who were best buddies in the military. The boys wanted us to become pen pals so we could comfort one another while they were deployed in the Middle East during the Gulf War.

Even though we lived 2,000 miles apart, it didn't take us long to become best friends, writing several times a week and pouring out our hearts to each other.

Since LaDonna lived in Iowa and I lived in Oregon, we didn't know when (if ever) we'd meet in person. She'd be thrilled to receive a video of our family's daily life in Oregon. Although we did send lots of photos back and forth, a video would be an extra-special surprise.

To my delight, Larry agreed to partner with me in putting together the video. He wasn't especially thrilled with being in front of the camera but vowed to give it his best shot.

It turned out to be a great idea and so much fun. I followed Larry around the farm and recorded him chopping wood, working with the tractor, and mending fences. He waved and talked to LaDonna and her husband, whose name is also Larry, interjecting funny little comments about me throughout the video. We also captured great shots of our donkey, pet pigs, horses, chickens, and the dog.

Inside the house, we filmed our lovely blue spruce Christmas tree, the kids' colorful stockings, and other festive holiday decorations. The cat reluctantly posed in her new frilly Christmas dress with a red bow in her hair.

The kids and grandkids were all included in the video, putting their personal spins on wishes for LaDonna and her family to have a merry Christmas and a happy new year.

I even took the video camera into our small town of Sandy to record places we frequented, such as the local stores, our park, the community library, and the kids' schools. I tried to include several clips of our gorgeous scenery including beautiful, snow-covered Mt. Hood, which is about thirty miles up the highway from our home.

Larry was such a great sport that it was difficult to discern whether he was simply trying to good-naturedly uphold his end of our Christmas gift agreement or was actually enjoying his acting debut. I was pretty sure I'd find out by the time we finished the video.

My answer came sooner than expected when, late on Christmas Eve, I was wrapping some last-minute gifts. I heard Larry go upstairs. Assuming he was getting ready for bed, I was surprised when I heard sleigh bells jingling in the living room. Upon investigation, I was startled at the sight of my six-foot-tall, full-bearded husband dressed in red long johns, green knee-high socks, and a red-and-green elf stocking cap! When I asked what he was doing, he replied, "I'm Santa's elf.

Thought our video could use a little more animation."

That was all the proof I needed to conclude that he was having a great time fulfilling my Christmas wish, and I looked forward to filming our kids and grandkids the following day.

The ending, which I planned to record late on Christmas night when the festivities were over, was well-rehearsed in my head, but I hadn't run it by Larry yet. I pictured the two of us sitting side by side on the carpet in front of the cozy brick fireplace in the family room, wearing the red plaid matching flannel nightshirts that one of the kids had given us for Christmas years earlier. It would be such a lovely finale!

Christmas Day was lively, and I got some good footage of our merriment to share with LaDonna. After the last of our guests left, I was overjoyed after Larry asked me if we were going to finish up the video. We giggled as we changed into our nightshirts but were able to regain our composure by the time I'd adjusted the camera and ran to take my place next to my husband in front of the glowing fire.

It was easy for us to talk to our friends while the gentle voices of Kenny Rogers and Dolly Parton set the mood with one of my very favorite Christmas songs: "The Greatest Gift of All." It was truly a magical moment that would live on in my memory forever.

LaDonna received our video late in the afternoon on New Year's Eve. She couldn't thank us enough for a gift that proved to be the perfect remedy to lift her spirits. We were both desperately missing (and worrying about) our sons while they were serving together in the desert. It was especially difficult during the holidays, and just as I'd hoped, our video offered my friend the comfort she needed.

Sadly, Larry passed away eight years later. While grieving his death, I found a hidden blessing in a saved copy of LaDonna's video, which will forever be a reminder of the deep love and respect that we shared throughout our thirty-seven years of marriage.

— Connie Kaseweter Pullen —

43

The Accidental Tradition

Creativity is thinking up new things.
Innovation is doing new things.
~Theodore Levitt

My mom had been hinting to Dad for months about a book she really wanted for Christmas. Well, Dad didn't quite get the hint, so Mom bought it for herself. She wrapped it up and put it under the tree with a tag saying it was from him.

Christmas morning finally arrived. I am the oldest of nine kids, so there were a lot of presents waiting to be opened. We started unwrapping our gifts when Mom opened her present "from Dad." We all erupted in laughter when my dad saw the gift and said, "Wait a minute... I didn't buy that. Where'd it come from because I sure didn't buy it!" My mom, through fits of laughter, explained to my very confused dad that she'd been hinting for months that she'd wanted that particular book. When Dad never took the hint, she took it upon herself to buy it. And thus was born a new tradition.

Now, over two decades later, everyone in the family buys one present that they really want, wraps it up and puts it under the tree. Most of my siblings have families of their own now, so we send pictures by text showing the present we bought for ourselves. From the accidental tradition that started with a "Wait a minute... I didn't buy that," twenty years later, it has become the most beloved tradition in the family.

I tell young couples of the tradition that started by accident, and they all laugh. I smile when I see them happily buy a gift for themselves to put under the tree, knowing our accidental tradition will live on for another generation.

— Celia Reeves —

44

Chicken Soup for the Soul

Fitting the Pieces Together

Creativity is intelligence having fun.
~Albert Einstein

"Honey, hear me out. I've got a fantastic idea!" I said. My husband raised one eyebrow, looked at me with the dread of a man who'd endured two decades of my half-baked ideas, and waited for me to explain my latest and greatest inspiration. "I know we can't all get together for Christmas this year, but what if we sent everyone in the family the same puzzle and had a contest to see who could finish it first?" Eight families, eight puzzles, and a month of friendly competition across the miles. It was genius.

Once he heard that my idea did not involve adding another pet to our already busy household or a long-overdue project to his to-do list, he exhaled, smiled warmly, and agreed. Even after twenty years together, I could still surprise him.

The Covid Christmas of 2020, as I'm sure it will be remembered by many, was an exercise in acceptance, flexibility, and creativity. That year, there would be no Christmas Eve at my sister's home. No excess of appetizers and desserts. There would be no Christmas Day at my in-laws' house packed full of cousins and sports on TV. I knew I wanted something that linked us all that year, and with puzzles being the quarantine pastime, my plan was born.

I ordered eight identical puzzles with a winter theme and had them delivered to every household in our family. I set a start date and offered a small prize to the winning household. With that, our competition began.

As the days ticked by, my little family worked on our puzzle on the table in the basement, so we could leave it out undisturbed. At first, the boys were motivated and loved the family time together. They dug right in, separating pieces by color and pulling out the edges. The boys raced to find missing pieces and celebrated each section we completed.

It wasn't long before the novelty wore off.

"Mom, this hurts my eyes."

"Mom, can we be done now?"

What had started as a fun diversion had turned into a task. So I did what any self-respecting modern mother would do: I bribed them with an assortment of Christmas cookies. Piled high on the holiday platter were peanut-butter cookies with chocolate Kisses, chocolate cake with mint melt-away topping, and snowballs rolled in powdered sugar. I turned on the TV and played *Elf*, the hands-down greatest holiday movie ever made. Even with Christmas spirit smacking them in the face, at nine and twelve, they'd had enough. Their little heads rested heavily on the snowy white IKEA table.

I might have gone into the puzzle competition with tinsel-colored glasses, envisioning a season of playful rivalries and socially distanced togetherness, but real life isn't a curated Christmas card. I discovered that I couldn't fit all our traditional family fun into 1,000 pieces of laser-cut cardboard. But I could fit some, and some was enough.

So, I tempered my competitive side. I did not want to let a fun family activity turn into a chore. For my little group, it took a bit more time and patient dedication to fill in the whole picture.

We didn't complete our puzzle first. The winning puzzle was completed in just one day. It took our little family a few days, but within no time all eight had been finished. In that time, we all sent photos back and forth with our progress and turned our eight individual puzzles into one cohesive family success. With a little effort, each puzzle was composed in its own time and in its own unique way. In the end, we all had the same finished product, regardless of how we went about it. More importantly, we all had a shared goal that kept us in touch, no matter how we chose to go about our challenge.

In the midst of uncertainty and isolation, a new tradition was born. Although we were back to celebrating a traditional Christmas, I bought new matching puzzles for last Christmas. This time, I thought a beach theme would be nice; winters in the Midwest usually leave us longing for summer. I piled up the cookies once again, and made some fancy hot chocolate complete with marshmallows, whipped cream, and silver sprinkles. You can be sure we had *Elf* playing in the background.

And we made more memories together as a family. I let the moment be what it was and did not cajole everyone into the moment I had envisioned. I appreciated each of my loved ones for the unique and authentic pieces they are. In return, I hope they found time to revel in their own uniqueness. I hope they appreciated each piece in this big family puzzle.

Hopefully, this is the start of a tradition that my children will pass on to their families one day. I look forward to seeing the unique puzzles they create for themselves.

—Jill Ann Robinson—

45

The Southern Desert Pine

*The best Christmas trees come very close
to exceeding nature.*
~Andy Rooney

Wintertimes come, and wintertimes go,
But there is one I remember so.
That year, with our kids so tender,
We set out on a great big venture.

We left from the north, moved six states south,
To a land that was dry, nearly in drought.
Gone were the seasons that changed by month,
Gone was the snow that filled the yard out front.

My husband's job took us south to a town,
Where the land wasn't green, just all shades of brown.
There, the breeze seemed ever too warm,
And the dirt often swirled into thick, dust storms.

We'd moved to the edge of a big desert bowl,
Where longhorns grazed and tumbleweeds rolled.
Where evenings burst with colors so pretty,
But I always felt gloomy, not thrilled with the city.

One day, I noticed the date and gasped.
Christmas, soon, would be in the past.
The big day approached, fun for our squirts.
But I was still focused on the heat and dry dirt.

Moving south was a big change of plan,
But my longing for home was now out of hand.
It was time I got happy for my munchkins, three.
The holiday loomed. It was time for a tree!

Oh, of trees, I knew my most favorite look —
Stout blue spruce, filled with holiday balls and hooks!
My husband favored pines that were tall.
I did a little dance. What fun for us all!

Next day, we loaded up our young sirs,
And went to assess the selection of firs.
The more we drove, the hotter the sun.
Right then, tree shopping was far from fun.

How I missed the cold snow on my face!
Of the winters we'd known, there wasn't a trace.
I longed to zip the boys' coats and boots,
And make a snowman, always a hoot.

I was hot, and I needed a breath.
I craved cool air on my face and my neck.
My husband reached and patted my knee.
Then, like an angel, he cranked up the AC.

And so continued our vast tree quest,
Where next to venture for the tree that was best?
At one store lot, the trees looked silly.
All that flocking on limbs seemed too white, too frilly.

Our oldest son soon started to mope,
And the youngest was at the end of his rope.
"Why is that tree so dry and little?"
Grumbled the one who was born in the middle.

Fake trees filled a row, most amusing.
To me, not a one seemed right for the choosing.
And then I spotted a slim desert pine.
"Let's just get it!" our little boys whined.

We paused to study it, then walked around it.
It was tall, even comely, I had to admit.
But small lights glowed from the branches in white,
A shortcut that, to me, didn't seem quite right.

I knew that I needed to get with the program,
And find a way up and out of the doldrums.
Could a girl from the north ever learn to cope?
Then, thankfully, came a glimmer of hope.

I saw that the southern pine proffered great joy.
They all truly liked it, my hubby and boys.
It came to me then that the pine and the dust
Were things to live with. I knew that I must.

Wow, finding a tree in the south was rough!
And the price was high, did I like it enough?
For sure, the pine was a rather strange brand,
But could it, like the desert, be sparse yet grand?

I glanced around and suddenly felt
That I didn't need snow. It would simply melt.
I had four guys, the gleam of my eye,
And above, all around, was the gorgeous hued sky.

I helped heft the tree to our car roof.
Of my change in attitude, that was the proof.
Once in the car, we sang, "Joy to the World."
I smiled, then laughed, my humor unfurled.

We lugged the faux pine in from the car.
It had lots of cones but still needed a star.
In a jiffy, the slim tree was up.
Our new tree was lovely, the right southern touch.

A youngster reached and flipped off the light.
My heart expanded. How grand, what a sight.
I fell in love with our new desert pine.
So spare, so beautiful. So perfectly fine.

— Clara Brummert —

46

Joy for Loss

Christmas is most truly Christmas when we celebrate it
by giving the light of love to those who need it most.
~Ruth Carter Stapleton

Donna and I had been friends for a long time when she lost her husband of thirty-one years. As the holiday season approached, Donna grew depressed. She opted not to decorate, refused invitations to holiday parties, and retreated into her sadness. "I don't know how to get through it," she told me repeatedly. "I'm just trying to endure it."

But then, on December thirteenth, everything about that first Christmas without Harvey changed. An unknown someone visited Donna's home for twelve nights, well after dark. Her doorbell would ring, and she would find a gift with a message attached on her porch. The messages were based on the historical implications of the "Twelve Days of Christmas" carol. The note explained that this was more than a song. It was the way Christians had communicated the gospel during times of persecution. The partridge in the pear tree represented Christ on the cross, and a bowl of pears accompanied the first message. Similar gifts and messages came for eleven more nights.

Donna admitted to trying to catch the giver. She would flip the porch light randomly through the evening. She left the door open and stood by half-opened blinds. She spent hours trying to discover her benefactor and accused friends, family, and co-workers. Nevertheless, she said, "It's made all the difference. It's something to look forward to."

I was not the original giver, but Donna's experience would catapult us into extending these twelve days of giving to other women over the next few years — women like Donna who had lost the love of their life and couldn't fathom a holiday without him.

Donna and I had many adventures during these escapades. We drove without headlights to avoid detection. Neighbors of our recipient eyed us suspiciously and called the authorities on occasion. More than once, we flattened ourselves against the side of a house while a widow on the porch called out, "Hello! Thank you!" One night, in a dense fog, I inched the car forward, attempting to pick up Donna from a drop. For several minutes, I drove into the blackness. I finally stopped, and Donna startled me by jumping into the car, breathing hard. She had been chasing me for a block!

Our first expedition of this ongoing adventure turned out to be the most eventful. The widow of a pastor and her two young sons lived on a cul-de-sac, which presented a problem. We had to park on the through street, sneak around the cul-de-sac, and hide until we could approach the door undetected. After ringing the doorbell, we had to hide between houses until we could safely walk back to the car.

On the first night, Donna wedged herself between a tree and the side of the house. A visiting friend came out on the porch with his firearm to investigate the late-night doorbell ring-and-run. Upon finding the message, he went back in and presumably assured the widow there was no threat.

On the fourth night, Donna came face to face with the widow. They had a staring contest until Donna walked off the porch without speaking. Two nights later, I parked in the driveway of a darkened neighboring house. It was lightly snowing and freezing. I pulled as close as possible to the garage door. Donna had almost made it across the lawn when the garage door in front of me flew open. A sedan pulled into the driveway, swerving to avoid hitting me. The driver jumped out of the car yelling. I rolled down the window and whispered my explanation. He encouraged me to pull into the garage for better hiding and became our co-conspirator for the rest of the days.

Another Christmas, our beneficiary lived at the end of an unpaved country road in the middle of nowhere. I had to get creative. I placed each day's message and gift in individual gift bags numbered one to twelve. The bags went into a huge basket with a letter explaining to open one each night beginning on December thirteenth. The basket "mysteriously" appeared in her church lobby on Sunday morning with the help of a mutual friend.

Neither Donna nor I attended her church, but I was invited to a Christmas program there the following weekend. I sat chatting with my friend while waiting for the program to start. The widow happened to slide into the pew in front of me.

"Look, look," she said, pointing at her lapel. A familiar pin of a glittering drummer boy twinkled. She began to tell her friend about the basket of twelve bags that was turning her sorrowful holiday into a joyful one. I concentrated on the program in my lap and hoped that my face didn't betray me. "I have no idea where it came from," she said.

"We'll find out," her friend assured her. "I'll help you." But they never did.

Over the years, I've finessed my list. I shop after Christmas in anticipation of another opportunity to change someone's sorrow into joy. I add a personal note on Day Twelve with a memorial to the lost loved one. It isn't an enjoyable project. The nature of it means that a friend has become a widow. I can't stop the outcome by pretending it didn't happen. I can only offer a little joy when there's an empty spot around the tree.

— TonyaAnn Pember —

Chapter
6

The Joy of Giving

47

Sweet Gift

My idea of Christmas, whether old-fashioned or modern,
is very simple: loving others. Come to think of it,
why do we have to wait for Christmas to do that?
~Bob Hope

I was walking to my friend's office in the city to bring him and a few other people some festive cookies. As I approached the historic downtown building on Washington Avenue, a man lingered by the door. He was layered in dirty clothes, and desperation darkened his face.

He stepped forward. "You got any spare change?"

"Sorry, I don't." I was pretty broke at the time, but the plates of cookies piled in my hands may as well have been shouting to go with this man. I grabbed a plate and held it out to him. "But I do have some cookies, if you want."

His eyes went wide. "Cookies!" he shouted as if he were a little boy. "God bless you. Thank you so much."

I laughed at his giddiness. We were suddenly like old friends instead of strangers. But before I could say, "You're welcome," he rushed off. I was twenty-two or twenty-three years old and working multiple jobs to make ends meet, but experiencing this during my winter break made me appreciate the fact that I had work. It also inspired me to stop and think back to the brief time when I was homeless myself.

I've never been without a place to sleep, but when I was eighteen, my sister and I were couch hopping before we landed on our feet. Our parents were unstable. Things snowballed fast, and we were on our own before I finished high school. It was a horrid feeling not knowing where we were going to sleep. I would never wish that uncertainty on anyone.

Even before then, whenever I saw someone down on their luck, I wanted to help. I've handed out more money than I probably should. But after I shared cookies with that man on Washington Avenue, a new tradition began.

I started whipping up extra cookies during the holiday season. I bagged them and drove around looking for people begging on street corners or sleeping under overpasses.

When I married my husband, he started coming along. He was nervous at first. He sat in the passenger seat staring out the window. "I just don't know what to say. It's hard looking at someone who's obviously going through something."

"Just smile and wish them well," I said. "That's what I do. It'll be fine."

He stuttered a bit at first. Sometimes you meet someone who is so grateful that it makes you cry. They are heartbreaking moments, but I like one-on-one interactions with people where we can discuss life or just bring a new sense of hope to each other. I've always found the best people in the worst places.

This also gave me a soft spot for veterans. A lot of shelters only take women and children. They have capacity limits and regulations that must be followed. During the pandemic, many shelters were even more limited (if they were opened at all), so there were more men left on the streets than ever. We witnessed that firsthand.

It hit my husband hard. He suggested we do more. "Why don't we give them something more substantial like sandwiches?"

"I still want to give them a festive treat. Something to include them in the holiday season…" We were working with limited funds, but I was also worried about all the vets with bad teeth. I wanted to offer something soft with good nutrition that was still a treat.

That led us to fruitcake. Even the nuts soften when you bake them in, and they're good protein for someone who truly needs it.

Fruitcake gets a bad rap because it's traditionally full of hard, candied fruit, but I make mine with fresh pineapple, cherries, raisins, and Craisins. Add in some chopped walnuts and pecans, and it's like a bread meal—something with more nutritional value than just cookies.

The more I share this story, the more people reveal their own charitable acts of feeding the homeless in their communities. It's such a simple gesture, handing someone food or offering them a blanket on a cold day. And it all comes back to us. Just as I had people who looked out for me when I had nowhere to live, there are others out there who can benefit from simple acts of kindness.

During the summer, handing out sandwiches is a fun gift, but when the holidays approach there's nothing like handing out fresh fruitcake. My husband and I pack up the children and display what the season is really all about. We've met families, loners, and everyone in between—people of all colors from all walks of life. And it all started with one man who was so happy to receive a plate of cookies that I wanted to give more.

—Jessica Marie Baumgartner—

48

The Christmas Fund

Do what you can, with what you have, where you are.
~Theodore Roosevelt

In early December, the check from a Missouri bank arrives in my Indiana mailbox. Though she has been gone several years, Mom's bank account still saves up money for a special Christmas fund, just like when my brother and I were growing up.

Dad and Mom insisted on paying for everything with cash, despite us not having much cash at all. Dad was mainly employed in outdoor jobs an hour commute from home. He called them "good-paying jobs," like construction projects or long periods of time on a river barge or the railroad. Mom worked at a factory job in our small town. When the electronics factory closed, she got hired at the toy factory, a forty-five-minute drive away.

During the winter, Dad would be laid off until the weather was better. Certain major bills always came due in October and November, which took most of the cash Dad and Mom had saved up. While Dad did odd jobs for relatives, Mom became the breadwinner for those months leading up to the holidays.

As a preteen, I worried myself sick before and during Christmas. I was the anxious one in our family, especially during the winter. No job for Dad meant less money coming in to pay the bills. I was nervous about the financial strain. Mom noticed my chewed-down fingernails and heard my restlessness at night. She was worried about me.

Out of necessity, Mom started our Christmas fund by cutting a slot into the lid of a juice can, emptying it, and turning it into a piggy bank. Mom and Dad would throw their extra change in there. We never knew how much was going in, since neither Dad nor Mom counted the money before dropping the coins into the can.

When Mom earned extra money, those folded bills would go into the can. She never considered holding some back for herself. All the extra money was for Christmas.

When Dad was laid off from his job, there wasn't much folding money going into the can. I only heard a few clinks from the coins. We could only hope we had added enough to the fund during the prosperous months.

After Thanksgiving, all of us would gather at the kitchen table as Mom removed the top with the can opener. My brother and I sorted the coins, while Dad and Mom did the folding money. No one ever guessed the correct total. We were always amazed by how much had accumulated. The best part for our parents was knowing the amount of cash they could spend on presents, having no debt to repay later. The best part for my brother and me was revising our lists, either adding on more items or narrowing them down, according to how much money was in the can.

Under the tree on Christmas morning, we found what we expected from our lists plus surprises from Santa. The Christmas fund also provided presents for neighborhood children who needed a gift or two.

Mom continued the Christmas fund until my brother and I were teenagers. When Dad passed away, she kept working as a custodian at the local school. Her greatest joy was helping children who needed winter coats.

My financial planner advises me to consolidate my mother's estate into more lucrative mutual funds. But, for sentimental reasons, we keep my mother's Christmas savings account, accumulating interest in the bank rather than a can. Many local organizations have benefited from the funds that come in each December — the food pantry because Mom enjoyed cooking and baking at Christmas, the local toy drive, the angel tree, and the Humane Society because Mom loved spoiling her dogs. Growing up, we knew Dad, Mom and Santa would fulfill anything on our wish list. Now others in my community see their wishes fulfilled, thanks to the Christmas fund.

— Glenda Ferguson —

49

Who Cares About Christmas?

The giving of love is an education in itself.
~Eleanor Roosevelt

He was an angry seventh-grade boy when his grandmother brought him into my office in the Academy that fall. She begged me to enroll him because he had been expelled from yet another school. I looked at his school records, and they were horrendous. He had received multiple referrals for classroom disruptions, insubordination, profanity, fighting, and walking out of the classroom. I was very hesitant to take him into our little, quiet church-school family.

But then I looked at him, with his diminutive stature and sad brown eyes. He was sitting beside his grandmother in my office with his head down and his hands in his lap. He didn't look so menacing sitting there, and I definitely couldn't picture him disrespecting staff. I asked him his name, and he responded hesitantly.

I asked if he wanted to come to this school. His grandmother started to answer, but I stopped her and told her I wanted James to answer. At first, he was silent, but then he said slowly and deliberately that he wouldn't mind coming to the school because he knew a couple of boys who attended, and he thought they were kind of cool. I asked him about his discipline record, and he shrugged. I told him that we couldn't have anybody in this school acting like he did at his other schools. He looked up at me with those big eyes and said, "I would like to try." I accepted him into the school that same day.

A month after James joined the Academy, I came into my classroom and found a single rose sitting in a vase on my desk. It was a beautiful, aromatic red rose, and as soon as I drew near it, I could smell the fragrance. I asked the other teachers if they had given me a rose, and they said someone had put a rose on their desks as well. We were all puzzled and started asking students if they had given us the rose. Everyone denied it.

Then, one of the older boys approached me before class started and said quietly, "I know who the culprit is." ("Culprit" had been one of his vocabulary words that week.) I told him that I certainly didn't consider the person a culprit since it was a wonderfully kind gesture. He whispered in my ear that it was James, but he added, "Don't tell him I told. He wanted it to be a secret."

Later that morning, when James went to the bookroom to get some extra books, I met him in the hallway and said, "Thank you."

He looked up at me and said, "I made it a whole month without getting in trouble. Thanks for letting me come to this school."

"You're welcome," I said. "Keep up the great work." We never mentioned the rose by name.

It was December 15th, ten days before Christmas. James had been in the school for two months by then and had not had one incident of misbehavior. As a matter of fact, he was a model student. He wasn't the best reader, but one of the teachers, Ms. E, was working with him to help him improve his reading. James was helpful, friendly, cooperative, and hard-working. The students and staff liked him a lot. He was a natural leader, and the boys were quick to follow him.

I noticed that, as we got closer to Christmas, he got quieter and more withdrawn, whereas the other students became louder and more animated. I constantly asked him if everything was okay. He continued to say everything was fine. I asked some of the students in class if they knew what was wrong with him, but no one knew.

I told James that every year we had one student serve as the emcee for the Christmas program, and this year I wanted it to be him. I reminded him that this was a big honor since it was the biggest and best-attended program of the year. He retorted in a rather angry voice, "Who cares about Christmas?" and walked away.

Later that evening, I called his grandmother and told her about the incident. I mentioned that I was concerned about James and wanted to know if everything was okay. She explained that his mother had abandoned him at Christmas when he was just five years old, and he didn't have a relationship with her. Needless to say, he wasn't a big fan of Christmas, even though she (the grandmother) said she tried to make it special for him each year.

I started thinking about what the school could do to make the holiday special for James. Some of the students shared their ideas. I talked to the other teachers, and we developed a plan.

We had convinced James to be the emcee for the Christmas program, and he did a spectacular job. He was funny, articulate, had excellent timing, and made all of us so proud. As the program came to an end, James did his final thanks and turned the program over to me. When I got up to give the final remarks, I called James to the stage. He looked puzzled but came up anyway.

When he approached the stage, I began talking about how Christmas is all about love because love was what Christ showed in being born into this world. Then, I told the audience that James had joined our school in October. During that short time, he had made a very positive impact. We wanted to let him know during this Christmas season how much we appreciated and loved him.

At that time, students began coming to the stage and presenting James with gifts, cards, hugs and handshakes. I looked down at James, and he was crying. I put my arm around his shoulder, and he looked up at me and said, "This is not just a school but a school full of love." I looked over to his grandmother who was sitting in the audience, and she was a puddle of tears. This was one of the best Christmas programs ever.

James remained at our school until he graduated in eighth grade, and he was a blessing the entire time he was there. I was so glad that I had given him a chance.

— Barbara Carter-Donaldson —

The Joy of Giving | 159

50

The Souper Christmas

To ease another's heartache is to forget one's own.
~Abraham Lincoln

I t was a hard year for me and some of my family; we had financial troubles, and I felt like I couldn't participate in giving at Christmastime. I was a fairly new widow, out of work, and sharing a home with my son and grandson. I felt like I was a burden. And I was lonely.

We went to a wonderful family dinner on Christmas Eve and watched the young kids there open their gifts. We enjoyed the family time and great food, but the joy of being able to give was still missing. If only I could give my grandson some sort of gift.

We got home around eight and were all just sitting around when my son asked, "How long does it take you to make a pot of soup?" Thinking he might be hungry again, I said it only takes about thirty minutes to fix potato soup. Then he suggested that we make some soup and coffee and take them downtown where there were several homeless folks.

What a grand idea! He started making coffee and filling the thermos pots while I fixed sausage-potato soup. My grandson put together cups, spoons, and napkins, and even went to get the candy his mother had sent him for Christmas to give away. Suddenly, we were all excited to see how much we had to give.

We drove for several minutes but didn't see anyone. We wondered if the cold night had them tucked away in building alcoves to keep warm. Then, on a corner, we saw a man with a cardboard sign. We stopped and asked if he would like a cup of soup and some coffee. He said he would.

As we got out to dish up the food for him, another man walked up, so we fed him, too. They thanked us, and we wished them "Merry Christmas" as we drove away. A few blocks later, we saw a couple of women walking down the street with packs and bedrolls, so we stopped and gave them a warm meal, too, complete with crackers and candy for dessert. By the time we ran out of soup and coffee, we had fed about a dozen people. All seemed very blessed by the warm meal on a cold night.

We returned home feeling the true spirit of Christmas, and I thanked my son for giving me the best gift he could have given. All three of us were excited and shared how blessed we felt to be able to bring some joy to others.

As we set out to bless others, God blessed us as well. As for my family and me, we had a truly souper Christmas Eve.

— Beajae Carman —

Facilitating Christmas Cheer

Never doubt that a small group of thoughtful,
committed people can change the world.
Indeed, it is the only thing that ever has.
~Margaret Mead

I was so excited! I was finally chosen for something important, or at least it felt important to me. I was going to be a peer facilitator at my school. Peer facilitators act as student counselors for their peers when they have a problem or need someone with whom to talk. This was huge for me because it was my senior year, and the first few years of high school had been anything but happy for me.

I attended a school that didn't value me or my contributions. I had endured a lot of difficulty in the first few years, but I had finally found my way. I had friends with whom I spent time, and now I was going to be able to help others not have to go through what I had experienced. I would be someone they could talk to when things were not going well. I was going to make a difference.

As Christmastime drew near, I decided I really wanted to do more to make life better for someone. I loved to write, and I had written a story where the main character, a young girl named Tracey, had changed someone's life by bringing a down-on-his-luck man home for dinner with her family. I knew that my parents would not likely allow me to bring a homeless stranger home with me, so I needed to keep thinking.

That afternoon, I happened to be at my friend Angela's parents' store. It was the only Christian bookstore in our town. I heard them talking about a family that wouldn't have money to provide much of a Christmas for their children that year. I had heard about families that struggled, but it wasn't something with which I was very familiar. I had been very blessed to have a family that could always meet my needs and most of my wants.

I thought it was sad that a mom and dad would have to worry about providing for their children at Christmas. I didn't say anything then, but a thought was forming in my mind. What if this was how I could make a difference? What if this was how I could help change someone's life? But how? How could I, with no real money of my own, help this unfortunate family? I wasn't sure, but I knew in my heart that it was what I was supposed to do.

I talked to my friend's mom, Mrs. Saunders, and told her what I wanted to do. I asked if she would be willing to give me the family's name and contact information. The next day, I made an appointment to talk to the school's guidance counselor because she was in charge of the peer facilitators' group. I told her I wanted it to be a group project for any peer facilitator who wanted to take part. There were ten of us, I think.

After I got permission from the school to do the project, I sat down and thought about all the things I would like to be able to do for the family. I wanted them to have a tree and ornaments. I wanted the children to have gifts, and I wanted to be able to provide food for them. We would need wrapping paper, bows, and tape to wrap the gifts. I created a schedule and decided to put each grade in charge of one area. I got permission to go into one class in each grade and tell them about the project and what was needed. We had one grade in charge of collecting everything needed for wrapping, one collecting food, one collecting toys for the children, and a couple of grades collecting clothing items. All the students were very helpful and interested.

I loved art and had a good rapport with our art teacher, Mrs. Norcross, so I shared the project with her, and she allowed the art students to spend part of their class time creating ornaments for the family to hang on their tree. It was so much fun and the only time I really felt like I fit in at my school.

The peer facilitators had meetings to discuss how things were going and determine whether we needed to make changes. One of the most fun days was when the other peer facilitators came to my house for two afternoons so we could wrap all the presents. By the time the project was done, we had toys and clothes for the children, clothing for the parents, decorations for the tree, canned food, and fresh fruits and vegetables. We were even able to get gift certificates for them to buy a ham and turkey from our local Food Lion.

Finally, the day came, and we were allowed to leave school a little early to "play Santa" for this family. I think they knew we were coming, but I'm not sure if they knew all that we had planned for them. Four of the peer facilitators, including me, rode together. We all crammed into my little Toyota Tercel, loaded down with gifts.

When we got there, it was so much fun. First, we gave them the tree and all the decorations and ornaments. Then, we gave them the wrapped gifts and extra clothing items. I could tell they were touched but maybe a little uncomfortable, so we quickly wished them "Merry Christmas" and headed back to school.

This was truly the best school memory I have. Not only was I given the privilege of making a difference in someone else's life, but I got to see another side of my classmates and share special memories with them.

— Karen S. Hollowell —

New Is Nice

Without a sense of caring, there can
be no sense of community.
~Anthony J. D'Angelo

The day before Christmas, my wife Ellie and I brought our Christmas gifts to the residents whom we regularly called upon at the Glendale Nursing Home. We had been doing volunteer hospice work for over fifteen years. We had a list of residents provided by hospice, and we called upon them once or twice a week. We sat and visited with them, and brought cookies and small personal items.

At Christmastime, we took gaily wrapped gifts of lap robes, slippers, shawls and sweaters. Our last visit on this day was with Margaret and Florence, two elderly ladies who resided in the same room.

When we entered the room, we overheard Florence and Margaret talking about going to the resident Christmas party, which was scheduled that afternoon.

"Ray, I like your Christmas sweater and Ellie's, too," Florence said.

"You look all ready for this afternoon's Christmas party," Margaret added.

"Yes, and we can take you down to the party if you wish," I said to the two ladies, who transported in wheelchairs.

"That would be nice. And maybe you could take Alice, too," Margaret replied, pointing to the frail, little lady who was lying in the third bed. "She just came here a couple of days ago."

"I heard the nurse say that she had been living alone somewhere nearby and had come here after a short stay in the hospital," Florence added.

We walked over to the bed, and I introduced myself and Ellie to Alice.

As Alice sat up wearily in the bed, the facility's activity director announced over the speaker system that the Christmas party would be delayed for about an hour. She added, with a twinkle in her voice, "Santa just called. It seems that he is having trouble with his reindeer this afternoon."

We laughed at this comment, and I asked, "Would you like us to take you to the Christmas party, Alice?"

Alice glanced up sadly at my wife. Her voice filled with regret as she whispered, "I can't go with you. My pants fall down whenever I walk anywhere."

I suddenly realized that Alice did not have a wheelchair by her bed and apparently was able to walk with some help.

Ellie walked to the nearby closets and asked which one was Alice's. She opened it, looked inside and removed several of the hangers that had slacks and tops neatly hanging from them.

"These slacks look much too large for you," Ellie remarked.

Alice nodded. "Yes. I've been sick and lost a lot of weight. And those are all the clothes that I have now. I used to work as a buyer at Macy's in New York. I had a lot of nice clothes then." Her eyes filled with tears as this memory seemed to overwhelm her.

I walked over and whispered to Ellie, "You know, we have some time before the Christmas party starts. Let's head over to Walmart and see if we can find something for Alice that will fit."

At that moment, a uniformed woman walked into the room and approached us. "Hi, I'm Eve, Alice's nursing aide. It's time for Alice to get her shower."

Ellie looked at her and smiled. "Hey, that's great, Eve. My husband and I were just going out to get Alice some new clothes."

The aide nodded. "Alice just came in yesterday, and she brought very little with her. I'll wait after her shower to help her dress."

Ellie nodded in agreement and said to Alice, "We have to leave for a short time, but we'll be right back."

Alice replied quietly, "I'll be here."

When Ellie and I got to the front door to leave the facility, Ellie's cell phone rang. It was Judy, our hospice volunteer coordinator. "Ellie, I was hoping to catch you and Ray before you went to Glendale Nursing Home. I've got another lady for you to call on there. Her name is Alice."

"Oh, we are there right now, and we just met Alice. We discovered that she desperately needs some clothes, and we were on our way to buy her some slacks and blouses."

"I'm glad that I caught you then. Why don't you and Ray head over to the hospice thrift shop? They are open until 4:00 today. I'll call ahead and then fax them a copy of a voucher for you to buy her about thirty dollars' worth of clothes. That should be enough to give her a good start on a wardrobe."

We headed to the hospice thrift shop, which was about fifteen minutes away.

About thirty minutes later, we returned to the facility with several bags of clothing, including underwear, slacks, tops, nightgowns and even a robe.

As we entered their room, we found Margaret and Florence sitting in their wheelchairs, talking quietly. Alice was sitting on the edge of her bed wrapped in a large towel. The aide, Eve, was standing next to her.

I walked over to the bed and handed a package to Alice. "We bought a few things for you to wear for the party. Maybe Eve and my wife can help you get dressed."

After I left the room, they helped Alice into the new undergarments, slacks and top that we had purchased. Then, they combed her hair and helped her apply some lipstick and blush.

When they were finished, my wife opened the door to the room and called for me to come in.

I could not believe the transformation. Alice looked extremely pretty in her new blue slacks and a printed top with colorful yellow, pink and blue flowers. With the little bit of make-up, she looked much fresher and younger.

After the announcement came over the speaker system that Santa was due to arrive at the facility soon, we escorted the three ladies to the dining room for the party.

The activity director walked over to us as we helped the ladies get placed around a table. She welcomed us and turned to Alice. "My goodness, who do we have here? Is this really Alice, who just joined us here at Glendale? I hardly recognize you. You look so lovely. And I just love your blouse and slacks."

Alice smiled sweetly, turned to me and winked. "Yes, new is nice."

— Ray Weaver —

53

Twice Recycled

*An effort made for the happiness
of others lifts us above ourselves.*
~Lydia M. Child

My mother worked as a housekeeper, and she was given myriad leftover things when clients sorted through their junk, including used toys as well as many other goodies. My older sister and I always loved sharing the recycled books and board games that Mom brought home. We fairly divided everything.

One December day, an old-model toy car arrived in the load of goods. It was as long as my forearm and took both hands to lift. My sister didn't want it, so it was all mine. I immediately began scrubbing it clean and polishing it to a bright candy-apple red. It was a thing of beauty, and I glowed as much as it did from pride of ownership.

Our relatives from France came to visit that Christmas, and my young French cousin fell in love with that wonderful, shiny red automobile. He'd been unlucky so far in life, suffering severe, life-threatening illnesses as a child and hurting himself badly earlier in the year when his bicycle careened into a plate-glass window. Already on this trip, he'd managed to break his eyeglasses when he accidentally slipped and fell on the icy sidewalk.

By now, everyone knew how I felt about the car, so nobody dared suggest that I give it to him. But, deep down, I knew it was the right thing to do. So, when they left, my red car went with him. Though I was crushed to see it go, my heart sang when I saw his beaming face as he tightly clutched it.

I still think about that car and miss it to this day. But with that beloved recycled Christmas gift, I bonded with my cousin for life.

Giving that gift showed me for the first time that it is better to give than to receive. It was the first gift that I gave that keeps on giving.

— Sergio Del Bianco —

54

Our Annual Cookie Club

When we have a circle of friends, we have more fun.
We get more done, we feel and are stronger, and we
really do celebrate the power of our "us."
~Mary Anne Radmacher

It all began when the daughter of a dear friend bought a "cookie club" book at a local yard sale. As she handed me the book she said, "I thought of you when I bought this book. If anyone will do this, I know it will be you!"

I read the book and I was hooked! I called twelve special ladies, gave them the date and the rules and they agreed to participate.

The rules were as follows: each participant had to make thirteen dozen cookies. Twelve dozen wrapped by the dozen in creative packaging, one for every participant to take home, and one dozen left open to share that night. No chocolate chip cookies were allowed. I supplied the appetizers and beverages.

The ladies' creativity in packaging was amazing. We had large coffee mugs, make-up bags, stockings, nutcrackers and of course the occasional cookie tin. It was a wonderful concept, as each participant went home with gifts for their hairdresser, manicurist, mail carrier, neighbors and hostess gifts. What could be better?

But by the second year the complaints started rolling in. The thought of making thirteen dozen cookies gave my baking group migraines. I gave it my best holiday sales pitch and we made it through another year.

I knew to get them back the next year something had to change. My daughter came up with the perfect solution. Everyone would make one full batch of cookies—at least a dozen. I would supply twelve containers. There would be plenty to share. And we would all bring an unwrapped gift for a child—to donate to a local residence for displaced children.

Our "cookie club" was back in business. We shared our cookies and we helped make Christmas better for children of all ages at a children's home that posted each child's wish list.

The purchase of a book from a yard sale by the daughter of a friend has left an indelible mark on so many lives. I look forward to those twelve women coming together each year, sharing their stories and adventures, and tasting their incredible creations. But most of all I love that a simple batch of cookies has led to an undertaking that puts smiles on the faces of so many children during the Christmas season.

— Kristine Byron —

55

Chicken Soup
for the *Soul*

A Christmas Star

*When we recall Christmas past, we usually find that
the simplest things — not the great occasions — give
off the greatest glow of happiness.*
~Bob Hope

One Christmas Eve, my seventeen-year-old son called me from the bakery where he worked part-time. He was on the evening shift with a couple of co-workers, and the store was about to close. The person from a local charity who was scheduled to pick up the leftover bread and pastries had not shown up.

He was worried about what to do with the food, so I suggested he call the manager to ask for advice. The manager told him to throw the leftovers into the garbage — approximately $1,500 worth of fresh baked goods.

It seemed utterly wrong for all this good food to go to waste, so we talked about where we could take it. A new homeless shelter had just opened in our area, so I called and asked if they could use a delivery of free baked goods. An excited staff member said, "Yes, please!"

I drove to the bakery and, together with my son and his co-workers, we loaded up the van and made our way to the homeless shelter. As we walked toward the entrance, a woman stopped and held open the door for us. Assuming we were staff, she thanked us for what we were doing and said she was really grateful for her new temporary home. She introduced herself and told us her street friends call her "Star." We chatted for a while on the sidewalk with light snow falling around us. She said that moving off the streets into the shelter had saved her life.

Star pulled a bottle of methadone out of her pocket and explained she was desperately trying to quit heroin. She told us she'd decided her job in life was to help and protect people. She spent her days looking out for those who needed help and trying to do kind things for others whenever she could.

Then she asked for a favor. She showed us a small Bible a friend had given her when she'd been living on the streets. His phone number was written on the inside. She'd wanted to tell him she was okay so he wouldn't worry, but she couldn't afford the long-distance call. I said I would be happy to pass on her message. She wrote his name on a scrap of cardboard from one of the boxes of cinnamon rolls we'd given her. Then she hugged us both, and we wished each other a merry Christmas.

Later that evening, my husband and I were chatting with our kids and sharing our favourite Christmas memories. We laughed about one unusual Christmas we'd celebrated on the beach in Australia with a cardboard cutout Christmas tree and fruit salad lunch. I told my kids they'd have a Christmas that was really special one day — one they'd remember forever. My son said, "I think I've just had that Christmas, Mom."

Meeting Star on Christmas Eve outside the homeless shelter, with the snow falling, was more than a little magical. My son and I will always remember that evening.

On Christmas morning, I called the number on the card, and a man answered the phone. I told him who I was and that I had a message for him from Star. His voice cracked with emotion as he thanked me for calling. He'd been distraught and was relieved to hear she was safe in the shelter.

A few months later, I was driving to a meeting. I saw a woman standing in the middle of the crosswalk with her arms stretched wide and a big smile on her face. It was Star. She was standing between the cars and an older woman with a walking stick making her way very slowly across the road. As soon as the woman had crossed the road safely, Star continued on her way. I smiled as I drove to my meeting, thinking about our neighbourhood "Star" doing her job.

— Gill McCulloch —

Family Fun

Following the Star

May you never be too grown up to
search the skies on Christmas Eve.
~Author Unknown

With two days left before Christmas, our town in suburban Chicago was covered with a pristine blanket of snow. My husband and I drew up a list of safe outdoor activities that would somewhat contribute to keeping the holiday spirit alive and our middle-schooler entertained as we lived through seclusion of the pandemic quarantine.

The following evening was Christmas Eve, and the three of us hopped in our car with flasks of hot chocolate, turned on old-fashioned Christmas songs, and set out to savor the Christmas lights and decorations in our neighborhood.

We had only driven past a few houses when we heard it. Next to us was a merry-looking tour bus playing Christmas music and containing a bunch of masked passengers. It sported holiday lights and a big star on top. It was the town's Christmas bus, and it would visit all the best decorated houses.

My husband grinned and said, "How about we follow the bus tonight? The tour bus will go to all the cool places in town!"

We followed the bus now, at a leisurely twenty miles per hour. Whenever we got separated we merely had to look for that big star and catch up. We stopped where the bus stopped, and so did the four additional cars that had lined up behind us!

Somehow, we all ended up becoming an unplanned, silent Christmas convoy. As we rolled through the old, historic districts we discovered majestically lit mansions and old buildings that had weathered time and space but told a thousand stories.

After taking in a dozen houses and traveling several miles, the trail came to a natural end. Just before parting, people honked in acknowledgement and appreciation to each other and the tour master, and then we each went our own way — with a little magic in our hearts.

— Amita Jagannath —

57

Wrapping-Paper Magic

Christmas is the keeping-place
for memories of our innocence.
~Joan Mills

"Stay, Hunter. Good boy! Just a couple more. Good boy. Stay!" I continued the positive words of praise intertwined with commands as I snapped as many photos as I could. My sweet Bloodhound sat at attention with a Santa cap atop his large head, doing all he could to maintain his composure as he stared with laser focus at the shiny Christmas present sitting on the area rug just a short distance from his reach.

It was Christmas Eve, and I could not help starting early with some Christmas presents for our special hound. Hunter loved unwrapping presents, more than any other dog I had ever had. We got a bunch of new toys for our spoiled fur baby, but we also wrapped up a bunch of his existing toys.

"Okay!" I gave him his release command, and Hunter went to town opening the present in mere seconds. Then he ran straight over to my husband, eagerly awaiting more gifts from the massive pile under the tree. My husband tossed him another, and then another. We had a Christmas paper massacre with crinkly, sparkly remnants strewn all about the house. Hunter had so much fun catching balls of wadded-up wrapping paper and zoomed around the house in childlike excitement.

When Hunter crashed early that evening after all his pre-holiday excitement, we snuck through the house and collected all the presents and wrapping paper. Then we discreetly re-wrapped all the toys he had just opened. We placed them back under the tree for safekeeping so we could bring them over to my parents' house for Christmas morning.

At my parents, Hunter once again became a wrapping-paper maniac and went bananas as we gave him toy after toy. We all had a good laugh as we watched Hunter tear through present after present. He would bring us his empty wrapping paper, and we would crumple it up and throw it to him like a wrapping-paper tennis ball. He would jump and catch it, and then he would run and zoom all around the house, quickly returning for more.

As we were getting ready to leave, Hunter was whining and slinking around, doing his best to evade us putting on his leash. He kept darting back to my parents' bedroom and hiding. We finally followed him back to the bedroom and were astonished when we saw what Hunter had been up to that Christmas morning. He had brought every single ball of wrapping paper we had tossed to him and stashed it on the bed that he slept on when he spent the night at my parents' house. We all giggled, but Hunter did not seem to find the humor as he lay down on the bed with all his wrapping paper.

"What do you think you need, silly boy?" I asked as I tried to put his leash on him once more. He rolled over onto his back, grabbing a wrapping-paper ball in his mouth as his tongue lolled off to the side. "Do you want to bring home all your wrapping paper, buddy?"

Thump, thump, thump! His tail beat happily on the floor.

"Okay, let me go get a bag for all of it," I said to see if that would help usher our stubborn hound into the car. And, sure enough, Hunter was thrilled once I started packing up his wrapping paper and promptly decided he would agree to join Mom and Dad and head home.

When we got home, Hunter was relentless at poking around at the trash bag full of wrapping paper, so we opened it up and let him have at it again. But he was not interested in playing with the paper balls now. Instead, he picked up pieces of the crumpled-up wrapping paper and set them dutifully near our Christmas tree. Then he began herding us to the bedroom for the evening.

"I could be a bit out there on this, but I think he is hoping that the wrapping paper will get filled back up with presents in the morning," I pondered aloud, not always quite sure what was going on in our clever hound's mind. So, we got in bed for the evening and turned on some Christmas movies. Once Hunter was snoring and sound asleep, we decided to humor our sweet pup for one more day. We cleaned up the wrapping-paper mess and then wrapped a few more of his already opened presents again.

Our precious Bloodhound was elated the next morning to discover newly wrapped, shiny Christmas presents under the tree. Once we gave him the okay, he tore into the wrapping paper for Day Three of holiday excitement. He played and played all day. As the day was coming to an end, he collected all his wrapping-paper balls and repeated his same behavior from the evening prior, placing them roughly near the base of the Christmas tree.

Hunter really latched on to the magic of the holiday season that first Christmas with us as a family, and his joy each year is just contagious. Like a little child, he gets so excited when our Christmas tree goes up, and he sees tubes of shimmery wrapping paper enter the house. Even for Hunter, it's not necessarily about what's inside the paper. It's the spirit of the holidays and all the enchantment of time spent together.

— Gwen Cooper —

Chicken Soup
for the Soul

It's In the Cards

The traditions we create will be the memories
our children will cherish in the future.
~Author Unknown

New Year's Eve. Some people travel to Times Square for the official countdown and ball drop. Some people attend elaborate parties dressed in evening gowns and tuxedos. And some people have simple gatherings with family and friends. For my part, I used to look at my husband a few days before and say, "I guess we should do something on New Year's Eve!" The "something" tended to be a quiet evening at home trying to fill the hours and stay awake until midnight. That is, until ten years ago when my friend gave me a simple yet profound Christmas gift.

It was a small box with 365 cards inside — one for each day of the year. The idea was to write on the cards daily like one would write in a journal. I have never kept a journal (nor had an inclination to keep one) but this little box inspired me. I decided that I would use the cards as a kind of "family journal" with a few highlights of each day. I did not have high hopes that I would keep up with this for a whole year, but for some reason I was highly motivated to fill up those cards. Before I knew it, I had faithfully completed a whole month's worth of cards. Then six months. Then ten months. And all the way to the last card in the box: New Year's Eve! What an accomplishment! I had successfully written something on every card on every day of 2012.

Now that I had completed it, my husband and sons, who were

then seven and eleven years old, were curious about what I had been writing all year. We came up with the idea that we would start with the first card and read all of them aloud together. We took turns reading a whole month's worth of cards before passing the box to the next person. It was the best New Year's Eve we had ever spent as a family! Instead of no plans for the evening, we had a plan! It takes a long time to read 365 cards chronicling your family life. Before we knew it, it was almost midnight. Some cards would say something simple like, "We took a family walk after dinner tonight." But others would say something important like, "We flew to Virginia this morning to visit with our family!" As the cards were read, we would make comments. "Oh, yes, that was such an amazing day," or, "Wow, I can't believe it has already been eight months since we went there!" It was a wonderful way to reminisce about the year that had passed and look forward to the new year that began at midnight.

We had officially started a new New Year's Eve tradition.

For ten years now, I have faithfully been filling this little box of cards with the highlights of our daily lives. And every New Year's Eve, we read the cards aloud as a family. Now, when we read the cards, each family member reads the cards from their birthday month when we get to it. When grandparents visit, they read their birthday month. When my son's girlfriend started joining us for New Year's Eve, she got to read her birthday month as well.

I never dreamed I could be this diligent about chronicling the lives of our family on little cards! I am so committed that I take the cards with me on trips so that I can fill them in while away from home. I now have a file box of the cards in order from the first one I wrote. I have been known to reference them when we have a family dispute about what year an event took place. It's all there in the cards!

This year, to celebrate the tenth anniversary of our New Year's Eve tradition, we have decided to read all ten years each month at our last family dinner of the month. That means each person gets to read ten years of their birthday month! We get to relive ten years of our life together. As we read through the ten years, we have been reminded of all the wonderful parties, vacations, weddings, concerts and graduations as well as the hard times and losses we have experienced as a family. It is like looking through a family album over the years but using words instead of pictures.

I am not sure if I will keep this up after our children leave home. But I think I know what I am going to give them as a gift when they leave: a box of 365 cards.

— Christina Peters —

59

The Seven Hours of Christmas

Dear Santa, I've been good all year. Most of the time.
Once in a while. Never mind, I'll buy my own stuff.
~Author Unknown

In the first hour of Christmas, we come back home from church —
don't step on Grandma's carpet with your dirty shoes!

In the second hour of Christmas, the cousins' car pulls in:
take the gifts, shake them, stick the biggest ones in front —
and, kids, don't walk on that carpet with your dirty shoes!

In the third hour of Christmas, we gather around the lunch:
close your mouth when you chew, gosh we ordered too much food,
take the gifts, shake them, stick the biggest ones in front —
and don't you dare walk on that carpet with those shoes!

In the fourth hour of Christmas, the living room is reached:
cameras start their flashing, children start unwrapping,
close your mouth when you chew, gosh we ordered too much food,
take the gifts, shake them, stick the biggest ones in front —
and get off the new carpet with those shoes!

In the fifth hour of Christmas, the gifts are all exposed:

batteries don't come with it, pretend the sweater will fit,
cameras are still flashing, the kids want more unwrapping,
close your mouth when you chew, gosh we ordered too much food,
take the gifts, shake them, stick the biggest ones in front —
and don't even think about stepping on that carpet with those shoes!

The sixth hour of Christmas is family dinner time:
pray if you are able (even at the kids' table),
batteries don't come with it, pretend the sweater will fit,
cameras are still flashing, the kids want more unwrapping,
close your mouth when you chew, gosh we ordered too much food,
take the gifts, shake them, stick the biggest ones in front —
and don't you dare walk on that carpet with dirty shoes!

In the seventh hour of Christmas, we all say our goodbyes:
use the bathroom one last time, Aunt Marge has a three-hour drive,
pray if you are able (even at the kids' table),
batteries don't come with it, pretend the sweater will fit,
cameras are still flashing, the kids want more unwrapping,
close your mouth when you chew, gosh we ordered too much food,
take the gifts, shake them, stick the biggest ones in front —
and what did Grandma say about those shoes?!

— Ana Reisens —

60

The Thanksgiving of The Incident

The moment may be temporary,
but the memory is forever.
~Bud Meyer

Our son Hyrum, his wife Cara, two small children, and one huge dog, Diesel, spent four days with us over Thanksgiving. Though my husband and I greeted them eagerly, our cat, Harley, was not as welcoming. She gave Diesel a disdainful sniff and stalked off.

"Harley's accustomed to being an only child," I joked.

Everyone laughed.

We continued to laugh at our pets' standoffish attitude toward each other until it happened: The Incident.

At sixteen years old, Harley had diabetes, which caused her to have "bathroom accidents" in various places throughout the house. One such accident left a steaming pile on the living room rug. Usually quick to spot such messes, I missed this one, too involved in playing with my grandchildren to notice.

When Diesel wandered into the family room, reeking of a foul odor, I jumped up, ran into the living room, and saw what I had feared: He had rolled in the pile of poop and spread it all over the rug, furniture, and everything else.

My cry of dismay alerted other family members. My daughter-in-law tried to catch Diesel, but he took the excitement as a signal to run through the house, slinging feces with every step. The grandchildren joined in the ruckus.

We were a household in chaos.

"Diesel, come here," Cara commanded.

Diesel skidded to a stop. The sudden movement caused more bits and pieces of excrement to fly from his quivering-with-joy body.

As for me, I was on my hands and knees cleaning up what would send most hardened crime-scene professionals into shock.

Cara took Diesel to the downstairs shower to shampoo his feces-matted fur.

Several hours and loads of laundry later, the family, including a chastened Diesel and an unrepentant Harley, gathered in the family room.

"We'll look back and laugh at this at some point," my husband said.

I wasn't so sure, but I knew that The Incident would be forever seared in our memories.

— Jane McBride —

61

The Card Guy

An uncle is a bond of faith that even time can't sever,
a gift to last all of our lives. An uncle is forever.
~Irene Banks

For many, Jesus and Santa are the two main guys of Christmas. They steal the show. And although Jesus is definitely the reason for the season in our household, there is another guy who is almost as important to our family during the holidays. It's the Card Guy.

We have a long-standing tradition on my dad's side of the family. We have a card contest. What started out as a friendly game of voting on which Christmas card was the best to be sent to my uncle and his family turned into an all-out fierce competition of judging, alliances, secret voting, song and dance, tears, fights, and carefully crafting the perfect and funniest card. We've had family members become the Griswolds, Kardashians, Joe Biden and Obama, and Ralphie and Randy from *A Christmas Story* — all in the name of the Card Contest. And, out of that, the Card Guy came to life.

The Card Guy is my uncle. On the eve of the contest, he transforms into a character wearing a denim vest full of Christmas cards from days of yore. The lights dim, the music sounds, and he bursts into the room almost magically, singing and dancing the opening number. It is usually a spoof on a popular song. It was oddly reminiscent of Michael Scott performing at The Dundies. Throughout his entire performance for the night, he does a spectacular job of hosting the contest. He divides the cards into categories: Nature, Religious, Plain Text, and the biggest, most coveted one of all — the Picture category. Then, he dazzles us with his jokes, wit, charisma, and charm until he ultimately crowns the winner of the night.

For a while, the Card Guy was on top of the world.

But, over time, we became greedy and hungry for victory. We pushed the Card Guy for more. More jokes. More songs. More pizzazz. And we razzed him when the contest dragged on for too long. We belittled him when our cards didn't win. We booed him when his jokes didn't land. We demanded he perform like he was some kind of show puppet and not a real person with real feelings. We couldn't see it, but the Card Guy was cracking. The pressure was too much.

Finally, he announced his retirement. Some family members made feeble attempts to encourage him to perform again, but he simply wouldn't do it. With the birth of children, weddings, surgeries, and the like, the family wasn't able to be together at Christmastime for the past two years. We made some tries to have the contest over Facebook, but it was missing something: the Card Guy.

With the past few years being so hard, we all needed something to unite the world during the holiday season — someone to bring peace and simplicity back into the homes of America again. We needed the Card Guy. But, more importantly, we needed the Card Guy because he unites our family. He makes us laugh. He makes us value family traditions. He gives us hope that, despite everything that has happened in the world, we will always have each other to lean on, fight and make up with, and ultimately create long-lasting memories with. Ones we can tell our children about. The year 2020 wasn't the time for traditions to be forgotten. It was the year for them to be remade, rebirthed, and restored in any way possible. It was the year that Card Guy returned.

— Lauren Barrett —

62

Jingle Bell Rock

Time spent with family is worth every second.
~Author Unknown

My parents had always loved to dance as long as I could remember. They married during the Great Depression, and they would go dancing every Saturday night for entertainment. My sister Gloria was fourteen years older, and she would tell me stories of their daring escapades. Sometimes, they would travel fifty to sixty miles on icy roads to find a dance hall in rural Wisconsin.

After I came along, they still went out for dinner and dancing on a Saturday night. That was their date night. When they got home, they would come into my room to kiss me goodnight with my mom carrying her spiked heels and humming. Then I would know that they had had a wonderful time dancing the night away.

As I grew up and married Paul, we would go to my sister Gloria's house on Christmas. She and her husband Ray had six kids. We had three, and there were various other relatives who would drop in. The evening started with presents and then a huge dinner, complete with ham and all the trimmings. After dinner, we would visit, laugh, and eat my mom's stellar homemade cookies and candy.

One Christmas, my mom confessed to me that there was a new song out, and it was her favorite: "Jingle Bell Rock." As one of her presents, I bought her the recording. That evening after Christmas dinner, my brother-in-law Ray put on his big-band music. Somehow, Mom slipped in her new record. She stood up from the couch and turned to my dad.

"Al, dance with me?" she said with a twinkle in her eye. My father was rather dumbstruck as he wasn't quite sure how to dance to rock and roll. Mom snapped her fingers in time to the music, and he knew she wouldn't give up until she got her way. They did the quickstep around the room, laughing. Pretty soon, we were all dancing, grown-ups and kids. Girl cousins grabbed shy boy cousins and dragged them onto the green shag carpet. That Christmas, a new tradition was born. Every Christmas after that, we ended up with the entire family dancing around my sister's house.

Many Christmases passed, and the kids grew up and moved into their own homes. Soon, there were tons of grandchildren joining us. Obligations to both sides of the married families split us up for dinners, but we all converged on my sister's house later for Mom's cookies and coffee. One of the grown kids would yell, "Put on 'Jingle Bell Rock'!" That's when the fun would begin. We did all the popular dance moves. Of course, my parents always went back to their own favorite, the quickstep.

Decades went by, and soon all the children, complete with grown kids of their own, scattered far and wide. It was no longer easy for them to travel many miles to be with us. We usually took flights to see them. My sister and her husband were off to their grandkids. But we always had my mom and dad for Christmas Eve dinner. On what would be their last Christmas together, Mom had me put on "Jingle Bell Rock." Age has a way of slowing people down, and Mom and Dad, now in their eighties, were no exception. I still saw that twinkle in my mom's eyes as they swayed to the music.

This Christmas, I was doing some shopping and found my feet tapping to a vaguely familiar song. I realized that "Jingle Bell Rock" was playing on the store's PA system. The past came tumbling back, and for an instant I went back in time, picturing my family laughing as they danced around my sister's living room.

— Sallie A. Rodman —

63

Chicken Soup
for the *Soul*

It Started with a Girdle

I love Christmas. I receive a lot of wonderful presents
I can't wait to exchange.
~Henny Youngman

O ur large family packed into Grandma and Grandpa Sommers' basement for our Christmas celebration. As we gathered on that late 1980s evening, little did we know that a strange family tradition would be born.

Exactly who wrapped the gift remains a mystery, but my bet is on Grandma. She was an organized, efficient woman who could have easily run a small nation, but for some reason she had decided to pull one over on straitlaced Grandpa. And that December night, we saw a different side of Grandpa. He opened the gift and started to giggle. Out of the box, he pulled a beige girdle from decades earlier. He shook the girdle from side to side and proudly displayed his gift to our family, who were now howling in laughter. This burly, old carpenter then did something no one expected. He put on the girdle! We barely kept our composure the rest of the night, laughing about Grandpa's gag gift.

The following year, we gathered again in the basement with the family. Cookies were eaten, and gifts were unwrapped one by one. It was the moment Grandpa had been waiting for. Imagine our surprise when a cousin opened a beautifully wrapped gift to find the girdle! But this time, it had bells sewn on it! With cheers and family peer pressure, the cousin also modeled the girdle, jingling all the way!

Thus, the tradition was born. A new person gets the girdle each year, adds an item to the girdle, and then gives it to an unsuspecting family member the next year. The recipient must immediately put on the girdle in front of the whole family. Thirty years later, the girdle is quite eclectic! Now attached to the girdle is gold underwear, a bra, a reindeer, and all sorts of things that dangle and jangle. Bodies very large to very small have somehow shimmied into that girdle to cheers and laughter.

Grandpa and Grandma Sommers are gone now, but the girdle remains. The children, spouses, and even grandchildren of those original participants still watch to see who will get the girdle each Christmas, and what new item has been added. We still laugh as a new victim tries to pull up the tight girdle over whatever beautiful outfit was worn. Who would have thought that a vintage girdle would be the gift that keeps on giving?

— Sharla Elton —

64

The Perfect Ornament

Gifts of time and love are surely the basic ingredients
of a truly merry Christmas.
~Peg Bracken

Christmas was always a big deal in my house. Even though I am an only child, and it was just the three of us, my mom decorated and baked as if she had ten children. And she took particular pride in assembling and decorating our artificial Christmas tree. She was meticulous in making it look as authentic as possible and took great care when hanging the garland and stringing the lights to make sure no branch was ignored. It was a work of art.

When I got a bit older, I asked my mom why we never bought a real tree. "They're messy, and they could catch on fire," was the answer. So of course, when I moved out of the house I bought a real tree for my first Christmas on my own. And I've been buying real trees ever since — even after having two children, despite how messy they are, and that yes, they could catch on fire. In fact, my wife and our two children, Max and Olivia, turned the tree-buying into a bit of an adventure… to find the "perfect" tree.

When Max was nine years old, and his sister Olivia seven, their mom and I divorced — a traumatic life event that unfortunately coincided with another, albeit less traumatic, life event for my parents — they were forced to downsize and move into an apartment in a senior community. Having to sell their home and their only child getting divorced were tough waters for my parents to navigate, but my mom especially struggled. So, as Christmas approached, it was understandable that she wasn't finding much joy in the season. In speaking with her, she sounded heartbreakingly defeated, and lacked the enthusiasm and conviction it took to decorate as she always had. In fact, for the first time in my life, she had no plans to put up a Christmas tree. She simply put a two-foot-tall ceramic Christmas tree atop a corner table and called it a day.

I visited my parents with the kids in the weeks leading up to Christmas, and Max noticed that the house looked and even smelled different than it had in past Christmas seasons. Less decorated, no smell of fresh-baked chocolate chip cookies, and no tree. He asked my mom why she didn't have a tree, and she told him that there just wasn't room in this new apartment for a tree, which was, of course, only a half-truth. She was just sad and clearly lacked her usual Christmas spirit.

When my children and I went shopping for our own tree, we wandered the lot for about a half hour before Max and his little sister agreed on a full nine-foot-tall Douglas fir. On the way out of the lot, Max came upon a small pile of trees, each only about four or five feet tall. Not quite in Charlie Brown shape, but close. He said that we should buy one for his grandmother. "We could give it to her on Christmas and help her decorate it." I felt ashamed for not thinking of it myself.

On Christmas we packed the car with presents for my parents, and the little four-foot tree we'd picked up for them. My parents greeted us at the door, as they always did, and Max anxiously jumped out of the car, ran to my mom, grabbed her hand, and took her to the back of the car as I popped the SUV's trunk. "We got you a tree Grandma! A real one! You can't have Christmas without a tree." Standing beside her, I whispered, "I know you don't like real trees, but he insisted." Her eyes welled with tears, and she gave Max a big hug and kiss, and said, "It's perfect."

Max and I went down to their storage space in the garage and carried all the ornaments and decorations upstairs. We cleared out some space in a corner, laid down the circular Christmas blanket, and together, with Olivia and my mom, decorated the tree.

An angel had always sat atop my mom's tree, but we found that the top branch was too flimsy to hold its weight. My mom said, "I have the perfect ornament for that." She moved an ornament from a lower branch to the very top—a hand-painted ornament Max had made in school. It was a picture frame, and in the center was a picture of him and my mom, with an eight-year old's painted words: "Grandma and Me."

—Victor Cataldo—

Through the Eyes of a Child

65

Imperfect Creatures

*Never ever doubt magic. The purest honest thoughts
come from children. Ask any child if they believe
in magic, and they will tell you the truth.*
~Scott Dixon

t has become apparent that there is something very wrong with
our Elf on the Shelf. Her name is Star, and she doesn't seem to
move at all. She'll sometimes go three days without moving an
inch, just perched in the upper half of our Christmas tree. My
daughter went so far as to sprinkle cinnamon on Star's head because
"that's what they say to do on YouTube." But even *that* didn't work!

"My friends' elves do all these funny things," my daughter complained. "Carson's elf wrapped himself up in a tortilla. Skylar's elf
spread shaving cream all over the bathroom mirror, like a snowstorm!"

That sounds awful, I thought, and shuddered inside.

"That's why I'm asking Santa Claus for a new one," my daughter
said.

A new elf?

I thought about this. "Sweetie," I said. "I think you maybe have
to accept your elf for who she is, right? Like, think about people.
Every person is different. Some people are just a little bit lazy. Some
people are just mellow or content. Some people are just a little ditsy
sometimes and forget to move themselves. Some people are more
introspective, like Star. Obviously, she likes to observe, and she found
the most perfect spot in the room. See? She found what works. And

that's wonderful! I applaud you, Star!"

"I'm asking for a baby elf, too," my daughter said.

"What I mean is," I concluded, "we all have our imperfections, and that's part of what makes us lovable and unique!"

"Well," my daughter countered, "I get how people are all different. That's why I am asking for a brand-new elf. Because I bet it will have a different personality."

Touché.

Two days into Star not moving, my daughter left some notes in the tree, right where Star could reach them and deliver them to Santa. Normally I wouldn't have touched them, but I wanted to make sure they got to the Big Man, since Star had clearly proven herself to be an unreliable ambassador. So, I ripped open the envelopes to see where I should address them.

Three of the letters were for Santa, asking individually:

1) Whether he is black or white or brown

2) For an iPhone (which she was not getting)

3) For a momma and a baby elf

Oh, boy, I thought. *Cue the overnight shipping.*

The last of the letters was for Star.

"Dear Star," it said. "Thank you for coming."

Thank you for coming: a precious reminder to open our homes and hearts for the holidays, and to *always* practice heartfelt appreciation for the ones we love, imperfections and all.

— Marissa Fallon —

66

Chicken Soup for the Soul

A Christmas Lesson

In the eyes of children we find the joy of Christmas.
In their hearts we find its meaning.
~Thomas Leland

A few years ago, my husband and I decided to dedicate our time around the holidays to families in our community that needed support. We reached out to a parish priest and a friend who was a pastor who ran a shelter in our area. We told them we wanted to start an annual anonymous sponsorship program and asked them both if they could put together a list of any families or individuals who could use some help around Christmas.

A few weeks later, we received e-mails from both men with their lists. We sent out e-mails and text messages to everyone we knew, asking them to help in any way they could, and we placed collection boxes in my husband's workplace and a few local businesses that agreed to help.

In the weeks leading up to Christmas, my husband began bringing home the collection boxes we had placed and the donations from our friends and family. We were overwhelmed with everyone's generosity. We had raised so much money and received so many items that every family on our list was going to get everything they needed and more.

I began sorting the donations into sections within our house, each room designated for a different family. Not really considering how much we had gratefully received and that this was a yearly program we wanted to develop, I got a bit carried away and distributed everything we had — saving nothing for the following Christmas.

As Christmas Eve arrived, we delivered everything to the church and the shelter so that the parents of the families could come and pick up all their food, gift cards and other items. As we made the final drop at the shelter, the pastor looked at everything we had brought and joyfully said, "You can't be serious. All of this?" We laughed happily, wished him a merry Christmas and headed home. Exhausted from the past several weeks, my husband and I slept soundly that night. Christmas came and went, and we enjoyed our holiday with our own family.

The week after Christmas, we received an e-mail from the pastor who ran the shelter. He had received a letter from one of the moms of one of the families that he wanted to share with us. She had written to tell him that this had been their family's best holiday ever. Something truly special had happened on Christmas morning in their house that would change them all forever.

Her seven children awoke on Christmas morning to find the gifts that Santa had brought them. The kitchen was filled with food and treats, and bags of new clothes and warm jackets sat by the front door. The youngest of their children, a five-year-old girl, had wandered into the kitchen after seeing everything they had and asked her and her husband if she could do something that left them speechless. She told them that their family was so blessed to have received all these special gifts, but she didn't feel that they needed all of them. She had a friend from school whose family could use some help, and she asked her mom and dad if she could take some things over to her friend's house and give them to her instead.

They were so touched that they sat down the rest of their kids and told them what their little sister wanted to do and why. As a family, they agreed that it was important to share with others in need even if that meant taking things away from themselves. So, they did just that.

She ended her letter by saying that their family received the best gift that anyone could ever hope for: the opportunity to share with others, which was something they would never forget.

Christmas through the eyes of a child is simple; it's uncomplicated and filled solely with love, compassion and kindness. They know only to share and give with no expectations. Imagine that a child so small could teach us all something so big.

— Nanette Norgate —

67

When the Tooth Fairy Met Santa

*Each day of our lives we make deposits
in the memory banks of our children.*
~Charles R. Swindoll, *The Strong Family*

My oldest child, Brayden, was seven years old that Christmas. Brayden had been wishing for months and months for a visit from the tooth fairy. He watched as all his classmates lost their teeth and regaled the class with the special treasures left behind by the magical tooth fairy. Brayden, too, wanted a chance to tell his class about a lost tooth.

Our family enjoyed a delicious Christmas Eve dinner prepared by my in-laws. My children were practically jumping out of their skins knowing that Santa was coming in a few short hours.

From the next room, my husband and I heard Brayden exclaim, "Mom! Come quick." We ran into the room to find Brayden with a smiling, bloody grin, holding a tooth in his hand. "Mom, my tooth just fell right out! I cannot believe it. I finally lost a tooth!"

"Mom, we need to go home and put the tooth under my pillow right away. Santa will meet the tooth fairy tonight!" This is something I had never pondered happening. Two worlds colliding... Santa Claus and the tooth fairy? How could this be?

After we read *'Twas the Night Before Christmas*, put on Christmas pajamas, and left out cookies and milk for Santa, the children were at last nestled all snug in their beds.

On Christmas morning, the children ran down the stairs ready to see what Santa had left. Brayden was the last to come down the steps — with a twenty-dollar bill in his hand. My husband laughed to himself as he realized that the tooth fairy accidentally mixed up a one-dollar bill and a twenty-dollar bill in the dark.

"Mom, the tooth fairy met Santa Claus and got Christmas magic. She wanted me to have a great Christmas." I smiled to myself as I realized that, through the innocent words of a seven-year-old, I was able to relive that Christmas magic yet again.

Brayden had quite the tooth-fairy story to finally tell his classmates when he returned from winter break. Every year, our family joyously retells our family and friends the story of "When the Tooth Fairy Met Santa."

— Danielle Hack —

68

Santa's Helper

Your children get only one childhood.
Make it memorable.
~Regina Brett

I t was Christmas Eve, and my husband Harold and I were watching TV before we started hauling presents down from the attic. We were about to start when we heard our youngest, seven-year-old Spencer, come down the steps. It was almost midnight, and I was hoping to get the presents under the tree so I could get some sleep before all five kids woke up at the crack of dawn to open them.

Rubbing his eyes, Spencer said he was thirsty and needed some water. We sat on the couch together while he took a few sips. He looked at the plate of cookies on the coffee table. "Why does Santa eat cookies in everybody's house? Doesn't he get full?" he asked with a tired voice. I told him Santa only takes a nibble to keep up his energy so he can deliver gifts, and he shares some with his reindeer as well. He started to ask his habitual "Why?" but there was a moment of silence, and he rephrased his question. "How does Santa carry all the gifts himself? Doesn't he get tired?" I took this opportunity of our quiet time to tell him how Santa delivers gifts all over the world in one night.

"Well, you see, Santa sometimes has special people helping him along the way." I paused and was about to continue when I heard Spencer gently snore.

Harold carried Spencer upstairs to bed, while I went to the attic to bring down some of the Christmas gifts that would be from us. We always wrapped our gifts with gold wrapping paper. The gifts that Santa brought were always wrapped with brightly colored wrapping paper. I was arranging our gifts under the tree when Harold told me he'd bring down the last of the gifts. Sitting back on the couch, I thought about the joy of the next morning and how excited the kids would be.

I was deep in thought when I heard a big bang, and then another, coming from the attic. I knew Harold must have knocked something over in the process of gathering the presents. Coming down the steps, Harold sheepishly whispered, "Sorry!"

As anticipated, the kids eagerly ran down the steps early Christmas morning. They always opened their gifts from Santa first. We loved sitting back and watching their joy. Our youngest daughter, Kimberly, gave a delighted yelp when she opened a much-desired gift. She looked upward and said, "Thank you, Santa!" All our children chimed in after her, thanking Santa for their gifts.

We continued our Christmas morning tradition with a big breakfast and the kids enjoying their presents.

It wasn't until the late afternoon that Spencer came up to me and announced, "I know who Santa chose to be his special helper!" He looked up at me with his large brown eyes full of wonder and cried out with an excited voice, "Dad!" I wanted to ask how he knew, but I didn't have to.

"I heard Santa and his reindeer land on the roof last night!" he said excitedly. "They woke me up!" He told me how he saw his dad pass his bedroom door, helping Santa carry gifts.

Then I realized that Harold's mishap in the attic was an unexpected blessing. It woke Spencer so he could witness his dad helping Santa deliver their gifts, a wonderful illustration of how Santa gets a little help wherever he goes.

— Dorann Weber —

69

Who Knew?

Santa Claus is believing in something greater,
believing in something magical.
~Vanessa Grimaldi, The Bachelor

There may not be any snow on the shores of sunny California, but that doesn't mean there is a lack of winter holiday cheer! While many are skiing in the mountains, my husband Baruch and I enjoy walking the Seal Beach Pier in mid-December while watching the swimmers and surfers ride the waves.

Before we've even finished our leftover Thanksgiving turkey, strings of lights dance above the city streets, and retail businesses suddenly turn into wonderlands of shopping specials! The neighborhood lawns sport manger scenes while Santa looks down from rooftops. Baruch and I contribute to the holiday cheer by putting a polished menorah in our front windows, anticipating the eight days of Hanukkah.

This time of year is a diverse mixture of family, culture and faith.

On one of those warm winter days, Baruch and I were in our local Trader Joe's, with the aroma of pumpkin spice wafting through the aisles. A young boy ran up to us, stared up at Baruch, and said, "S-s-s-anta?" His mother caught up to her son and apologized for his bold behavior. We were bewildered as to what to do next. It took us a minute to realize that this little boy thought he had found the real Santa accompanied by his missus!

Thinking quickly, Baruch bent down and, with a smile, spoke in his deepest, softest voice, "Have you been a good little boy this year?" The boy's eyes immediately flashed to his mother as his head slowly nodded up and down. Baruch then stood up, ruffled the little boy's hair, and proceeded to belt out a resonant belly laugh while projecting a thunderous "HO HO HO!" It caught the ears of surrounding shoppers and left the little boy's mouth wide open in awe.

This was only the first of many such occasions during the holiday season. It became apparent that we possessed the striking, jovial images that many children have come to know and love. Baruch has a long, curly white beard, twinkling blue eyes with miniature glasses perched upon his nose, rosy cheeks as big as peaches, and a generous belly that jiggles when he laughs.

As for me, I am short and plump, wearing long skirts and a kerchief upon my head. Yes, we could stand in for the real duo, no doubt!

It seemed after repeated incidents in public places that we had little choice but to play along. We became very proficient at recognizing the gaze of a child, and it became our treat to play along, having ample pocketfuls of colorful, foil-wrapped chocolate gelt (coins) to share. With a wink and a smile, Baruch asks a curious child if he or she has been behaving, ingratiating Santa with the little tikes' parents.

As Jews, Santa may not be a part of our tradition, but we are happy to oblige in spreading a bit of cheer into a child's life.

— Miryam Howard-Meier —

70

Natural Giver

*Every one of us comes into this life with lessons
to learn and gifts to give.*
~Shakti Gawain

Morning came in a rush as usual. I led Cabe sleepily into the bathroom to potty and helped him brush his teeth. He was not old enough to have loose teeth, but he always tried to see if his big-boy teeth were coming in. It was about the only thing that opened his eyes in the morning. I dropped him at the neighborhood babysitter's house, where he would get breakfast. We clung to each other for a minute, knowing I would not see him again until after dinner.

I drove off to my job as an Instructional Assistant at the elementary school in town, preparing for my morning with a class of special-needs children. I felt fortunate that day because I only had to do my evening paper route after school, and not my substitute clerking job on the third shift at the hospital's emergency room. I could not wait to finish my paper route so I could start on my Christmas surprise.

I took Cabe with me on the paper route, and we always had a fun time as he helped me "toss" the folded papers onto our neighbor's porches and front stoops. As soon as I got Cabe fed, bathed, and tucked into bed with a story and a kiss, I went to the storage shed and brought in a secondhand tricycle. It was in very sturdy riding condition, but it needed sanding and a good paint job. The little tricycle was missing a pedal, but I picked up an inexpensive pair of new plastic pedals. After spreading newspaper on the kitchen floor, I began sanding where I left off the night before. I would be able to paint it the next night.

The next day was like the day before, except that I had to put in four hours at the hospital. Picking up Cabe from the neighbor's, I started counting out my change to pay my neighbor for watching Cabe for the past month. She said, "Oh, no, dear. You should hang onto that for Christmas." But knowing that she had a family to buy presents for as well, I insisted that she have her payment in time for Christmas shopping. My sweet neighbor humbly took it and gave me a quick hug.

Dinner, bath, bed, and story for Cabe, and I was off to paint his "new" tricycle. It turned out beautifully. Shiny, clean and with new pedals and cute, fringed rubber handlebar covers, he would never be able to tell it was not a brand-new trike.

On Christmas Eve, Cabe and I had a day to ourselves, which we spent walking around our neighborhood, looking at the beautiful Christmas lights and decorations. We had gotten a little tree from a neighbor who said she found a bigger one that she wanted. I knew she was being nice, and I felt a little embarrassed, but I wanted Cabe to have it all. I found a couple of strands of lights in the basement of our apartment house that nobody wanted and was happy they all worked. Cabe and I baked cookies and decorated them with frosting and colored sugar. It was a wonderful Christmas Eve. I tucked my child into bed with smiles on our faces. He wanted to make sure Santa would come, so he went to bed very easily that night.

I snuck out to the living room early in the morning and turned on the tree lights. When Cabe saw the tricycle he squealed, looking back at me as if to get permission to ride it. My smile said yes! He hopped on and rode around the room.

He climbed onto my lap, all shivery and happy, and said, "Miss Sue said they were not getting any presents for my friend because they are poor. Momma, do you think Santa would let me give my tricycle to the poor kids?"

That was the best Christmas ever.

— Sheree Negus —

71

As Long as You Believe

Brothers aren't simply close; brothers are knit together.
~Robert Rivers

Late one Christmas Eve, while I was tidying up and waiting for everyone to have visions of sugar plums dancing in their heads, I watched our youngest son, Ben, who was seven at the time, scurry around the house with little pieces of paper and tape. I didn't know what he was up to, but he was making a stop in every room. And close on his tail was his brother, Jon, who was eleven. Jon was casual about his movements, visiting every place Ben had been, but keeping a close watch to make sure he wasn't spotted following his brother from room to room.

I followed them both, being drawn in by this interesting Christmas Eve mystery. I was trying to figure out what was going on without disturbing the process. When Ben's job was completed, he slipped off, climbing the stairs quietly to brush his teeth. I met up with Jon in the last location, giving him an inquisitive look. He just shook his head as he turned the piano bench over and drew a small "x" on the piece of paper taped there. I leaned down to see the paper. In small, second-grade handwriting, was written, "Santa, mark here if you are real." As Jon returned the piano bench to its position, he simply said, "Santa shouldn't have to do all this work. I'm helping him out."

I gave Jon a big hug and thanked him for being such a good brother. Then he headed up to get ready for bed. As long as you believe, Christmas magic is everywhere.

—Jesse Neve—

Chicken Soup for the Soul

Making Our Wish List

If you carry your childhood with you,
you never become older.
~Tom Stoppard

"I t's here, it's here!" I called to my sister Mandy, holding up the Sears Christmas catalog that had just arrived in that day's mail. In the 1980s, the Sears catalog was one of the highlights of most kids' Christmas season. My siblings and I spent hours looking through the toy section, circling items we wanted and folding down the corners of the pages.

Mandy and I loved to show each other the toys we'd circled, and sometimes we even coordinated our requests. "If you circle the Cabbage Patch doll stroller on page 47, I'll ask for the Cabbage Patch doll car seat on page 51," I said. "Then you can borrow my car seat when you need to drive Louisa May to the doctor, and I can borrow your stroller when I want to take Nellie Sue to the mall."

Mandy thought this was an excellent plan. "It's like a 'buy one present, get one free' deal," she said. "We should totally do that." I think we even shook on it.

Santa cooperated with our arrangement, and Louisa May and Nellie Sue did enjoy taking turns with their new stroller and car seat.

Yes, the Sears catalog was my favorite thing about Christmas — until the year when Santa got a little confused about which kid circled which toy.

On Christmas morning, when my brother opened the stuffed

Chewbacca doll I'd circled in the catalog, I burst into tears.

"I'm sorry," Mom said. "Chewy is from *Star Wars*, so I'm sure Santa thought your brother wanted him."

After significant negotiations, we worked out a visitation schedule to share custody of Chewy, but I could tell by Mom's expression that she planned to speak to Santa about his egregious error.

The next year, when the Sears Christmas catalog arrived, Mom laid down the new ground rules. "We're done circling things in the catalog and folding down the pages," she announced.

Mom took a piece of paper, wrote my brother's name on it, and then drew a grid. "Each of you will have your own paper," she explained. "When you see something you want in the catalog, you need to fill in the grid with the page number, the item number, if there's a certain color you want, and anything else Santa needs to know." She winked at me. "He wants to get things right this year."

The new system worked well, and Santa kept things straight from then on.

By the time my own children were born, the Sears Christmas catalog was a thing of the past. I missed it, but we developed our own tradition to make their Christmas wish lists. Each year, we took a "just looking" trip through Toys "R" Us. When the kids were little, I took a small notepad to write down the toys they seemed especially interested in. When I got my first smartphone, I let the kids take photos of the toys they wanted. They loved swiping through the photos when we got home, dreaming of the fun that was coming on Christmas morning.

Then Amazon happened, and my kids started making their wish lists online. It was convenient to shop with a few clicks, but I missed our old traditions.

Then, a few years ago, something wonderful came in the mail. Amazon started sending out a printed toy catalog. When it came, I flipped through it and could hardly believe how great it was. The smart people at Amazon had made the Sears toy catalog even better because they'd added a sheet of stickers for kids to use to mark the items they wanted.

I showed the catalog to my youngest son, Nathan. His eyes got big as he flipped through page after page of Lego sets.

I showed him the stickers and said, "You can use these to mark the toys you want. When I was little, I used to make my Christmas list with a catalog like this, but we didn't have stickers back then."

"This is so cool," he said. "Can I put the stickers on the pages right now?"

I nodded. "I'm going to start dinner. Go ahead and mark the toys you like with a sticker, and then we'll look through it together in a little while."

As I cooked, I could hear him muttering to himself about the awesome toys on every page. I smiled to myself, wondering if he was going to run out of stickers.

After dinner, Nathan was anxious to show me the toys he'd marked. But when he opened the catalog, I saw that he'd placed the stickers directly on top of the toys he liked, completely covering each item.

"Baby, I can't see the toys you like because you covered them up with the stickers," I said.

His shoulders slumped. "You said to mark them, so that's what I did."

He was right. I obviously didn't explain it well enough. We tried to peel back the stickers, but the paper ripped. When I looked at Nathan, he had tears in his eyes.

"This was special to you because it's like when you were little, but I messed it up," he said.

"No, you didn't," I said. "It's actually funny if you think about it. I mean, I thought Amazon was so smart for including stickers, but maybe they aren't such a great idea after all."

I called my mother-in-law, who lives just down the road, and asked her if she'd gotten an Amazon toy catalog in the mail that day. When she said yes, I told her what happened and asked if we could have hers. Of course, she said yes.

I grabbed two Popsicles from the freezer and told Nathan to grab his jacket. As we walked to my mother-in-law's house, we ate the Popsicles.

When we got back home with my mother-in-law's catalog, Nathan grabbed a piece of paper and drew a grid, just like my mom had done after the Chewbacca debacle. "I'll use the stickers for something else," he said as he wrote down the page numbers for the toys he liked.

I don't know if Nathan will remember the Amazon catalog as fondly as I remember the Sears one, but helping him make his wish list from that catalog became one of my favorite parts of Christmas once again.

— Diane Stark —

73

An Unmatched Lesson

Selfless giving is the art of living.
~Frederic Lenz

Some Christmas stories are as sweet as hot cocoa topped with melting marshmallows. This one is not. All the same, I would not trade it for the world—or even for a toy Matchbox car.

The year was 1966, wintertime in central Ohio, and I bit my quivering lip trying with all the strength a six-year-old can muster not to cry. I felt like I had just found a lump of coal in my stocking.

I was in first grade in Mrs. Bauer's class at a time when "holiday parties" were still called "Christmas parties," and elementary schools held student gift exchanges. I was to swap toys with Paul, a boy I knew little about because he was not in my circle of recess friends.

I knew one thing, however: I would buy Paul a Matchbox car. After all, all boys loved the tiny metal cars, racers, and trucks. I seem to recall that Matchboxes cost about a dollar, which was probably the price limit for our gifts.

Mom took me to the local five-and-dime where my two brothers and I spent our allowance money. We got a nickel for each year in our age, so I received thirty cents weekly as a first grader while my older siblings got forty-five and fifty-five cents. They spent it on trading cards, comic books, and Matchboxes.

I do not remember which car I picked out for Paul, but my best guess is a Mustang since that is what I would have wanted for myself.

Paul did not reciprocate with a Mustang or any other Matchbox. Nor did he give me a rubber baseball, a Frisbee or a few packs of football cards.

No, the gift I opened at our class party was a plastic Santa Claus, slightly larger than a coffee mug, on green snow skis. A bag for toys on Santa's back was empty, although it had probably held candy canes when originally purchased. Even filled with candy canes or Hershey's Kisses, skiing Santa surely cost less than my weekly allowance.

In other words, I had swapped a shiny and cool Mustang for a lump of plastic coal.

As Paul and my best pals, Dan, Bob and Bill — boys did not go by Daniel and Robert and William in the '60s — enthusiastically raced their new Matchbox cars around the classroom's long windowsill and across desktops, I blinked back hot tears and tried not to sniffle noticeably.

Despite selfishly feeling sorry for myself, I started racing my skiing Santa alongside the Matchbox cars. Truthfully, I was not trying to erase any embarrassment Paul might have felt for giving such a crummy gift. I simply did not want to feel left out.

When the recess bell rang, Mrs. Bauer asked me to remain behind for a moment. I sat nervously at my desk having no idea what I had done wrong. When we were alone, my teacher knelt beside me at eye level and said, as I remember it: "I'm proud of you for not showing your disappointment. That would have hurt Paul's feelings. You gave him a very nice toy that made him happy, and you should be happy about that."

Mrs. Bauer's message, which I did not fully comprehend at the time, was that it truly is better to give than receive.

Before the school year ended, I became friends with Paul and spent a few nights at his house. I remember his socks always had holes in them. He shared a tiny bedroom with two sisters, and his dad had died.

Skiing Santa was not stupid, I came to realize many years later. It might have been all Paul had to give. That perspective has been a far greater gift than a Matchbox Mustang.

— Woody Woodburn —

Through the Eyes of a Child | 219

Chapter
9

The Perfect Gift

74

My Mother's Everlasting Gift

When I'm weak and unpretty, I know I'm beautiful and
strong. Because I see myself like my mother does.
~Lauren Alaina, "Like My Mother Does"

Everyone receives gifts they don't want, like the fuchsia shirt my mother gave me one Christmas. The tag on it called the shade raspberry, but no bush ever grew a fruit that color. Mom wrapped the shirt in a gold box that once contained a gift set of her favorite perfume, and the strong, sweet scent spilled out as soon as I lifted the lid.

That shirt reflected my mother's love of the vibrant, exuberant, and joyous splash that stood out in a crowd. What it did not reflect was *me*. I preferred flying under the radar.

Not only did the color shout, but the shirt fit tighter than what I usually wore, hugging extra curves I liked to keep hidden.

I thanked Mom as I refolded the bright sleeves and tucked it back inside the perfume box. I didn't tell her that I would probably never wear it.

My mother had enclosed a gift receipt, but for one reason or another — the chore of returning it to a department store I rarely visited or being overtaken by everyday life — I never returned the shirt. Instead, the box lay untouched in the back of my closet. It was still lying there the following Christmas after my mother died unexpectedly during the summer.

Her passing transformed that forgotten gift. When I felt sad, I could lift the lid to breathe in her perfume, letting it wrap me in her presence. When I figured as the family villain in my teenager's eyes, I peeled back the green tissue and remembered that my mother had considered me a vibrant woman who should never hesitate to stand out in a crowd.

And when I wanted to touch the past, I buried my face in the shirt and inhaled from the cotton knit the same scent my mother wore.

A decade later, the hurt from Mom's passing has eased. Now, I more often think of her when I hear a funny story and imagine my mother laughing with me.

But I still keep that box in the closet. The gold gleams, even if the tissue paper within is crumpled and torn. Mom's perfume still drifts through the air when I lift the lid. And sometimes, when I sit in my room wrapping presents for Christmas, I like to unwrap again one that my mother chose for me.

I become someone's daughter once more when I open that box, remembering how it felt to sit with my parents beside the tree on Christmas morning. Nestled inside shreds of green tissue paper lies the best unwanted gift ever, from a mother who believed her child was capable of anything, even wearing an unnatural shade of raspberry.

—Susan Lendroth—

75

Christmas Past, Present and Future

Carve your name on hearts, not tombstones.
A legacy is etched into the minds of others
and the stories they share about you.
~Shannon L. Alder

When my aunt died in 2005, many boxes that she had stored came to my house and were stored again. Those were virtually untouched when they were joined by more boxes from my parents' house in 2012.

I had become the "Keeper of Family Things" and was overwhelmed by the sheer magnitude of decisions about what to keep and what to let go. I put it all in a room and closed the door until the air-conditioning unit above that room developed a leak. Boxes got wet. Everything had to be pulled out, dried, sorted and repacked into plastic bins. I was finally seeing much of it for the first time.

In one box, I found three phonograph records labeled as "glass." They bore paper labels, "The Voice of Your Man in Service," with my father's name, dated 1943. Sadly, one was broken in half.

Internet research told me that during WWII, the Pepsi-Cola Company operated three centers for military personnel — Times Square, San Francisco and Washington, D.C. — with free showers and message services, a lounge and a low-cost sandwich bar with free Pepsi. The centers also had recording booths so that servicemen and servicewomen could record a greeting that would be mailed to their families. Several very scratchy recordings were reproduced on YouTube.

I could only imagine how thrilling it must have been for my grandparents and aunt in Arkansas to receive the records in the mail, play them on a 78 RPM record player, and hear my father's voice from across the country as if he were there in the room with them. I couldn't wait to hear them myself. But how?

I didn't want to risk mailing them anywhere, so I was excited to find a place nearby that could transfer the recordings from the two intact records to a thumb drive.

The result was disappointing. Although labeled with my father's name, they didn't quite sound like him. In 1943, he would have been twenty-three, with an Arkansas accent. It was hard to make out exactly what he was saying.

I was distressed that the third one was broken in two. What message from my father was I holding in my hand, now lost forever? I studied the break; it looked clean. So, on a whim, I went back to the store and asked if there was any way they could glue it together to find out what was on it. They did!

I held my breath as I plugged in the thumb drive. There was my father's voice, clear and distinct. It began, "'Twas the night before Christmas, and all through the house..." Tears sprang to my eyes. I listened to him read the whole story, recorded eight years before I was born, just as he had done every year throughout my childhood.

How I wished I had known of these records while he was alive to talk about recording them! They had been hidden away, first at my aunt's house and then at mine. I could imagine the fun of hearing him describe learning of the Pepsi booth, deciding what to say and his excitement in sending the recordings home. We think nothing now of voice recordings, but in 1943 it would've been magical. I wished we had been able to hear my grandparents and aunt talk of their excitement to receive the records and hear Dad carrying on the family tradition as if he were actually there.

The recordings are all now safely saved on thumb drives, and the original records are packaged in bubble wrap and a plastic box. Every Christmas, my children and grandchildren will hear my father read *'Twas The Night Before Christmas* just as I did.

— Carol Randolph —

A Christmas Wish Fulfilled

*For those who are willing to make an effort, great
miracles and wonderful treasures are in store.*
~Isaac Bashevis Singer

E very Christmas Eve, from the time I turned six, I prayed
for a horse. Not just any horse. I wanted a white Arabian
stallion, one with a silver mane and tail, just like the picture I tore out of a magazine while my mom and I sat in a
doctor's waiting room.

I plastered the walls in my bedroom with pictures of horses. I
taped a poster of a big black Friesian horse above my bed. Just imagin-
ing the power in the Friesian breed made tiny goose bumps rise up
on my forearms. I often imagined I rode on his back with my arms
outstretched while embracing the wind in my face. The picture of an
enormous black-and-white Gypsy horse, with its shaggy white feet,
took priority in a frame on my small, cherry antique dresser that my
grandpa Pop had given me.

I wrote stories about horses. I drew pictures of horses. My bedtime
prayers always ended with the words, "Please, God, all I've ever asked
for is a horse. Please? Amen."

Every book about a horse that graced my three-foot bookcase
had tattered corners from the many times I had read and reread it. I
had to tape the front and back covers of my absolute favorite book,

Black Beauty. I could never read through it without a box of Kleenex at my side. Thank goodness, it had a happy ending!

And so, Christmas came and went each year. A horse never appeared under my Christmas tree or in my back yard. The best I could do in all those years was to muck stables as a teenager to earn the privilege of riding the stable's rental horses. That was, until everything changed.

I taught tennis at a resort nestled in the heart of Scottsdale. A lady approached me one afternoon in the tennis shop. She held the hand of a blond little boy. "Good morning, I have a proposition for you. A friend told me that you have always wanted a horse. How would you like to give my son lessons, and we can barter? In exchange for tennis lessons, I will give you an Arabian foal that one of our mares is expecting any day now. Would that work for you?"

After I got over my shock, I stuttered, "I… I don't know what to say. I don't have a place to keep a horse, much less feed it."

She sat down on a chair in front of me. She pulled her little boy onto her lap. "No problem. We will keep him at our ranch and feed him. We have our own tennis court, so you can teach there and then spend time with your foal anytime you want."

We spent the next hour talking about the details, including the wonderful friend who had made the connection. The kind lady explained to me that the colt (or filly) soon to be born, because of genetics, would be born dark gray, but as the foal matured, it would turn snow-white, with a flowing silver mane and tail.

— Alice Klies —

77

The Last Ceramic Tree

Christmas is doing a little something
extra for someone.
~Charles M. Schulz

I couldn't believe it. Christmastime was here again, and everywhere I looked, ceramic Christmas trees were popping up — on shelves, in the stores, in my friends' Facebook posts, at the antique shops where the vintage versions had exorbitant prices. I spotted green glazed trees with snow, green glazed trees without snow, completely white trees — all with colorful, miniature bulbs glowing from their branches.

I despised ceramic Christmas trees.

Sometime during my childhood in the 1970s, my mom took up ceramics as a hobby. The kitchen table was her workshop where she carefully cleaned the greenware and meticulously painted each piece. In the early years of her craft, she took her projects to a ceramic shop to be fired in a kiln. But soon, she owned her own kiln and fired her own pieces. Then, she glazed them and returned them to the kiln for a final firing.

When it came to ceramics, Mom was a perfectionist. There was nothing she hadn't painted, and there was nothing she painted more than ceramic Christmas trees. Anyone who knew my mom well had received one of her trees, easily identifiable by her trademark signature painted underneath the base: her initials DD and the date.

By the time I moved out in 1987, I had no desire to see another ceramic Christmas tree. Within a few years, the tree trend ended. But now, more than thirty years later, the trees were making a comeback.

But something surprising happened. When I saw a tree for sale at Target, or on display in the dentist's office, or scrolled past my co-worker's ceramic-tree collection on social media, my disdain slowly turned to nostalgia. Mom had been gone a little more than a year, and now I was surrounded by imitations of the many masterpieces she had created. It was the single ceramic item that I associated with her most — the Christmas tree. Suddenly, I wanted one — *needed* one. If only I hadn't been so foolish when I left home all those years ago without one! I was determined go to any length to find a ceramic Christmas tree with her initials painted underneath.

I brainstormed a list of people who might have one. Sadly, I realized many on the list had passed before Mom, but I had a few good leads. I reached out on social media, sent notes in the mail, and made a few phone calls. No luck.

So, I went to Target and bought the last ceramic tree left on the shelf — a plain white one. Mom never made white. What skill did that take? A couple of firings and a coat of glaze. Her trees were green, shaded lighter here and darker there for richness and depth. I displayed the substitute tree in my kitchen, a little happy and a little sad, and posted a picture on Facebook along with the story about my failure to locate an original of Mom's.

For two Christmases, I flipped the switch on the bottom of that white tree, and it dutifully illuminated its colorful little bulbs. Then, this past summer, my sister-in-law Cindy walked into my house with a white cardboard box, obviously aged, with shredded newspaper poking out the top. It was just like the ones my mom used to pack her ceramic trees.

Cindy handed the package to me. "I found this in the basement and want to give it to you."

I took it cautiously. Excitement and fear tugged my emotions in opposite directions. Could it be? But… what if it wasn't?

Slowly, I pushed the yellowed strips of paper aside and dug into the box. Ceramic. Definitely ceramic. I pulled out a Christmas tree.

Cindy was smiling, but I was still reluctant to believe it. This could be any tree, a gift to her from someone other than Mom. Maybe Cindy didn't realize I didn't want just *any* tree. I reached back into the box and pulled out a white base with a single light bulb mounted in the middle. By now, my hopes were high. I turned over the base, and there it was: DD 1994.

This year, Mom's ceramic Christmas tree is the centerpiece on an antique table in my living room. Often, before going to bed at night, I turn off all the decorations except her tree. When I look at its colorful lights glowing in the dark, Mom doesn't feel so far away. I remember her searching the shelves of the ceramic shop for her next project. I see her sitting at the kitchen table turning a dull piece of greenware into a beauty. And I hear her asking all those years ago, "Would you like a ceramic Christmas tree?"

This time, I answer, "I would love one."

— Karen Sargent —

78

The Christmas Exchange

A mystery item, right under the tree… It says,
"secret Santa" but who could that be?
Open me up and take a quick guess…
when you see the new gift that you do possess!
~Author Unknown

"It's traditional fun!
"It's a Christmas Exchange!
"We'll give gifts, steal them back.
"It will be a nice change."

"My new in-laws are great!"
Said Bill, an idealist.
Of his new tribe he's fond,
But his mother's a realist.

We all drew a number,
From a brown paper sack.
Picked a gift in our turn,
Then unwrapped it, leaned back.

And the stealing began,
The purloining of gifts.

Moans and giggles ensued.
Trades were final and swift.

But my number was "one"!
And the problem therewith.
I just hoped some man craved,
The gift I'd been stuck with.

By mistake I had picked
Billy's dad-in-law's gift.
He did not shop at Kohl's,
If you're getting my drift.

When I opened it up,
He bragged, "I scored mine free!
"From the store Harbor Freight."
I said, "Wow. Lucky me!"

Expectant, I waited.
But a theft never came.
My laughs grew dishonest.
My good humor, the same.

But with thanks, said goodbye,
To my son and his gang,
With my holiday gift,
A voltmeter. Oh, dang.

—Leslie C. Schneider—

79

Red Ryder Christmas

The best of all gifts around any Christmas tree:
the presence of a happy family all
wrapped up in each other.
~Burton Hillis

My dad didn't get excited about receiving presents when I was a child, and he really didn't care about shopping for others either. "Most people have what they need, and when they don't, they buy it themselves," he'd say. He didn't care about opening gifts. "I don't need anything," he'd say in the weeks leading up to Christmas. "And I guess you'll have to return those pants you got me," he'd tell my mom after the holidays.

It would not be accurate to categorize my dad as a Scrooge, though. He enjoys the Christmas season and all its beauty and religious meaning. He likes Christmas music, particularly the crooner classics, and he likes holiday movies. In recent years, we have watched *A Christmas Story* together at least once per season. We own a copy of the DVD, but my dad jokingly prefers to watch it "live" when the twenty-four-hour marathon airs on Christmas Day. We quote the movie throughout the other months of the year, and we reference our favorite parts: the Bumpus hounds, the leg lamp, and, of course, the Red Ryder BB Gun.

This year, my dad asked me if he could give my son Evan a big present. "How would you feel about me giving Evan his first BB gun?" my dad asked. "I'll be going over some safeguards with him and showing him how to use it." I told him I thought it was a great idea. Evan had asked Santa for a Red Ryder, but I knew it would be even more meaningful if it came from my dad.

In mid-December, my dad made arrangements to get the wrapped BB gun to my house and hidden away under my bed. His plan was for it to be the last gift by the tree on Christmas morning. He wanted it to be as much like the movie as possible.

While my dad orchestrated his Christmas surprise, I wondered how he had transitioned from someone who didn't care at all about gifts to a man who couldn't wait to give my son a present — his first BB gun. The answer turned out to be pretty simple: He became a grandparent. He went through the most incredible metamorphosis a person can experience!

On the day of our family celebration, we ate lunch and opened gifts. At the end of the present extravaganza, one gift remained. The nametag read: "To Evan, From Pop." Evan ripped off the paper and revealed a Red Ryder starter kit. "Thanks, Pop," Evan said. Evan looked confused, though. "This will be nice when I get a BB gun one day!"

While Evan read a little more about what the starter kit contained, we brought down another package from upstairs, and my dad handed it to him. This package was a little more obvious, and though Evan was eager to open it, we made him read the card first:

I hope you have as much fun with your first BB gun as I did with mine. Love, Pop

Before we could even clean up the wrapping paper, Evan and his grandfather were on their way outside to try out the Red Ryder.

Even though I still have not touched or held the BB gun, it is one of my favorite presents, too. It may not have been for me, but I have the gift of watching my son and my father enjoy something special together. It doesn't get much better than that.

— Melissa Face —

The Best Christmas Gift

Christmas is the season of joy, of holiday greetings
exchanged, of gift-giving, and of families united.
~Norman Vincent Peale

From the moment we took turns holding her in our arms, we were love-struck. She was our first grandchild, and we were both overwhelmed with emotion as we celebrated her birth. Leia was born in July, during our summer visit with our daughter and her husband. We only spent a week with her before we returned to our home in another province, and we wouldn't see her again until our next visit in September.

Several months after Leia was born, we asked our daughter and her husband to consider celebrating Christmas at our home in Vancouver rather than their home in Calgary. When they graciously agreed, my husband and I were ecstatic and quickly made their flight arrangements to seal the deal.

All of a sudden, the pre-Christmas season became magical. To celebrate our granddaughter's first Christmas, we decided the house had to be decorated from top to bottom. I sewed a new Christmas stocking for Leia, and my husband purchased additional sets of exterior Christmas lights to add more sparkle to the front of our home. The gears were in motion as we purchased gifts, gifts and more gifts, arranged the Christmas dinner menu and organized our dinner guests. We booked tickets to the Festival of Lights for Boxing Day and made arrangements to visit relatives on the North Shore during Christmas week.

On the day of their flight's departure to Vancouver, our son-in-law thoughtfully sent us a photo as they left their home for the trip to the airport. We received an e-mail with Leia in her car seat. Subject: "On her way." The next photo was taken by our daughter while Leia's daddy held her next to the window after boarding the plane. Subject: "Happy to be on the plane!" I took the final photo as soon as we saw the three of them at the airport's arrival area. We had unintentionally captured Leia's first trip to her grandparents' home step by step.

Christmas with Leia brought back so many wonderful memories of years gone by. On Christmas Eve, when I took a photo of our daughter sitting by the Christmas tree holding Leia, it brought to mind memories of our daughter's first Christmas. It was like looking in a mirror and seeing a young mother new in her role, reflecting pure and nearly perfect love for the beautiful child she had brought into this world.

The excitement of Christmas morning brought back even more memories of Christmases past as we watched our daughter and her husband take delight in Leia's reaction to the crinkle of paper while they helped open her gifts. It reminded me of a similar scene with our own daughter at that age, and I thought about how the addition of a new generation is a renewal of family.

Our Christmas morning with Leia was full of laughter and the making of many new memories, proving that the magic of Christmas is not the tangible gifts. By agreeing to celebrate Leia's first Christmas with her grandparents, our daughter and her husband had provided us with the gift of a link to our past as well as our future. The anticipation of the joy our role as grandparents would bring us in years to come was the best Christmas gift of all.

— Kathy Dickie —

Dear Santa

The stockings were hung by the chimney with care,
in hopes that St. Nicholas soon would be there.
~Clement Clarke Moore

This year, for Christmas, I would like:
- a self-cleaning toilet.
- hair that looks like the shampoo bottle promises I will have after using it.
- just one night as a back-up singer with somebody on a stage somewhere.
- Hallmark to call and say, "We loved your script! We're gonna turn it into a movie!"
- teal-blue carpet in my living room. (You may have to bribe the rest of my family.)
- chin hairs to cease and desist.
- to feel refreshed and renewed after a night's sleep. Please????
- three or four more hours in every day; at this rate, I am never going to catch up.
- the pine trees behind my house removed so I can see the mountains from my kitchen window.
- 20/20 vision because I'm too chicken for Lasik.
- *Boston Legal*, *Northern Exposure*, and *Little Men* back in active production.
- a full-time gardener, or even a once-a-week gardener. Heck, I'd be grateful for a once-every-six-months gardener. You choose.
- my favorite make-up products to be around when I run out and want to buy more. Do I just keep picking weird things, or is this an

evil plot to make women crazy?

- a white fur muff like the one I had when I was five.
- a red dress with embroidered white snowflakes like the one I had when I was five. (Five was a very good year.)
- to swim with dolphins. But then there's that whole fat white thighs/bathing suit thing. Sigh… never mind.
- Internet service that never goes down.
- Mars bars to go back into production. The real American original version.
- Captain Kangaroo and Mr. Rogers back on TV. We need them. Badly.
- a donkey. Maybe a giraffe. No, a meerkat! Definitely a meerkat.
- all of us here on Earth to get along, be kind, and use proper grammar.

I think that'll do it, Santa. Of course, you know I'll still be grateful even if there's nothing under the tree except socks and underwear. But, hey, a girl can dream.

—Jayne Jaudon Ferrer—

The Spirit of the Season

Welcomed Back Home

Christmas is a day of meaning and traditions, a special
day spent in the warm circle of family and friends.
~Margaret Thatcher

My heart was beating fast as we pulled up to the house of my aunt and uncle. I was excited, nervous, and sad that it had taken this long for me to finally get here. Mom happily got out of the car, and Dad got up from the driver's seat. I followed them both quietly to the house. We rang the doorbell and waited.

Ten years. It had been ten years since I had been at a family holiday gathering and eight years since my grandfather's funeral. I hadn't seen most of my uncles or aunts and none of my cousins. I had disappeared, stubbornly isolating myself from those who loved me unconditionally. What were they going to think?

Uncle Nigel answered the door, and the surprise was written beautifully on his face. It was my cousin Jules who first exclaimed, "I knew it was you!" He smiled and laughed. I almost cried every time I hugged anyone, especially the cousins who I had not met before. They were all so happy to see me, but I was full of regret.

I had missed the birth of three young cousins. Abby was almost done with high school. Jules had graduated. I hadn't seen my aunts in years, and I'd never responded to their e-mails or phone calls, yet they hugged me and chatted with me. My four uncles welcomed me, too. And Mama, my grandmother, sat quietly and ever so proper with tears in her eyes. I was so glad I could tell her that her prayers for me had not been in vain.

As much as I wanted to cry, I wanted to laugh even more because there was so much joy in the house, so much noise and so much food! It was Christmas Eve, after all, and what I had secretly longed for so much was finally all around me: family. Oh, how I had missed them! I remembered crying while watching Christmas movies and wondering what was wrong with me. So fierce had been my pursuit of independence that I had found myself alone. I had lived for so long to please someone else, and I had been painfully taken advantage of. After years of abuse, I had lost myself; I hardly knew who I was. But here among family, I could name a feeling that I had not felt in more than a decade: belonging. I finally fit.

The food was tasty, but I was much hungrier for the building of relationships I had missed out on. I sat between my cousins, enjoying their presence. I listened to their stories about school, friends, what they liked and disliked, their hobbies and what they wanted to become. I watched my mother celebrate every moment and knew in my heart how special it was to her that her daughter had finally come back home. I talked with my uncles and aunts as friends, not as enemies. They forgave me faster than I could forgive myself. I soaked up the warmth and closeness that family brings, especially at Christmas. I had been so desperate for it!

We made plans to be in each other's lives again. I was the cousin, or niece, or granddaughter who was not going to disappear. I would stay and be a part of this family who had never stopped loving me and hoping for my return. I will never forget that Christmas Eve; it was a milestone in my journey of healing. I had been gone for ten years, but I was welcomed back in an instant.

— Alarica Reichert —

Scripelles

Cooking is at once child's play and adult joy.
And cooking done with care is an act of love.
~Craig Claiborne

December 24, 1954. "You have to roll it nice and tight so the cheese stays inside." My mother's strong fingers guided my chubby, five-year-old hands as we rolled the delicate crepe into a thin tube.

"Like that?" I asked.

Mom examined the scripelle and nodded. "I think you've got the idea. You know, I was your age when my mother taught me to make scripelles." She peeled another crepe from the stack, placed it on the clean kitchen towel in front of me, and sprinkled it with a handful of grated Parmesan cheese. Then she wiped her hands on her apron and stood back. "Now, try one all by yourself."

Eager to take part in this annual tradition, I studied the crepe, determined to get this right. A recipe brought to America by Italian ancestors, these "scripelles" would be served with Mom's homemade chicken soup as the highly anticipated first course of our Christmas dinner. I didn't know then that they would also form a bond connecting four generations and spanning more than sixty years.

Each Christmas Eve, Mom would hurry into our tiny kitchen and turn on the boxy radio that sat on the counter. While the voices of Perry Como, Bing Crosby, and Mario Lanza sang carols, she'd beat eggs, water, and flour into a thin batter, pour a ladleful into a hot, cast-iron skillet and, with a quick twist of her wrist, coat the bottom with the liquid. After a few moments, she'd carefully pull out a golden circle by its edges, turn it over, and return it to the pan. Then she'd lift the pan and flip out an airy crepe that would flutter down onto a waiting plate. I'd watch as she repeated this routine until the batter was gone and the plate held a pile of perfect scripelles. While my mother worked, we'd talk about all manner of Christmas-y things — what I thought Santa would bring, who would be joining us for dinner, whether there'd be snow. The cooking smells, mingled with the piney scent of our Christmas tree, created a fragrance that would always conjure up happy holiday memories.

I took a deep breath, lifted the lacy edges of the crepe, and slowly rolled it, trying to duplicate the actions of my mother's skilled hands. The result was an elongated log that loosely resembled the one she had made.

"That looks good, Jackie!" Mom smiled and placed a stack of scripelles in front of me. "Now, let's get to work."

December 24, 1981. "You have to roll it nice and tight so the cheese stays inside." My mother, now a grandmother, closed her hands around my daughter's fingers as she demonstrated how to roll the crepe.

"Your Nanny is the champ when it comes to rolling scripelles," I called from the stove. "I still can't get mine as tight as hers."

Luciano Pavarotti was singing "O Holy Night" from a new eight-track tape player, an early Christmas gift from my husband. I flipped a scripelle onto a plate.

"Marian is doing a great job." My mother spread a handful of cheese on another crepe. "I wasn't nearly as good when I was six."

"Look, Mommy!" Marian held up a finished scripelle, grinning with pride. "I did it."

"It looks perfect," I said. "I hope Santa is watching. Maybe he'll bring you that Cabbage Patch doll you asked for."

Mom pointed at the window. "I hope Santa's reindeer can make it through all this snow."

Marian surveyed the feathery flakes fluttering from the leaden sky.

"Oh, Nanny, don't worry," she said with a shrug. "He's got Rudolph."

As we laughed together in the cozy, aromatic kitchen, with the snow falling silently outside, I was overwhelmed by a sense of déjà vu. Suddenly, the years fell away, and I was a child again.

December 24, 2015. "You have to roll it nice and tight so the cheese stays inside." My mother's gnarled fingers curved around my granddaughter's tiny hands as she painstakingly rolled the scripelle.

My daughter sat across the kitchen table dusting another scripelle with cheese. "Watch Nanny carefully, Jocelyn. Nobody can roll scripelles like she can."

Mom chuckled and kissed Jocelyn's cheek. "You'll be just as good as Nanny when you've been rolling scripelles as long as I have. Maybe even better."

"I don't know about that, Mom." Batter sizzled as I ladled it into the old iron skillet. "It's been over fifty years, and I still haven't mastered your technique."

Jocelyn held up the scripelle. "Like this, Nanny?"

My mother clapped her hands. "That's perfect, Jossie. Show your grandmother."

Jocelyn waved the scripelle at me. "Look, Grammy. I made a crispell!"

I looked at this little girl, a miniature version of my own, wondering how I had gone from Mommy to Grammy in what seemed like the blink of an eye. "Good job, Joss. With all these scripelles to roll, we really need your help." I surveyed the two sizeable stacks, thinking of how they'd grown over the years as our family welcomed new in-laws and grandchildren

Bruce Springsteen's "Santa Claus Is Coming to Town" blared from my daughter's iPod. Jocelyn's head bobbed to the beat. "Mommy, can I make a crispell for Santa?" she asked. "And some for his reindeer?"

"Maybe one for Santa," Marian said. "We'll stick with carrots for the reindeer. Lots of people are looking forward to eating those scripelles tomorrow."

Mom gave Jocelyn a hug. "Someday, you'll be teaching your little girl how to make scripelles. Do you think she'll be able to roll them as well as you?"

Jocelyn thought for a moment, and then shook her head. "No, Nanny. You'll have to show her. You're the champ."

Mom tucked a stray strand of hair behind Jocelyn's ear, her eyes wistful. "Jossie, there's nothing that would please me more."

December 24, 2021. "Did I roll it tight enough, Nanny?" Jocelyn held up a perfectly rolled scripelle.

Mom sat at the table, her ninety-nine-year-old eyes dimmed by the ravages of dementia. She gave Jocelyn a vague smile. "That looks good, Jackie."

As Jocelyn kissed my mother's wrinkled cheek, I swallowed the lump that caught in my throat, knowing Mom had returned to that long-ago kitchen where she first handed the tradition down to me.

Sixty-seven Christmas Eves had passed since that day. The Earth turned. Seasons changed. Friends came and went. Some loved ones departed the Earth; others arrived. Outside, the world had become a very different place. But in the warmth of this kitchen was something eternal — a priceless gift passed from mother to daughter, grandmother to grandchild, great-grandmother to the great-granddaughter she lived to see. It was a bond that transcended time and change, an unbreakable chain with links forged by precious memories, enduring traditions, and fragile scripelles rolled by loving hands.

— Jackie Minniti —

84

A Busy Elf

Always laugh when you can. It is cheap medicine.
~Lord Byron

The year I got married, I drew the short straw and was scheduled to work on Christmas Eve at the hospital where I was the newest member of the nursing-school faculty. You might think that would dampen my spirits, but I was still basking in newlywed euphoria and enjoying every aspect of my life — ugly little apartment, low-budget meals, and makeshift furniture included. It didn't matter. It still made me smile to be called by my married name.

There were students on duty throughout the hospital that day, their last day before a week-long break. Because of the holiday, I was the lone instructor for all of them. So, they were told to work as much as possible on their own and page me when they needed help. I hustled from one patient room to another and from one hospital department to another. The hours went by quickly.

The mood on the wards was jolly, which surprised me. The patients didn't want to be there, and the staff didn't either. But those of us working did our best to maintain some holiday spirit. Although the school didn't allow students the privilege, some of the nurses and techs wore jingle bells around their necks, sparkly candy-cane earrings, and Christmas tree socks with their white uniform shoes. We wished one another "Merry Christmas" or "Happy holidays" as we passed in the halls.

There'd been a decent attempt to decorate the hallways with paper doily snowflakes hanging by suture material from the acoustic tiles in the ceilings. Little snowmen and Santas in various poses sat on the counters at most of the nurses' stations, and a crèche had been set up on every floor. Lots of visitors came and went all day with poinsettias and boxes of chocolates for their loved ones. Any patient who could be sent home had already been discharged, so the students had extra time to spend with the remaining ones, to offer comfort and encouragement along with necessary medical procedures.

For me, it was beyond hectic. I covered students with varying degrees of experience and competence on six floors. Some needed lots of help; others, only a little. By the end of my day, I was worn out.

I was standing with a group of nurses on the third floor, nibbling reindeer- and star-shaped sugar cookies and drinking hot ginger-spiced tea sent up by the kitchen staff, when once again I heard myself paged overhead, called to the sixth floor.

They rolled their eyes. "You must be nearly dead," one of them said. "I've been hearing your name all day. Are you about done in?"

I checked my watch. "This may be it for me," I told her. "I'll see what it's about, and then I'm going to round up the students and have them give report so they can go home. Merry Christmas, everyone!"

On the sixth floor, I saw my student pacing, wringing her hands and watching for me. "I'm not sure how to handle this one," she said, obviously in a lot of distress, chewing her bottom lip. "He's so upset."

"With you?" I asked.

"No, I think he's just so frustrated to be here at Christmas that he's yelling at everyone."

I could understand that. "Let's go talk to him."

The two of us geared up for a substantial rebuke and walked into the patient's room. He'd had an emergency gallbladder removal two days prior. Back in those days, the surgery required a front-to-back surgical incision under the right rib cage and a long recovery with a lot of post-operative pain.

He was sitting with the head of his bed raised, a bulky dressing covering his abdomen, and a murderous look on his face.

The Spirit of the Season | 247

"I'd like to know why everyone is so cheerful around here," he said, starting right in as soon as he saw us.

"It's rough, isn't it, being in here this time of year," I said.

"Yes, it's rough. I expect it to be 'rough.' I'm okay with 'rough.' What I don't expect, what I'm not okay with, is all the horsing around and shenanigans going on. This is a hospital! First the third floor, then the sixth, then back to the fifth. What is it, a contest to see who can be the most annoying?"

While I was still trying to get my head around his complaint, he clamped his hand over his forehead and sighed dramatically. "Everybody gets so cute around the holidays. Don't you people realize we're sick? We're not in the mood for stupid jokes!"

"I'm lost," I said. I looked at the student, and she seemed just as confused. "Can you help me out here?"

"I'm trying to get some rest, and they keep monkeying with the PA system."

"Really?" I hadn't noticed anything unusual myself, but I'd been busy. What had I missed?

He must have seen my bewilderment. "Haven't you been listening? All day long, they've been joking around, making fake announcements calling for some Christmas elf. First one floor, then another. It has to be a prank. One person getting that many calls in one day? Not possible. So, yeah, I get it. It's Christmas! Very funny."

"Ahh." I bit my lip and raised my hand to point to my name tag.

He leaned forward and read it. "It was you!"

I nodded, kept a straight face as much as I could, and said, "I'm the only teacher assigned to students today. I have to be everywhere at once. That's why they've been calling me."

"Did your parents really do that to you?"

"I got married."

Putting his arms across his bandaged belly for support, he let himself laugh, then grabbed my hand and held on tight. "Well, I think I just won the Old Grouch Award. I'm sorry."

"It should quiet down now. The students and I are finished for the day. We're headed home."

He raised my hand to his lips for a courtly kiss. "You're doing a good job. Thank you." Then, as we left the room, he called out, "Merry Christmas, Holly Green!"

—Holly Green—

85

Thank You, Santa

A wise lover values not so much the gift
of the lover as the love of the giver.
~Thomas á Kempis

t was the first Christmas without my husband, and my determination to keep busy during the holidays prompted me to visit the local travel agent. One look at a poster of palm trees and blue ocean had me handing over my credit card for a ticket to Florida. All the flights were full, but she found me a seat on the train. Having never ridden on Amtrak before, I looked forward to the adventure.

On the day of travel, it must have been obvious that I was confused by all the tracks, and the trains loading and unloading. A man standing behind me asked if I needed help. His salt-and-pepper hair was neatly trimmed, and his smile made his brown eyes sparkle. I decided he was a blessing sent and held out my ticket.

"Yes, please. I'm on number 317." I pointed to the silver passenger car that towered over both of us. "Is this it?"

"No, don't get on that one. That goes to Canada," he laughed. "I'm on train 317, too." He inclined his head toward the other end of the station. "Come on, I'll walk you down."

He kept up a friendly chatter as I fell into step beside him and pulled my case down the long concrete platform. We stepped through a whirlwind of holiday activity. By the time we reached the correct car, I had learned that his name was Tom, that he was retired, and that during the winter months he lived on his boat in a marina close to where I was staying.

After my husband had passed, I had shied away from the thought of dating again or getting involved with somebody. But today, for the first time, I found myself wishing the walk had been longer. As he extended his hand to help me manage the first steep stair off the platform and onto the train, his hand proved warm and strong.

"What time are you assigned to the diner car?" Tom craned his neck sideways to peek at my ticket. "Ah, 6:30. I'm in luck," he grinned. "So am I. I'll see you at dinner then." I followed the porter down to my compartment.

The train rolled out on time, and soon we were passing over rivers and through long stretches of farms and woodlands. The snow was deep in spots, as it was winter in New England, and I settled back and enjoyed the view. We passed small towns where children pulling sleds waved at me and large cities that sparkled in the sunlight. Soon, it was time for dinner. Dinner with Tom. I fussed with my hair and rummaged in my case to find a pretty blouse. My racing heart brought out some color to my cheeks, and I decided to put on a touch of lipstick. I hadn't used it in so long that I had a hard time finding it. I smoothed my slacks with a nervous hand and then made my way to the dining car, arriving on the dot of 6:30 only to find Tom seated beside another woman.

"There you are." Tom gestured to me to take the chair across the table. "Let me introduce Collette." He nodded to the lady next to him. "She doesn't speak much English. Do you speak French by any chance?"

"No, I don't," I said. "Sorry."

He bent his head toward Collette and began to explain the menu. I couldn't help but notice how he patted her hand and gave her a huge smile. My heart sank. He was taken. I had read more into the first meeting than I should have. Oh well, it was still nice to have company for dinner and not be by myself on Christmas Eve.

The food on the train was simple but tasty. Collette mostly kept quiet, and when she spoke, she spoke only to him and in French. During dinner, Tom talked about life on the water and entertained us both with funny boating stories. When he talked about leaping off the side and into the ocean for a swim, his face lit up. I wondered how Collette managed living on the water in the sun for months with her light skin tone. I couldn't picture this shy woman jumping off a boat.

"You speak French quite well," I commented to Tom as we drank our after-dinner coffee.

"I'm from Quebec. Everyone does there." He smiled. "Are you coming to the lounge later to watch the movie?" He seemed quite disappointed when I said no, which I found a bit odd.

Later that night, I realized that the man on the train had felt like a promise, and I had finally opened myself to believe that such things were again possible. Traveling by myself to Florida on the train was brave, but opening up to new possibilities would be even braver. Was I ready for a new relationship? I decided it was time I got back into life. As I settled into bed, I whispered to Santa, "Bring me something fun this year. I'm ready."

The next morning was Christmas Day. At breakfast, Tom looked pleased to see me and waved me over to his table. "I saved you a place."

We were now in the South, and it was sunny and green, with palm trees and riots of bright red poinsettias dotting yards and patios of the homes we passed. The tables were decorated with holiday greenery, and the car smelled wonderfully of fir.

"Where is Collette?" I asked, settling in the seat by the window.

"I saw her a few moments ago in the lounge car. From the sounds of it, she's talking to her husband."

"She's married?" I didn't know quite what to think of that.

"Why, yes, I believe so."

"And you two —" I let it hang. It really was no business of mine.

Tom laughed. "Oh, no, Collette just happened to get seated at our table last night."

"But you said we love to live on the boat, and I thought —"

"I meant Links and me. My dog. I sent him down by plane to my brother two days ago. Big black Lab. Loves the water." He handed me the menu. "I speak a fair amount of French. Collette was nervous traveling alone."

"A damsel in distress?" I gave him my best smile. "Do you always help women on trains?"

"Only the pretty ones." He fiddled with his napkin. "You know, I was nervous myself last night around you. Later, I realized I had talked all through dinner. I'd love to hear more about you."

"You would?" I was delighted at this turn of events.

"Yes, I would. For instance," he said with a twinkle in his eye, "how do you feel about dogs and jumping in the ocean?"

Thank you, Santa.

—Jody Lebel—

86

Why I Love Boxing Day

I think holidays come in all sizes —
sometimes you just need to relax.
~Kate Garraway

When is boxing a gloves-off, punch-free event? When it's Boxing Day in Canada, that's when.

I haven't always been the biggest fan of Christmas. Don't get me wrong. I enjoy the warmth and fellowship of what is essentially a family holiday. Having friends and relatives come from far and wide to join in the traditions of the season is always worth experiencing.

But there are aspects of the Christmas season that don't endear it to me. As the calendar turns to December, I can feel my stress level rising. Christmas ads and decorations pop up like mushrooms in stores and malls throughout the city. And, all of a sudden, the music of the season seems to be everywhere.

The commerciality of Christmas is its least endearing quality. I don't mind planning and preparing Christmas dinner. I don't even mind helping decorate the house and the tree. But I take little joy in the annual stressfest known as Christmas shopping. I have to somehow divine what everyone wants and then face hordes of shoppers to find the desired gifts. Plus, I have to come up with gift suggestions for myself, even though at my age I have pretty much everything I want.

Once the presents have been purchased, wrapped and labeled, I can start to relax and enjoy the season. The worst is over, and the best is ahead.

And the best part of a Canadian Christmas is not even Christmas; it's something called Boxing Day. It's a holdover from our British roots, a day historically set aside right after Christmas to present gifts or "Christmas boxes" to household servants.

Today, it has transformed into something else: a day full of year-end sales to end all sales. It is the culmination of a month full of shopping distilled down to one single crazy madhouse retail day. It is as if Americans combined the worst of Christmas shopping, Presidents' Day sales and Black Friday.

But that's not why I love Boxing Day. For someone who dislikes the whole Christmas shopping exercise, a day at a mall filled with crazed, bargain-hunting shoppers is not my idea of fun.

No, I love Boxing Day because I don't have to shop. It gives us Canadians two days off in a row—sometimes three if it falls on a weekend.

Thanks to that double or triple helping of days off, I can truly enjoy the holidays. All the work, planning and preparation are over, and I can finally sit back, rest and relax.

Let the bargain hunters have their 6:00 A.M. door-crashing specials, two-for-one offers, and seventy percent–off sales. I'm happy to have a day of quiet time at home. Some time to reflect on the joys of family and the joys and sadness of Christmases past.

Boxing Day for me is a time to slow down and decompress. It's a time to catch up with visiting relatives and revisit the past. It's also a time to quietly watch a movie, read a book or just snack on all the accumulated Christmas goodies.

I'm not sure why our Canadian forefathers decided to add Boxing Day to the holiday calendar. After all, it's not as if we had inherited the rigid class structure of our motherland. Few of us ever had servants who had to work Christmas Day and then needed a post-Christmas celebration.

But, whatever the reason, I'm sure glad they did. Boxing Day may

The Spirit of the Season |

have been transformed into a commercial holiday for most of us but not for me. In fact, in some ways, Boxing Day is my real Christmas.

—David Martin—

87

Hanukkah at the O.K. Corral

The spirit of Hanukkah, the Festival of Lights,
is shared by all people who love freedom.
~Norma Simon

"I am so glad we're here," my eleven-year-old daughter mused as she gazed out the car window, squinting at the rows of stately saguaro cacti lining the dusty road like prickly green soldiers standing at attention. "But it's too bad we won't be able to celebrate the first night of Hanukkah."

"Why not?" came the unanimous response from the four adults in the car—my sister and brother-in-law, and my husband and me.

"Duh!" declared my six-year-old niece. "We are in Tombstone, Arizona! Who celebrates Hanukkah here? The cowboys?"

"We celebrate it wherever we are," I announced, rummaging in my purse and producing a tiny, travel-size menorah, barely four inches high. Everyone burst out laughing.

"Where did you find such a teeny menorah?" the girls squealed. "And what kind of candles would fit in that? Even birthday candles would be too big!"

"I got that covered," I assured them, producing a box of extra-thin candles.

My husband, daughter and I had left the cold and snow of New Jersey, where we live, to spend the last week of December visiting my sister and her family in Arizona. As part of our joint vacation, we embarked on a two-day excursion to Tombstone and the Kartchner Caverns. Hanukkah happened to fall during our trip, and I expected it would provide a pleasant reminder of the many East Coast Hanukkahs my sister's family and mine often celebrated together before their move to the Southwest.

The menorah returned to my purse, and the six of us spent the day exploring the town of Tombstone, which involved observing men dressed as cowboys re-enact the famous shootout at the O.K. Corral and chase one another down the streets for the entertainment of the hordes of tourists. We visited stores and restaurants that re-created the décor and ambience of saloons. We took a stagecoach ride and heard the history of the town's founding, which is credited to a prospector who, in the late 1880s, discovered silver ore in this area.

As the stagecoach wheels rumbled beneath us and the cowboy-actors shouted and brandished their guns on every corner, our stagecoach-driver-guide regaled us with tall tales of the numerous battles that took place when Tombstone was a lawless frontier. His main story focused on the most famous fight of all: the O.K. Corral shootout involving the legendary Wyatt Earp. The children's ears perked up at the mention of that familiar name.

By the time we swaggered back to the car at day's end, pointing imaginary guns at one another, we were thoroughly immersed in the atmosphere and mythology of the town, and could imagine the gambling houses, saloons, and brothels that once lined the streets.

That night, on the drive to our motel, we admired the glittering outlines of the giant saguaros lit up against the dark sky, as if painted on a black canvas. "Those are Christmas lights strung around the cacti," my brother-in-law informed us. "I don't think you'll see that in New Jersey."

"Cool!" my daughter breathed, mesmerized, and I reached into my bag to feel for the little menorah.

In our motel room, as I cleared off the desk to set up the menorah, the girls rushed to close the drapes.

"We can't let anyone see us," they explained.

"Why not?" I asked, reopening them.

"Mom," my daughter droned, hooking her thumbs into the belt loops of her jeans and assuming the hip-jutting stance of the cowboy, "I don't believe there are too many Jewish people in these here parts."

"It would be kind of… weird… if anyone else here sees us do this," my niece added.

"We do live in a country where we have freedom of religion, don't we?" my husband asked.

"Not like the Maccabees," my sister pointed out. The deeds of the brave Jewish Maccabees around 165 B.C.E., who refused to give up their faith when ordered to worship pagan gods, and who took to the hills to launch a three-year, guerilla-style war against their powerful Greek-Syrian rulers, are what we celebrate every year on Hanukkah. The saga of their dedication and struggle, their ultimate triumph, and their cleansing and rededication of the Jewish Temple, which had been defiled and vandalized, capture the imagination and pride of Jews everywhere.

"Yeah, our people were fighters, too," my brother-in-law pointed out, fingers laced through his belt loops. "Way before there were cowboys roaming these here parts."

"In fact," I took the opportunity to explain, "I did a bit of research before we came here. You might be surprised to know that Wyatt Earp's wife was Jewish."

"What?!"

"It's true. Her name was Josephine Sarah Marcus. An adventurous spirit, Sadie, as she was known, left home for the Arizona Territory as a teenager and met Earp here in Tombstone in 1881. She was his common-law-wife for forty-six years until Wyatt's death. In fact, both of them are buried in a Jewish cemetery in her family's plot in California."

My daughter pulled the drapes open. "Let's light the menorah," she said.

The following day, with the menorah ensconced in my purse once again, we headed to the newly opened Kartchner Caverns State Park near Benson.

"Hey, didn't the Jews secretly study inside caves when they were persecuted by the Greek-Syrians?" my daughter remembered.

"And a few of them stayed outside as sentries, playing dreidel," my sister reminded them, referring to the spinning-top game popular on Hanukkah.

"Is that why we are visiting a cave now — because of the Hanukkah theme?" my niece joked.

Hanukkah, as it turned out, was the last thing on our minds as we stepped into the chilly, immense cavern. Conversation instantly ceased. We knew we had stepped into another world, a nature haven, a magical kingdom of contortionist icicles. Giant stalactites dripped from above, and spindly stalagmites sprouted upward from the ground. The formations from above often merged with the ones from below, icicle arms linked in a dance. More bizarre formations could not be imagined.

But what captured our imaginations most powerfully was the history of the cave. Two college friends discovered it in 1974 when they investigated a sinkhole they noticed on Kartchner property. They realized their find was an unexplored treasure and kept it to themselves for fourteen years, secretly visiting when they could. They named it Xanadu.

They feared that publicizing their discovery would lead to its abuse and ruin. When they finally went public, they devoted themselves to obtaining guarantees from the Kartchner family and the government of Arizona that the natural condition of the cave would be protected.

Outside after the tour, dazed and blinking in the bright sunshine, we marveled at the love and perseverance of those two young men. My daughter whispered that the place felt "holy."

"Tonight is the second night of Hanukkah," my niece dreamily remarked as we staggered through the parking lot. The connection did not need to be put into words. Inspired anew, we were ready to re-dedicate ourselves to preserving what was beautiful and special to us.

And to proudly proclaim it to all, with the drapes wide open.

— Ruth Rotkowitz —

The Scent of Christmas

It is amazing how much love and laughter they
bring into our lives and even how much closer
we become with each other because of him.
~John Grogan, Marley & Me

Have you ever noticed how certain smells can call up particular emotions or memories? A whiff of perfume or aftershave recalls a favorite person; the yeasty fragrance of warm bread tickles the taste buds. Think about newly mown grass or how the air smells after a thunderstorm. Burning leaves on crisp fall days always remind me of football Saturdays.

Perhaps the aromas that surround Christmas carry the most memories. The fresh green scent of pine; the brown fragrances of cinnamon, nutmeg and cloves while cookies are baking; hot chocolate and wood smoke around the crackling fire.

But the smell I associate best with Christmas and winter is wet dog.

Our dog was mostly an outdoor dog and was often drenched in the rain. We tried to dry him off as soon as he came in, grabbing the old, dirt-encrusted towel from the peg by the door. He usually shook himself before we could catch him. The walls of the back entry were splattered in brown dots all winter.

He had also encountered a skunk or two in his life. Try as we might, we never could completely get rid of that smell. It lay hidden deep in his fur and skin.

We brushed him regularly in spring and summer when winter

fur fell out by handfuls, but baths were rare. So, of course, his smell built up over time.

The distinctive odor of wet dog was a reminder of the Christmas vacation when I was twelve, and the cousins from Ohio were visiting. We had gotten shiny, slippery flying saucers as gifts and were also blessed with fresh snow. The four of us spent as much time as possible sliding down the short hill to the creek. Naturally, we tested the ice on the irrigation pond the first day, and we knew we could slide across it and lengthen our ride.

On the third day of our festivities we were so eager to play that we did not check the ice or the temperature. A few degrees of warmth added a small layer of water to our slide, increasing our speed and excitement. My brother Peter slid gaily down the hill and on to the pond. Seconds later, he was floundering in the icy water. Peter was only eight and not a good swimmer, especially bundled in a winter coat and boots.

We all screamed. I skidded down the treacherous slope to reach him, but the dog was faster. He jumped into the water, grabbed Peter by his flailing hand, and pulled him to shore. The cousins and I were able to finish pulling Peter out of the frigid water.

You can guess the rest of the story. We managed to wrap Peter in our coats and get him back up the hill and to the house in record time. Sipping cocoa by the heater, we patted and hugged that wet dog.

The dog took all day to dry out. His wet-dog smell lingered longer and returned often, reminding us of his heroics and our own Christmas miracle.

— Gretchen A. Keefer —

89

The Case of the Missing Santa Hats

Perhaps the best Yuletide decoration
is being wreathed in smiles.
~Author Unknown

"What on earth happened to the Santa hat I placed on our concrete dog?" I asked my husband. We had spent the previous day outside putting up Christmas lights, garland, lighted stars, and wreaths of various sizes. The weather, in the seventies and sunny, gave us a perfect day for decorating the exterior of our new home.

Every year, we went all out on decorating. But this was our first Christmas at our new home in a retirement neighborhood in Texas. We'd moved down from cold Minnesota. We weren't sure what the protocol was for putting up Christmas decorations, so my husband decided to go ahead and do our normal decorating. If it turned out wrong, we hoped someone would tell us.

I had shipped most of our Christmas decorations with our furniture, so when Christmastime approached, I climbed into our attic and carried down the boxes. Included in the boxes were red furry Santa hats. We always wore Santa hats when entertaining for Christmas. I wondered what to do with the Santa hats this year. Since we didn't know anyone in the neighborhood, there would be no invites to parties or open houses. I had found two life-size replicas of our current dogs, Springer Spaniels, at different garage sales, and we'd put them outside the house — one in the yard and one by the front door. We decided to double-stick tape the Santa hats onto the two concrete dogs. They looked so cute with their Santa hats, and I thought the neighbors would enjoy seeing some creative decorating.

The next day, I took the dogs for their normal walk around the park. As I walked down the driveway, I glanced at our decorations and noticed the dog located by a tree in the yard was missing its Santa hat. When we returned from our walk, I started a tour around the house, looking for the missing hat. I thought it might have blown off and was in our yard or a nearby neighbor's yard.

I did not want to blame the neighbors — yet. So, I started a sneaky neighborhood search by walking up and down the street, glancing between the houses and in the front yards. Since the row of homes where we lived bordered on a ranch, there were no backdoor neighbors, so I walked the fence line as a final search for the Santa hat. How could I miss a big, fuzzy red Santa hat?

No luck. I was perplexed. Then I thought maybe my husband had removed the hat to play a joke on me. After all, he was a jokester and had played pranks on me before.

He said, "No," but laughed that I was so upset over the missing hat.

"Okay," I replied. "I still have another hat. This time, I'll make double sure the hat stays secured to the dog."

I used twice the amount of tape for the second hat. The next morning, the hat was missing again. The statue was right below my bedroom window. Surely, the dogs would have heard someone outside. After all they went crazy even when our many squirrels were up and about.

"I give up," I said.

So, the dog went hatless through Christmas. After Christmas, a new neighbor came over to introduce himself as we were taking down the decorations.

We talked for a few minutes, and then I mentioned the mystery of the missing Santa hats and that I couldn't believe any of the neighbors would have taken them.

He looked up at the tree, which was finally losing it leaves for winter, and said, "You mean that hat up in the tree?" He pointed to a crook in the tree where a squirrel had made its nest using both the Santa hats.

"What!"

"Yeah, the squirrels around here will find anything colorful and take it with them to make a nest."

Our next-door neighbor drove by and pulled into her driveway. I walked over to her and pointed out the missing Santa hats I had mentioned to her earlier. "Doesn't surprise me," she said. "I had a nice chair on my porch. The squirrels came and chewed the fabric off the chair and carried it to their nest."

This was so unbelievable. Here, I had suspected my neighbors, and the squirrels were the culprits all along. However, in retrospect, they did have a nice warm home for winter.

—J. A. Rost—

90

Music Soothed My Soul

The best way to spread Christmas cheer
is singing loud for all to hear.
~Will Ferrell, Elf

The news I'd received at the doctor's office shook me to my core. Tears blurred my vision, and a few blocks after leaving the clinic, I realized I shouldn't be driving.

Fortunately, the hospital clinic was near a large maritime museum, which was basically closed for the pandemic, and I got off the highway and pulled into their ample and nearly empty parking lot.

There were numerous ocean-going freighters out on the water, along with the usual commercial fishing boats, river pilot transfer vessels, and Coast Guard patrols. I blew out a deep, shaky breath, and it totally fogged up my windshield.

"Geez, Jan," I said aloud. "That was dumb."

Since I have a habit of talking to myself when in the car alone, I wasn't surprised when no one answered. I simply turned the key back on and powered down my window.

I drew a huge breath of salty air and felt my nerves begin to steady. The sun peeped through the dark December clouds and illuminated selected spots on the waterway. I tilted my car seat back and closed my eyes.

"Accept the things I cannot change," I whispered. "So, how do I find the courage to change the things I can?"

There were medical decisions to be made, but they didn't have to be made that day. I could research the options, make a list of pros and cons for each course of action, and then solicit advice from friends and obtain a second opinion from another doctor. I smiled. As a retired teacher, I always feel better when I have a tangible lesson plan.

Suddenly, I became aware of saxophone music. The melody was not something I recognized, but I was pretty sure it was being played live, and it was coming from somewhere out there along the riverbank.

I opened my eyes and sat up, scanning the walkway along the river. Yes! My eyes, almost blinded by the increasingly bright winter sunshine, zoomed in on the source of the beautiful music.

A young man, wearing a heavy coat partially unzipped to expose a brightly colored college hoodie sweatshirt, was coaxing a gentle tune from his saxophone. The instrument's case was open on a park bench, and a water bottle was lying on the grass near him.

His next song was one I easily recognized. It was "In the Mood," an old standard of the 1940s made famous by the Glenn Miller Orchestra. Funny what memories our brains keep tucked away.

My grin deepened. I wondered if the young man would take requests. I thought I might be able to gather myself together enough to walk over and ask him to play "Misty" for me.

As I got out of the car and navigated carefully over the trolley tracks, I realized that "Misty" was a song a former boyfriend — from over forty-five years ago — used to play for me on his sax. Oh, dear! That would never do! Much too melancholy!

I had my pandemic mask firmly in place as I approached the musician. He, of course, couldn't play with a mask on, and I kept my distance. He acknowledged me with a nod and finished the song he was playing.

When he finished, he picked up his water bottle and took a big gulp while I inquired about requests.

"What would you like to hear?" he asked self-consciously. He did not look me in the eye, keeping his head tilted downward.

"Do you know any Christmas songs?"

He bobbed his head, still not looking directly at me.

"And would you mind if I videoed the song with my phone and

put it up on Facebook for others to enjoy?"

He thought a moment. "I guess that would be okay."

I pointed to the college sweatshirt he wore. "Do you go to school there?"

His brow furrowed, and he looked momentarily confused. Then, he looked down at his chest before he shook his head. "No. I got it at the Goodwill. It's warm."

I wasn't sure if he was uncomfortable talking to me or just embarrassed at the unsolicited attention, but as soon as he started playing, he became oblivious to his surroundings. He turned his back on me, and he played only for the birds and boats out on the water, just jamming with nature.

My hands shook as I recorded his song: "Chestnuts roasting on an open fire, Jack Frost nipping at your nose, Yuletide carols being sung by a choir, And folks dressed up like Eskimos…"

A hard lump formed in my throat as the tears rolled down my cheeks, but I managed to capture the whole song. When he finished, I thanked him and attempted to hand him a twenty-dollar bill.

He shook his head. "No. I'm just practicing."

"Me, too!" I countered. "I'm practicing being nice to people and spreading Christmas cheer. Please help me do that by accepting this money."

He grinned, gave me a quick sideways look, and echoed his previous answer to my request for a song. "I guess that would be okay." He took the bill and crammed it into his jeans' pocket.

"Merry Christmas," I said, hurriedly heading back to my car. I didn't want him to see me getting all emotional; I was afraid he might think he didn't play the song well enough.

But the song had been perfect. We had shared a moment. As the music had wafted out over the water, it had also washed across my soul. And, in my heart, I knew my earlier pity party had been unnecessary.

I was suddenly absolutely sure of three things: 1) My health would be just fine; 2) the pandemic couldn't last forever; and 3) the world could become a kinder, softer, gentler place if each of us embraced our "moments" of true human connection, one small saxophone kindness at a time.

In other words, my 2020 musical Christmas gift was one of hope.

— Jan Bono —

91

Almost Stolen

*Gratitude can transform common days into
thanksgivings, turn routine jobs into joy, and
change ordinary opportunities into blessings.*
~William Arthur Ward

"Well, babe," said my fiancé, tossing his work-worn hat and coat in the entranceway. "I just talked to Mom. She and Dad are having Christmas dinner with my sister and her family because they've been quarantining."

My heart went out to him. As the eldest son, it has always been important for him to be there to look after his family. It was a duty placed on him since childhood, which he'd carried out with pride for the past fifty-four years.

"Unbelievable," I sighed. "First, we are booted out of Tuesday and Sunday dinners, and now we are banned from Christmas — as if Thanksgiving wasn't hard enough."

"I know, but you and I are essential workers, and we are around people at the hospital and job site all day." His shoulders were drooping, tired from lifting heavy materials all day. Gray dirt made the lines around his eyes more prominent. I wished I had the power to take away Covid, knowing that his time with family was what greatly motivated him and carried him through his busy days.

We both knew the safest thing to do was stay away from our

loved ones, especially the elderly and those with health issues, but the distancing had been taking a toll on us both. Thankfully, we got to spend a bit of time with our children now and then, but we all were being cautious about gatherings.

Christmas arrived. I went to work at the hospital while he plowed snow for the neighborhood and rental properties. After hot showers, we brought gifts to our parents and left them on the steps, waving and talking from the driveway. We didn't stay long as the New England weather bit at our skin, chasing us home. In cozy clothes, we ate a non-traditional meal as we both were too tired to cook. But our tummies were full as we snuggled on the couch and took turns opening our gifts to each other.

"You know what, babe?" I said as we looked into each other's eyes. "This was actually really nice just to sit here and relax and enjoy our time together."

He nodded. "I was just thinking the same thing."

New Year's Eve came and went. Even though we worked during the day, we partook of a beautiful dinner while social distancing at a fine restaurant. Again, we were surprised by how much we enjoyed the slow and private pace of it all.

The next day, while relaxing as I scrolled through my social-media account, an uneasy agitation welled up inside me as I read one negative post after another. People were saying goodbye to "horrible" and "awful" 2020. As I read those posts, I felt as though some unseen force was creeping in and trying to steal all my beautiful blessings from the previous year. So many wonderful things had happened to me, and I was suddenly overjoyed, knowing I must share them with my friends online so they might also remember their own good fortune.

I wrote with new hope, saying: *I am so thankful for the year 2020. Here are some of the beautiful blessings that came my way: I got engaged to the love of my life; We and our children are healthy; I have a job; I am becoming a nurse at the age of fifty and taking classes online; My parents are alive and active; I have a new family to add to my list of loved ones. I am keeping my eyes and ears open to see what new and exciting blessings are waiting for me in 2021.*

"You know what, babe?" I said after sharing my post. I snuggled deeper into his side. "2020 was one of the best years of my life."

— Lindy Tedesco —

After a Loss

92

A Little Holiday Scheming

When your mother asks, "Do you want a piece of advice?" it is a mere formality. It doesn't matter if you answer yes or no. You're going to do it anyway.
~Erma Bombeck

My five-year-old daughter was the first person to notice. Well, at least, she was the first one to say anything about it. "They taste funny, Daddy."

"What tastes funny?"

"The peppernuts you made for Christmas. They taste funny."

She was right, of course, although I was reluctant to admit it, having already produced two cookie sheets full of the tiny cookies.

"It's your grandmother's recipe," I insisted, showing my daughter the step-by-step directions.

My daughter closely scrutinized the handwritten recipe.

"It doesn't taste right," she quietly insisted, unimpressed with the recipe she couldn't read.

The recipe had been written out for me and my two sisters by my mother during her last Christmas with us. Making cookies, particularly the pfeffernusse, or peppernut cookies as we liked to call them, was a long tradition in our family and one that my mother took seriously. Every December, she would recruit her grandchildren and convert her kitchen into an assembly line, turning out sheet after baking sheet of the small, sweet cookies.

And it was a tradition that Mom had insisted we keep up when she delivered copies of her handwritten recipe to my sisters and me on Christmas Day.

"It's my last Christmas with you," she firmly stated after pulling the three of us aside.

We objected, of course, insisting that she'd be around for many Christmases to come.

"No," she clearly reiterated, as if the matter was settled. "The doctors have spoken. You know what the tests showed as well as I do. Now then, I've got a few things to make clear with the three of you."

My sisters and I sheepishly nodded. While we were in our thirties and forties, Mom wielded a strong hand when it came to matters of our extended families.

"First, make the cookies," she stated in a clear voice that belied any hint of weakness or infirmity. "I make them every December. It's a good warm-up for the holidays, and it teaches the grandkids about the importance of tradition. Not only that, they love making the cookies as much as they do eating them."

"Second, get everyone together on Christmas Day. Your dad and I started that tradition, and just because I'm not there doesn't mean you can skirt around the importance of getting our family together on the most important day of the year."

The three of us looked at each other and shrugged.

"I know, I know," Mom continued. "You've got families of your own and all kinds of obligations. But there's nothing more important than the three of you getting together with your spouses and my grandchildren on Christmas Day."

Mom finished her speech and folded her arms, resolute and unmoving. She had made her point.

Now, here I was almost a year later, fumbling around in my kitchen with Mom's handwritten recipe, doing my best to fulfill one of her wishes. And, apparently, botching the whole thing.

It was obvious that I needed help, so I called one of my sisters.

"Hey, Betty, I'm having a little problem with the peppernuts. They're not turning out right."

"What do you mean?"

"Well, they taste… funny."

"That's weird. I had the same experience, and so did Carol. The kids won't touch them. Carol's stopping by after work tonight. Why don't you drop by, and we'll try to figure out what we're doing wrong."

Although we lived in the same city, my sisters and I rarely got together. And, sadly, we had made no plans for this Christmas despite Mom's insistence to do so. Seems that between in-laws, uncles, aunts, cousins and friends, getting together on Christmas Day just wasn't going to happen.

At least, maybe we could get the peppernut cookies right.

"Okay, for starters, let's take a look at Mom's recipe," I began, spreading my copy out on the kitchen table. "Mine starts with ½ cup molasses, ¼ cup honey…"

"Hold on there," Betty chimed in. "I think you've got that backwards. Mine says ¼ cup molasses and ½ cup honey."

"No, no, no," Carol countered. "He's got it right. That's what mine says."

The three of us looked at each other and then at our recipes, completely befuddled.

For the next hour or so, the three of us went line by line through our respective handwritten recipes, discovering that none of us had a completely accurate recipe. Two of us would have one measurement (four eggs) while the third had something different (two eggs). And the directions, whether combining ingredients, heating or stirring them, were different as well. It was only by meticulously comparing our recipes that we were able to patch together what we determined to be the correct one for peppernuts.

Hoorays and high-fives punctuated our accomplishment. But then, our euphoria gave way to the obvious question. Why?

"It's not like Mom," Betty observed. "Her recipes were sacred to her."

"She'd never make a transcribing mistake like that," Carol added.

We were silent, mulling this over, when I had a sudden revelation.

"She did it on purpose."

"What?" both of my sisters exclaimed.

"She did it on purpose, knowing we'd have to get together if we wanted a complete recipe. But it's not really about the recipe or the cookies. It's about Christmas. More than anything, Mom wanted us to be together on Christmas Day, and this was her way of reminding us."

"Well, it worked," Betty observed with a smile. "Smart lady, our mom."

"So, what do we do now?" Carol asked.

I grabbed both my sisters' hands and laughed. "Isn't that obvious?"

Three weeks and eight cookie sheets of peppernuts later, it was Christmas Eve. My wife and I were making last-minute preparations for what was to be an extended family gathering for Christmas Day. My sisters and their spouses and children would be there along with in-laws, aunts, uncles, cousins and friends dropping by throughout the day.

Oh, and the peppernuts? They were perfect. After all, we had Mom's recipe, a recipe for not only perfect cookies but for a perfect, old-fashioned family Christmas, as well.

— Dave Bachmann —

A Christmas Miracle Right Before My Eyes

*Sometimes, healing moments take forever to arrive.
At other times, they fall in our laps with sheer grace,
like a feather from an unseen bird.*
~Kristina Turner

I haven't looked forward to the holidays since my son's death. It seems the harder I try to suppress my feelings, the worse it becomes.

A few years ago, I was working as a part-time bookkeeper at a church. The church is a sponsor for the Salvation Army's Angel Tree Program. One of the church volunteers, Marge, was looping a string on the Angel Tree tags to hang them on the Christmas tree. Curious, I asked, "What are these for?"

"They are Angel Tree tags for the Christmas tree."

"Why do they have names written on them?" I asked.

"The Salvation Army's Angel Tree Program helps children from low-income families. Each tag has a child's name with information such as age, favorite color, their needs, clothes and shoe sizes, along with their Christmas gifts wish. The tags are hung on the church's Christmas tree in the narthex for members and friends to select, purchase the gifts, and return the gifts to the Angel Tree. Two weeks before Christmas, we will take the gifts to the Salvation Army, and they will distribute them to the recipient on the tag."

It touched my heart to know there was such a noble cause. "Is it open to anyone or just the people attending church services?" I asked.

"It's open to anyone who would like to help a family," she responded.

I returned to my office but could not stop thinking about the Angel Tree. Memories of my children opening their gifts on Christmas Day flooded my mind. I could see their smiles and their anxious hands ripping apart the wrapping paper, eager to get to their gifts. I remembered the look on their faces when they received what they had asked for. To see them happy made me happy, and I needed nothing else. But to know that there are children who do not get that opportunity made me sad. I was already struggling emotionally with the holidays around the corner. So, I called my husband and told him about the Angel Tree and its purpose. We agreed that we wanted to take part.

We had been fortunate to always have gifts for our three children when they were young. That call left me thinking about my angel, Richie, in heaven. He was always on my mind, but with the holidays approaching, it heightened my emotions. So, I thought, *We can't get our angel Richie a gift, but we can get a gift for a young child and make his or her Christmas a happy one. We will do it for Richie.*

I returned to the reception area to ask Marge for an Angel Tree tag. She fumbled through the tags and said, "There are little girls here. Which name do you like?"

But my eyes were fixed on the first one on the top pile. The tag read "Ricardo." Not Richard or Ricky, but "Ricardo." It was staring me right in the face. I stared back in shock.

The volunteer was oblivious about what was happening. She said, "Well, I found a little girl's tag if you want it."

I responded, "You know what, Marge? I'm going to take this one right here. Look at the name: Ricardo. My son's name was Ricardo."

Marge smiled at me and said, "That's God's way of letting you know your son is always with you." She stood up and went around the desk to hug me. "Had I not been here to witness it, I wouldn't have believed it."

As tears filled my eyes, I felt that Marge's words were true: God was letting me know that Richie is always with me.

— Debbie Centeno —

94

Christmas Validation

Wherever a beautiful soul has been there
is a trail of beautiful memories.
~Ronald Reagan

E verybody told me the holidays would be the hardest. I'd
nod my head and feign understanding, but I didn't see
how anything could be harder than that fateful day in
August 2021 when I lost my wife Lynn to breast cancer
just shy of our thirty-ninth wedding anniversary.

As the holidays approached, my apprehension level rose as I
prepared to get through Thanksgiving. Thankfully, the pain of the first
major holiday without my wife was tempered by the outstanding job
my daughters did in preparing the meal that was traditionally Lynn's
domain.

It was a good day. I think being a part of the group was beneficial
for me. I was able to share some laughs, enjoy the Macy's Thanksgiving
Day Parade on TV, and savor the aromas that only the preparation of
a Thanksgiving feast can provide.

However, I knew the real test was lurking right around the corner
in the form of Christmas — a fact that was driven home when Santa
Claus did his traditional job of closing the Macy's Parade.

At first, I wasn't even going to put up a tree — or any decorations,
for that matter. Honestly, every box of ornaments, decorations, or
string of lights I looked at brought with it another memory I shared
with Lynn… and more tears to my eyes.

But, at the urging of my daughters, and in no small part for Lynn's and my first granddaughter, Mila, who had just turned one year old in October, I relented.

I went out and found a good tree. The next day, I even dragged out a ladder and ran strings of lights across the front porch and the bushes in front of the house.

So far, so good, but I knew the hardest part was yet to come.

After giving the tree a couple of days to settle, I dragged out boxes of lights, decorations and ornaments, as well as various wall decorations that we'd hang every year. I brought out the Christmas-themed shower curtain, rug, and soap dispensers for the bathroom. On the bathroom counter, I placed stuffed Christmas gnomes. For the kitchen, there was a "Countdown to Christmas" block set where we could change the blocks and count down the days to December twenty-fifth. Holiday window clings and a bell/mistletoe combination hung over the doorway.

In the living room and dining room, we had Christmas-themed Disney artifacts that we had purchased on our many trips to Walt Disney World. In addition to the tree lights, there were wall lights, faux flowers, multiple likenesses of Santa Claus and his reindeer, Mrs. Claus, angels galore, nativity sets, and a dancing Santa who shook his butt to "Jingle Bell Rock."

Yes, Lynn and I had everything covered. And, again, everything had a memory attached to it.

I saved trimming the tree for last because I knew it would be the hardest. As I opened the box with the ornaments and began taking them out, my eyes quickly welled up.

"Our First Christmas"… "Baby's First Christmas"… "One-Year Anniversary"… The memories went on and on.

There was an ornament featuring the likeness of our lovable Rottweiler, Leo, whom we had lost in 2016. Others were made by our daughters when they were in grammar school, stating, "Merry Christmas, Mommy and Daddy… I love you!" There were lighthouse ornaments and seashell ornaments in testament to Lynn's and my love of the Jersey shore.

The more ornaments I extracted from the boxes, the more tears streamed down my cheeks—until I came across one very special ornament.

It was a ceramic piece that depicts a pair of blue lovebirds cuddling together in a nest. Their eyes are closed, they're content, and they share a single red Santa hat pulled across both their heads. They're clearly very much in love.

Of course, this wasn't the first time I'd seen this particular ornament. In fact, I looked for it every year when we decorated the tree because it somehow resonates with me. And, each year, Lynn would help me find that "special" place on the tree for it. There are three criteria for its placement: First, it has to be nestled a bit back from the edges of the branches—a "pocket" of sorts in the tree to place it in. Second, it needs to be unobstructed and easily seen by someone admiring the tree. And third, it has to have a light nearby to highlight it.

Since the lights were already on the tree, I began looking for the perfect place for my lovebirds. Somehow, I sensed that Lynn was right there helping me as she always did.

Perhaps because this wasn't a typical year, it took a bit longer to find that special spot. But that was okay because I'd come to learn that things will present themselves when they're needed. It's like the old saying goes, "When the student is ready, the teacher appears."

And, sure enough, after a few minutes, that special spot on the tree presented itself.

I'm confident that Lynn directed me to it. It was perfect: The branch would easily support the weight of the ceramic birds, it was clearly visible with no obstructions, and there was a bright, white light right under it that would illuminate the birds perfectly.

As I reached up and into the tree to hang it, I found myself smiling. Honestly, most of my smiles since Lynn's passing were less than genuine, but this one was the real deal. I just knew that Lynn had once again helped me locate that special place on the tree for my lovebirds.

I finished decorating the tree with a new outlook. Sure, some of the ornaments had little or no emotional impact. Others, like the "Firsts" that I described above, and the ones our daughters made for us in grammar school, had significant emotional impact.

But the lovebirds took it to a whole other level...

Whereas I had approached this past Christmas season with dread, through those birds, I came through it with a newfound sense of knowing the connections to our loved ones never cease.

I will always miss my wife dearly. But Lynn let me know this past Christmas that everything's okay. She validated that she's still here and showed me that our physical passing is not the end but merely a transition to another realm where lovebirds can still cuddle together.

—John Torre—

95

My Christmas Memories Basket

Although a handful of years seems like a brief time,
they're blissful and long when spent cherishing
those who are worth every moment.
~Rhett Downing, Crocodile Tears

It began with the cutest Christmas greeting I received that year. Three adorable little angels grinned at me from the front of a semicircular die-cut card. Although I did not routinely save my cards from year to year, there was something so charming and unique about this one that I decided to use it as part of my Christmas décor the following season.

The card came from one of my dearest friends, Peg. Twenty years older than me, we had become fast pals when I lived in New England. When my husband was transferred to Florida in 1994, Peg promised that she would visit. She came that March for a grown-up spring-break bash. And, like college kids, we stayed up late, went to Disney World and laughed ourselves silly for most of the visit.

It was so much fun that we agreed to make it an annual tradition.

The following Christmas as I took out my decorations, I found Peg's card — but Peg was gone. She had left us suddenly that fall, thankfully not knowing how ill she was until near the end.

As I looked at the card, I thought about how fortunate I was that I had kept it. And, in that moment, I decided that I would keep all my cards until the following year. That way, if someone I loved died, I would have their last Christmas greeting to me.

I decorated a small wicker basket with a red velvet ribbon and a flat, golden wreath ornament, lovely and worthy of the special cards it was to hold. I named it my Christmas Memories Basket.

I am part of a large family with hundreds of relatives — first and second cousins, aunts and uncles, nephews and nieces. I receive a lot of cards every year. In the two decades since I began the Memory Basket tradition, seventeen of these beloved souls who were so special to me have departed this life.

When I put the basket on display each December, I read each card in the basket again and think about what the now deceased sender meant to me over the years. It is my favorite Christmas ritual.

My basket holds the last card from my Great-Aunt Rita who lived to be 100. Mentally sharp to the end of her amazing life, she was one of the most inspirational women I have known. She did not have an easy existence on the farm where she lived for sixty-five years, but she was a generous spirit who loved life and people. A woman of faith, she would always talk about how beautiful God's world of nature was to her.

There is a card from my cousin Cecelia, who signed every card with "love and prayers." She often encouraged me to "just offer it up" whenever I was going through challenging times. And I still laugh at the crazy dances she loved to perform for my delight.

Irene, my beloved godmother and middle namesake, was a part of my heart. One of the earliest photos of me is being cradled in her arms. Her name means "peace," which is what she represented. She was always agreeable and fun to be around. I have countless memories of golden hours spent with her.

My dear buddy, Chuck, a family friend, shared my love of ABBA and *Seinfeld*. His last card reminds me of the gag gifts he sent each year. The plastic sunflower singing "You Are My Sunshine" as it swayed in a flowerpot was a favorite.

Gladys, another older friend, was a talented artist and musician who survived the blitzkrieg attack on her hometown in England. Her twelve-year-old friend standing next to her did not. She was a gentle and caring soul of strong faith despite the scars of war.

My last card from Aunt Vicki mentions how much she was looking forward to coming to Florida the following month. It was to be the last joyous time that I saw her. She was my greatest lifelong cheerleader other than my parents. I wrote letters to her from the time I was sixteen, sharing tidbits of my daily life through the decades. How I miss her cards and notes with the most beautiful handwriting I have ever seen. The last of my father's sisters, she has left a hole in my life that will never be filled.

Finally, there is Nora's card picturing two young girls hugging each other. As I look at it now, my eyes are filling, as is my heart. My best friend since we were fourteen, she died after a ravaging three-year illness. This card makes me the saddest because it was not supposed to be in my basket yet. We were going to be old ladies together, laughing about unrequited high-school crushes and teenage antics. I could tell Nora anything, and we talked about everything during our fifty-five-year friendship. Even now, sometimes, when the phone rings after dinner, I think for a second that it might be her.

I cherish my basket and the memories each card offers me. It is also a significant reminder for me to enjoy every Christmas as it could be the last — if not for me, then for someone I love dearly.

My basket is filled with the sentiments of special people who have blessed my life in immeasurable ways over the years. And, as I look at it during the holiday season, I silently promise each one that I will always remember them with love for the rest of my life.

— Claudia Irene Scott —

96

The Little Tree in the Woods

*The joy of brightening other lives, bearing each other's burdens,
easing other's loads and supplanting empty hearts and lives
with generous gifts becomes for us the magic of the holidays.*
~W.C. Jones

Each December for the past five years, as our Great Pyrenees Scarlett O'Hara leads the way, my husband Michael and I have trekked out into the snow-dappled woods of Quail Hollow Park. Once there, we place tiny plaid mittens and hats, red bows, and battery-operated Christmas lights on a scrappy little pine tree. Next to the tree, we place a poster-board sign with a message and an attached Sharpie.

We call it the R.Y.A.N. tree, which stands for Random Yule Action Now. It honors Michael's son, Ryan, whom we lost in a tragic accident eight years ago.

Decorating the little tree has become a Christmas tradition, but it has become much more.

The tree was first introduced to readers in *Chicken Soup for the Soul: The Wonder of Christmas*, with a follow-up story called "A Small Miracle in the Woods" in *Chicken Soup for the Soul: The Blessings of Christmas* in 2021. After that story came out, I thought I was done sharing stories of our random decorating. But I was wrong. The sparkling tree in the Ohio winter woods has not finished touching lives or teaching me things.

This year, I am sharing five lessons that lonely little tree has taught me.

After the story came out in *The Blessings of Christmas*, we were walking in another area of Quail Hollow Park when we came upon a small tree on the right side of the trail wound with sparkling green beads. It wasn't a pine tree, but hanging from the branches on red ribbons were white ornaments that said, "Ho Ho Ho." I stopped and looked at each of the decorations placed with care on the bare branches, wondering if they held any special meaning for the people who had hung them there. Then I started dancing around on the trail. "I can't believe someone else did some random yule decorating," I said to Michael.

A couple of weeks later, on a Saturday afternoon, I received a direct message on my Instagram account from someone thanking me for my stories about the R.Y.A.N. tree. They shared they were hoping to do something similar next year to honor a loved one they had lost.

When I started sharing about this tradition, I never dreamed other people might hear the story of our little tree and be motivated to do some honorary decorating of their own.

Lesson 1: The one good thing you do today, no matter how small, might catch on. It might even be the beginning of something much bigger.

In January, when it was time to undecorate the little tree, all three of our children were here in Ohio for a visit. So, on a frosty morning, I grabbed my stepdaughter Madison and my daughter Alexa and we headed out to the trail, with Scarlett leading the way. As we inched closer, I could see that people had written on the sign. I smiled in relief as we'd been so busy that it was Christmas Eve morning before we had decorated it this year.

The first year we ever decorated the tree, I had no thoughts of a sign. It was all Michael's idea, and he writes the message each year. Those signs have become the most special things about this random act of decorating we do. We've kept them all folded up and tucked away in the bag with the decorations we use each year until it's time to visit the little tree again. When people take the time to sign their name or write a message on our sign, it is one of the sweetest blessings of the little tree.

Lesson 2: Don't be afraid to invite people into your celebrations, your sorrow, or your life. Given a chance, they just might surprise you.

This year, there was something more. When I pulled the sign off the tree and began scanning the names and messages, I noticed that someone had written that they look for our tree every year, and they love seeing it in the winter woods.

Lesson 3: Even when you do not know it, the little things you do might mean something to others. People remember the good things you do, so don't quit.

It was very special to have the girls along with me that year. Our children are scattered in different states — Ross in Iowa, Alexa in Illinois, and Madison in South Carolina — so none of them had yet been able to experience Ryan's tree up close. They'd only seen it in pictures and read the stories. Back at the house, we propped up the sign on the kitchen island and gathered the family around so they could see it up close and personal. As Madison was reading the messages, her eyes filled with tears. She was very moved that people wrote messages and visited this small tree in memory of her brother. She and her dad both had wet cheeks as they shared a hug. It was a beautiful moment. It reminded me to hold a place for her grief over losing her only sibling. Later that afternoon, we all gathered back at the park to have our family pictures taken. Madison held a framed photograph of one of the last pictures taken of Ryan.

Lesson 4: Make room for the memories — even if they might make you cry during happy times.

When you lose a child, it's hard to find your way through the forest of grief. Five years ago, the tree was just a small, Charlie Brown-looking tree. This year, when we decorated it, I had to reach up to place the bow on top as it is taller than me now. As it's grown, so have the lessons it's taught me.

Lesson 5: Healing comes when you share your grief journey with those you meet along the way.

We plan to decorate the little tree for many years to come. Sometimes, the things that seem random turn into traditions, and those traditions lead to a legacy you never knew was possible.

— Amy Catlin Wozniak —

97

The Spirit of Christmas

Christmas is the spirit of giving
without a thought of getting.
~Thomas S. Monson

As the calendar changed to December, I waited for that magical Christmas feeling that I felt every year. But, for some reason, it didn't come.

I decided my Christmas spirit needed a little help to get going. I decorated my nine-foot Christmas tree with shiny silver and red ornaments as Christmas music played softly in the background. But nothing changed.

I tried wrapping gifts instead. I pulled the presents I'd been buying all fall out of the boxes and bags I'd stashed them in. I chose the perfect bows and ribbons to match each wrapping paper and waited for that Christmas feeling to hit me. Still nothing.

Maybe baking would do the trick. I pored through old recipe books and baking blogs until I found the perfect Christmas desserts. I made batches of fudge, dozens of cookies, and a couple of pies. There were enough sugary sweets to give Santa a toothache. But nothing changed.

I guess things are just different when you're in your twenties, I finally decided. *Maybe that all-consuming Christmas spirit stuff is for kids. Maybe it's something you outgrow.*

By December tenth, I'd given up entirely. That night, a tornado ripped through my area. My family's house was spared, but people thirty minutes away were left with nothing but the clothes on their backs and whatever they could pull out of the rubble that used to be their homes.

The next afternoon, my family drove to the store and loaded down the back of our SUV with juice boxes, crackers, and cookies. We dropped the supplies off at a local church so they could distribute them as needed. In a matter of hours, churches and businesses had so much that they had to ask everyone to stop donating until they could sort through everything. "That," my mom said as we looked at Facebook pictures of donated bottled water and shampoo stacked high, "is the spirit of Christmas."

The day after that, we took a generator and heater to our family friends. Thankfully, their house had been spared from the storm, but they didn't expect their power to be turned on for several days. They came to the door bundled up in coats and gloves, thanking us for helping them out. "Helping others like that," my mom said as we drove away, "is the spirit of Christmas."

We swung by McDonald's for soft drinks on our way home. As my dad tried to hand his debit card to the teenager at the first window, the boy shook his head. "No need. That guy in front of you just paid for your order." We didn't know the man, and by the time we got through the second window, he was gone. "I know I keep saying it," Mom said, "but doing something kind for someone you don't know — that's the spirit of Christmas."

That evening, I stood outside the courthouse for a prayer vigil with over 200 people I didn't know. The pastor reminded us that no matter our race, denomination, or circumstances, we were stronger together. We were one. The service ended with a worship song. A couple of people began to sing along, and then a few more, until the whole crowd joined in. Mom didn't even need to say a word this time. That Christmas feeling hadn't been found in trees or gifts or cookies, but in unexpected places. "This," I realized, "is the spirit of Christmas."

— Mara Cobb —

98

The Return of Mrs. Claus

*Six years later my mother's absence remained
in the air around us, a deafening silence that
I had not yet learned to stifle with words.*
~Carlos Ruiz Zafón

I t took six years and Covid-19 for Mrs. Claus to return. She hadn't visited my family since my mom passed away more than six years ago. And now, much to our delight and surprise, she stood, all twenty-four inches of her, in the middle of my dad's empty dining room.

This life-like doll had entered our lives more than thirty years ago when my mom had spotted it at a Christmas sale and my dad dutifully purchased it for her. My dad was like that; he always bought the little things my mom desired. And the battery-operated Mrs. Claus mesmerized my mom. So, every holiday season, it was the first decoration to come out of storage.

When my parents downsized and no longer decorated a tree, Mrs. Claus held steadfast, and brightly wrapped gifts were placed at her feet. She became the center of attention, our "O Tannenbaum."

When my mom died, my dad's life shattered. They'd been together for sixty-five years, and she was his world. He sank into a deep depression, which exacerbated his other health problems. As determined as Mrs. Claus was, hunkered down in her well-worn box in the storage room, she couldn't brighten my dad's spirits during the holiday season.

Christmas was no longer joyous for my father. Without my mom's encouragement, he couldn't pick out cards or gifts for us. December twenty-fifth was a day of grief-filled nostalgia for the holidays we once celebrated, a time to amplify the sense of loss that Dad felt all year.

Meanwhile, Dad had given away or donated the decorations that he and my mom had collected during their years together. Whether they held little or too much sentimental value for him to keep, we didn't know.

Several times over the years, he'd asked us if we wanted Mrs. Claus. And every time, for whatever reasons, we declined the offer. It was too "hokey" for my adult household; other family members were transient or didn't have the space to store her all year. Eventually, she was forgotten, and we assumed that she had been sold at the seniors' centre garage sale or given to the thrift shop. After all, Dad had already sold his dining room table and chairs, donated the spare bed, and emptied out my mom's china cabinet. He planned to ensure his family wouldn't have to get rid of the lot when he passed away.

Then Covid-19 hit, days after celebrating my dad's eighty-eighth birthday. He was physically healthier than he was in the first years after my mom had died, but the rest of the family was concerned for his wellbeing during a pandemic, so we shopped for him and ran his errands. We dropped off food, but we didn't stay at first. Then we were able to include him in our "Covid bubble" and visited him — but not often. Despite our best efforts, we couldn't spend adequate time with him. He said many times that he felt the walls were closing in. His age, forced physical isolation, and lack of social activities wore him down, and he was bored and emotionally exhausted.

After several months of trying our best to keep him occupied, alert, and happy, we started to dread another Christmas — this one without a rambunctious family celebration. We knew he was no longer excited about the holidays, but he always enjoyed a big turkey dinner with all the fixings — and spending the day with his kids, grandkids, and great-grandson. This was not about to happen in 2020.

Although I was working in a small clothing shop, we (and other retailers) were restricted as to where and when stores could be open. No one had been vaccinated yet, and the virus wasn't under control, so Christmas shopping as most of us know it — strolling through streets or malls, selecting the most appropriate gift at the appropriate price — wasn't happening. "Happy Holiday" or "Merry Christmas" greetings were wished from across the room or, in many cases, miles away, across a computer screen. No hugs, no kisses, no mistletoe. No extended family visits, no staff parties, no New Year's shindigs.

It could have been another dismal season for my dad, who was having difficulty with the "new normal." He wasn't exercising or getting the fresh air that always revitalized him. He wasn't connected to social media, so he couldn't Zoom or FaceTime. He was lonelier than ever, we thought.

But one cold December night, I received a text — and a picture — from Addi, my niece.

"OMG I am sobbing! Look at what Papa did! It's going to be Christmas again!"

I glanced at the accompanying photo.

There was Mrs. Claus, resplendent in her red velvet granny gown, her bobbing candle lighting the way. She was in the very center of my dad's empty dining room — where the dining room table had been. Where we'd shared meals and stories and family love. And now, the table and chairs had been replaced by... hope. At the end of a year when hope was in short supply, Mrs. Claus had returned. It's like she'd known we needed her.

My dad simply smiled and said, "I just thought it was time."

Now, I wouldn't be surprised if his decision was tough; I'm certain he battled his own still-tender grief to share something that had meant so much to my mom.

My niece and her brother had grown up knowing Mrs. Claus and anticipating her arrival each year. Both "kids" are in their thirties now, but Addi squealed with delight when she walked into my dad's apartment that night and excitedly explained to her young son, Chayse — who was eight — how important a role Mrs. Claus had played in her own childhood.

In 2020, many eight-year-old boys favored Minecraft, and Chayse was no different. He can spend hours playing computer games and waging war on digital fantasy foes. A thirty-plus-year-old mechanical Mrs. Claus doll would likely hold little interest for an eight-year-old boy, right? After all, it just does one thing, endlessly, and its movements are sadly unsophisticated. It's not exactly the type of robot a kid of today might be fascinated by.

But Mrs. Claus… she's a crafty one, coming out of hiding just when we needed her most, her lit candle a beacon through the fog of 2020. Chayse lay silent and wide-eyed at her feet as he listened to his Papa and Mommy sing Mrs. Claus's praises. When he finally spoke, he said she reminded him of Nana.

Update, 2021…

Thank you, Dad. Thank you for sharing this most wonderful gift on what would turn out to be your last Christmas here with us. Our hearts break a little every time we think of how we miss you. And although we are so, so sad, we're eternally grateful for all the special moments and love you gave us. How do we know when it's time to capture those special memories, to take mental and emotional snapshots of something we will hold onto forever? If we're lucky, we figure it out. Although Mrs. Claus has been resting comfortably in our new shed since October, this week she'll be on duty once again in her new home with Addi and Chayse.

— Catherine Kenwell —

Just Me

Solitude is where I place my chaos to rest
and awaken my inner peace.
~Nikki Rowe

My friends were worried about me after I told them about my decision to go on a Caribbean cruise alone over Christmas. "You're so brave." "Wow. I don't think I'd have the nerve to do it." "Are you sure? Won't you get lonely?"

To be honest, I had those same reservations. But this trip was more of a need than a want — something I had to do for myself, and *by* myself. I was newly divorced after an eighteen-year marriage. I was facing my first holidays as a single mom without my teenage son, Adam, who was spending two weeks with his father in Florida.

"So, what are *you* going to do?" he asked me, feeling guilty that he was leaving me alone. Good question.

I promised him I wouldn't stay at home feeling sorry for myself. I would plan something fun. Unfortunately, my parents were no longer alive. My two siblings both had trips of their own planned, so I didn't want to impose on them. I knew I could call any number of friends to ask if they could fit one more seat at the table, but I'd decided I'd rather be alone than face a day of family togetherness with someone else's family. I wasn't ready for that.

"Have you decided yet?" Adam asked me again a few days later.

My answer surprised both of us. "I think I'll take a cruise."

It wasn't such a far-fetched idea. I needed time to process what had happened to my marriage and how I could best support my son, who was, at sixteen, at a very transitional stage of life. I had to figure out what I wanted my life to be like after he was on his own — and I was on *my* own. I needed to do this without distractions, to-do lists, or any advice except what I felt in my gut.

A cruise, I thought, would give me space, let me exhale a little, and help me find the woman I used to be: fun-loving, curious and adventurous. "Your mother's lost her sense of humor," I heard my ex tell Adam once. Well, I wanted it back. Within an hour of my decision, I had a confirmed reservation for a week-long Caribbean cruise from December twenty-third to the twenty-ninth. I knew if I didn't commit right away, I might back out.

In the days leading up to the cruise, I was a little anxious and uncertain but mostly excited. My anxiety began to heighten on my way to the airport to catch my plane to Miami, where I would board the ship. *Seven full days? I won't know a soul. What was I thinking?* Thoughts like these raced through my mind. I became conscious of what others might think. "Poor thing," I imagined them thinking. "She doesn't have any friends. She's desperate."

When my parents died — my mother from breast cancer when I was twelve and my father five years later from a heart attack — the thing I hated most was the look of pity from others. *Don't feel sorry for me,* I wanted to scream. I longed to be just like everyone else, to be "normal." Apparently, that same feeling was just as strong some twenty-five years later.

"Where are you headed?" the cab driver asked me as we arrived at the airport.

"To Miami to catch a cruise to the Caribbean," I said.

"My, my!" he replied. "What a nice Christmas for you! Are you meeting some friends inside?"

"Nope, it's just me."

And that became my mantra for the rest of the trip.

The shuttle bus that met me at the Miami airport to take me to the cruise ship was filled with chatting, mostly middle-aged vacationers.

"Are you meeting your traveling companions in the airport?" the woman next to me asked.

"No, I'm traveling alone. Just me." *Awww, too bad,* her look said.

By this time, my anxiety was slowly becoming a meltdown. I wasn't sure I could take those looks for an entire week. "Look," I wanted to tell this woman who knew nothing about me. "I chose to travel by myself. I intend to relax and celebrate my independence. I don't need your pity." Instead, I told her to have a wonderful time, and I would look for her on the ship.

As I walked up the ramp to the ship's entrance, it started to rain, and I started to cry. I was relieved because others couldn't tell my tears from the raindrops. A photographer was waiting to take pictures of the passengers as they boarded. "No, thank you," I told her, wiping my eyes with a Kleenex. "I'm fine."

"No, really," she said. "You'll want this picture as a memento of the trip. Where is the rest of your party?"

"Just me," I told her. When I look at my face in that picture today, the word that comes to mind is "overwhelmed."

Finding my state room was exhausting as I got lost for about thirty minutes weaving my way through the lower levels of the ship. Finally, I flagged down a steward to ask directions, and he showed me to my room.

"How many people will be in your cabin?" he said.

JUST ME.

Dinner was served at 7:00. I left my state room around 6:30 so I'd have time to get lost, which, of course, I did. When I got to the dining room — accompanied by another steward as my guide — I was the last to arrive at a table already filled with other passengers. This was to be my dinner-table assignment for the week. I sat down, nodded hello to everyone, and immediately the man to my right said, "Are you traveling alone?" It had been a long day, and I was tired. I fought the urge to be snarky. Instead, I smiled and told everyone my story. "You've got a lot of courage," the man told me. If any of my table mates felt pity, they didn't show it that night.

On Day Two at sea, I began to loosen up. I took out the book I had brought with me: a 366-page biography of Eleanor Roosevelt. She has always been a role model of mine, and I was looking to her strong example to help me navigate through all the uncertainty I was going through. "How would Eleanor handle this?" I asked myself to feel braver and surer of my future.

As the week progressed, I kept busy. When I wasn't reading, thinking, or gazing at the sea, I attended workshops on jewelry-making and feng shui. Toward the end of the week, I went on day-long tours of our ports of call: St. Maarten and St. Thomas. I learned St. Maarten is actually two different countries: The southern half is Dutch (Sint Maarten), and the northern half is French (Saint-Martin).

When he finished the tours, our guide left us with a joke: "On the Dutch side, you have casinos; on the French side, you have nude beaches. Either way, you lose your shirt." Most of the group groaned at the humor, but I laughed hard—not so much because the joke was that good (hardly) but out of relief. It was a release of all the uncertainty bottled up inside me. I realized I was beginning to de-stress. As Mrs. Roosevelt once said, "You must do the thing you think you cannot do." And I did. Just me.

—Diane Hurles—

The Family Tree

From home to home, and heart to heart,
from one place to another, the warmth and
joy of Christmas brings us closer to each other.
~Emily Matthews

Days after our honeymoon and years before pre-lit trees were invented, my new husband brought the artificial Christmas tree in from the garage. He stood it in the corner in front of the window, and slowly spread its branches, careful not to break the tiny light strands he had painstakingly wired to each of them. I watched from the floor, feeling love and compassion for the man whose favorite Christmas memories included the scent of pine needles. He had married a woman with tree allergies.

As soon as Mike finished the tree, my two children, Michael and Amber, started emptying the two large boxes of our ornaments. In our eight Christmases before Mike, we had collected a trove of ornaments. As they unpacked them, the kids told the story of each one. The felt turtle was a package decoration from Michael's first birthday present from my mother. No one remembers the present, but the turtle remains. The twelve glossy and identically uniformed wooden soldiers were a gift from his other grandmother the year he played a soldier in his kindergarten *Nutcracker* production. Amber showed him her angel collection, the "gold one and the silver one," and two tiny Hallmark houses that my mother got for her.

I studied Mike's face as he smiled and listened intently and tried to imagine how overwhelming this must feel.

Once our ornaments were on the tree, the kids opened Mike's box. Inside were lights, candy canes, six short strands of gold bells, and an unopened package of icicles. Wrapped neatly in a package inside the box were seven exquisite ornaments: stars, bells, and balls made from Styrofoam and covered with elaborate ribbons, sequins, and beads.

"Whoa, these are beautiful," Amber said, holding one of the bells up to the light.

"Cindy made those," Mike said quickly, as though he was surprised to see them.

"Who was Cindy?" Amber asked, as she hung it on the tree. And there it was — a conversation we hadn't anticipated so soon.

In the six months we had dated, my son and daughter learned a lot about their future stepfather. They knew his parents, his sisters and their soon-to-be cousins.

They knew he liked to fish, rode a motorcycle, and was taller than anyone they knew, but Cindy was news to them.

I nodded my head to assure Mike it was okay.

He took a deep breath. "She was my first wife," he said.

"Where does she live?" Amber continued, in the non-concerned voice of a child with multiple families.

"She died," he said quietly.

"Died?" Amber repeated. "I am so sorry."

"She spent so much time making those, I just couldn't throw them away."

"Oh, we are never going to throw these away," Amber said. And, just like that, Cindy's ornaments became part of our first Christmas tree.

That night, after the kids went to bed, Mike and I sat on the sofa and admired the afternoon's work.

"I'm sorry about Cindy's ornaments," he said. "We don't have to keep them."

I chuckled. "Don't be ridiculous. You heard Amber. We're never throwing those away."

From that first Christmas, our tree was a visual reflection of people and things that mattered in our lives. Among my favorites: a shiny red globe (with his name in glitter) from Mike's third-grade Christmas party; two Eskimo fishermen from a tree my mom once decorated entirely in gold and silver lamé; and a family of hand-painted wooden ornaments that Mike made for our second Christmas together.

One year, a twelve-inch Popeye's coupon printed on an image of a fried-chicken leg went straight from the mailbox to our tree. I still shudder at how many Christmases that chicken leg reappeared, despite how many times I threw it away.

Year after year, we collected souvenirs from vacations, hobbies and passions and saved them for the tree. By the time the kids were in high school, we had filled a twelve-foot tree of our lives together. Putting the tree up each year and reliving those memories was my favorite part of Christmas.

Twenty Christmases later, our life as empty nesters was happening at a pace too frantic and staccato to be represented on a tree. In just one year, Mike and I decided to build a new house, Michael started a career in another country and got married, and my mother died. I spent my last Christmas with her in fifteen-minute visits spread over four hours of waiting outside her intensive-care unit.

The following December, the first in our beautiful new home, the boxes with our tree and ornaments sat in the garage for days before Mike asked me if I wanted a tree that year at all.

While the house was being built, I dreamed of the day that big tree would sit in the living room, beneath the tall ceilings and in front of the picture windows. But, even though the kids would both be home for Christmas, I felt no joy in what was once my favorite Christmas ritual.

So, I told Mike I wanted the tree, but I would decorate it when I was ready.

With that, he brought the boxes into the living room. He took the tree out of the box and set it in front of the window, spreading the branches and tweaking the lights the way he always did, while I did other things around the house and tried to not feel guilty.

When he finished, he came and hugged me. "No pressure," he assured me. "It's all there when you're ready."

The next morning, after he left for work, I took my coffee into the living room and opened the first box.

As I began the process of unwrapping each ornament, I was glad the kids no longer lived at home to see how little I cared.

There were no chuckles or smiles as I unpacked the soldiers and houses. No happy memories — just a darkness that wouldn't leave.

At the bottom of the first bin was the small gold box where I kept the oldest and most fragile: an Eskimo fisherman, a collection of crystals from my mom's last tree, and the Lady of Guadalupe ornament I had taken to Mom when I visited her in the hospital last Christmas. I held the box on my lap, mustering the courage to remove the lid.

Sure enough, poking his head through the purple tissue paper was the Eskimo. But stacked on top, each wrapped in shiny paper, were Cindy's ornaments, and I cried at the healing moment I never saw coming.

Immediately, I remembered how easily these sparkling ornaments became part of our first Christmas and lovingly anticipated every Christmas since. Unwrapping each one was like being with an old friend. And when I lifted the Eskimo from his tissue, I did not feel pain but joy in all the good memories associated with him.

And, once again, I felt blessed that Cindy was part of our family tree.

— Karen Ross Samford —

Christmas in July

Happiness can be found in the darkest of times,
if one only remembers to turn on the light.
~J.K. Rowling,
Harry Potter and the Prisoner of Azkaban

"It's January fifteenth, El. Can we take down the Christmas tree?" my husband John asked as he crossed his arms. The tree had been up since mid-November.

"Let's leave it up a little while longer. The tree isn't in the way, and I like looking at it." The tree and the memories it held brought me joy from happier times. My fifteen-year-old daughter Cassandra was battling complications resulting from cancer treatments she had received as a toddler. She was medically fragile; her lungs were deteriorating, and she relied on oxygen around the clock.

At the end of January, Cassandra's health worsened, and she was rushed to the emergency room with dangerously high levels of carbon dioxide. She was admitted to the pediatric intensive care unit with a guarded prognosis. There were times during the lengthy stay when the medical staff warned she might not make it home. But after three difficult weeks, Cassandra and I returned home from the hospital. As we walked past the living room, our artificial Christmas tree was there to greet us. It was now the end of February, and my husband asked, "Can we take down the tree now?"

"I will get to it." There was no time to think about removing the ornaments and storing the tree. Cassandra needed constant care, and follow-up doctors' appointments and home tutors needed to be arranged. Not to mention, I enjoyed looking at the tree and revisiting the happy memories it displayed. I needed those happy memories.

Before I knew it, March came and went, and then April. Next, May and June had passed. My husband was persistent. It became a weekly question. "When are we going to take down the tree?" he would ask as he tapped his foot with growing impatience.

I continued to answer, "I will get to it." It seemed silly to take down the tree with December twenty-fifth less than six months away. The next time my husband asked about the tree, I smiled and said, "I am planning a special celebration, and I need the tree to be up." Cassandra had good days and bad days—days when she was strong and days when she was weak. There were weekly appointments at the hospital to receive intravenous steroids in addition to doctors' appointments and medical tests. We needed a break. We needed something to look forward to. Cassandra and her nine-year-old brother John enjoyed the holidays and gathering with friends and family. We were going to have Christmas in July.

As July twenty-fifth approached, I pulled the Christmas tree from the corner and dusted it off. A holiday ham and presents were purchased. Friends were invited. The children were very excited. Cassandra looked forward to having friends visit, especially since she could no longer go to school.

Finally, it was July twenty-fifth, and even the weather cooperated; it was an unusually cold summer day. Cassandra had a morning doctor's appointment that took a bit longer than expected. Afterward, we rushed home to finish preparations for our Christmas celebration. We streamed holiday tunes and turned on the tree. The tree lights twinkled shades of green, red, yellow, and blue. We illuminated the nativity scene with a light. While Cassandra took a much-needed nap, I moved to the kitchen where I peeled potatoes and carrots and placed the ham and Christmas cookies in the oven. Soon, holiday aromas filled the air.

The table was set with festive snowflake placemats and an arrangement of silk poinsettias. Elf hats were hung on the chair backs. Presents were placed under the tree. I dressed the family pets in their holiday apparel. The pig had a Mrs. Claus dress, the Dachshund wore a Santa sweater, and the Pug sported an elf collar.

With the preparations complete, I woke up Cassandra, and we sat in the living room by the tree to wait for the doorbell to ring. Our celebration was about to begin. One by one, our guests arrived bearing gifts and wearing Christmas sweaters and hats. After greeting our guests with hugs, we caught up for a bit while gazing at the tree. The ham was done, and it was time to sit down for our holiday meal. We took our places around the table and said thanks to God for the meal and for each other. The meal was delicious, and the conversation was lively. We shared stories of favorite Christmas memories and our times together.

After dinner and dessert, we went to the living room to listen to holiday music and open presents while the tree twinkled behind us. We shared inexpensive gifts that had infinite value to our hearts. There were funny eyeglasses with mustaches attached, pocket tissues, rubber bracelets, and princess headbands. Cassandra received a special mermaid shirt. We took pictures with each other and the pets. We laughed as we watched the pets run around the tree in their holiday finery. We celebrated Christmas in July to its fullest. We made great memories around the tree. I was grateful it did not get put away.

A few months later, in November, my daughter passed to eternal life. What had started out as a fun way to deal with the Christmas tree still being up turned out to be Cassandra's last Christmas on Earth. We were blessed to spend that last holiday with her and each other. We created memories that will warm our hearts for many years to come. That is the greatest gift we all received that cool summer day when we celebrated Christmas in July. It's a gift that I will hold in my heart forever.

— Eleanore R. Steinle —

Meet Our Contributors

Amy McVay Abbott is a journalist and author who writes about all the ties that bind or unwind us. She enjoys writing opinion columns, essays, and is the author of several books.

Dave Bachmann is a retired teacher who taught English to special needs students in Arizona for thirty-nine years. He now lives in Upland, CA, writing stories and poems for children and grown-ups with his wife Jay, a retired kindergarten teacher, along with their fifteen-year-old Lab, Scout.

Lauren Barrett graduated college with a degree in deaf education and her master's in reading education. She teaches DHH students and coaches cross-country. She is the author of a children's book entitled *Henry's Hiccups*. Lauren enjoys reading and writing. She lives in Raleigh, NC with her husband and son.

Jessica Marie Baumgartner is a reporter for *Go 2 Tutors* education news. She is the author of *Homeschooling on a Budget*, *The Magic of Nature*, and *The Golden Rule*. Her work has been featured in *The St. Louis Post Dispatch*, *Missouri Conservationist*, and many more.

Jan Bono recently completed a six-book cozy mystery series set on the SW Washington coast. She's also published five collections of humorous personal experience, three poetry chapbooks, nine one-act plays, a collection of twelve murderous short stories, and one serious novel. Learn more at www.JanBonoBooks.com.

Trish Bonsall has been married to her husband Al for over forty years and they reside in North Carolina, but she says she will always be a Philly girl. She enjoys cooking and says that the kitchen is her happy place. She and Al love to cruise and are finally fulfilling a bucket list dream this year with a cruise to Alaska.

Charlotte Bowling-Roth is a writer, meditation instructor, and perpetual procrastinator in Louisville, KY where she lives with her husband, two Havanese and ninety-two houseplants. Her writing draws from life growing up in Pineville, KY, a small town in the heart of the Appalachian Mountains. Her two grandsons and gardening fuel her creativity.

Theresa B. Brandt writes, cooks, gardens, crafts and is living happily in mid-Missouri. She shares her life with her three (almost) grown boys, the best boyfriend ever, a pack of furry friends and a wonderful extended family and group of friends. She writes articles for the local paper and is currently working on a novel.

Clara Brummert is a former high school teacher who now spends much of her time as a writer. Originally from Pennsylvania, she and her family are now happily settled in Texas. This is her second appearance in the *Chicken Soup for the Soul* series.

Nathan Burgoine is a tall queer writer of mostly shorter queer prose, though occasionally novels happen. His most recent release is the queer holiday romance novella *Felix Navidad*. He lives in Ottawa, Canada with husband Dan and their rescued Husky, Max. Find him online at nathanburgoine.com.

Kristine Byron retired from Tupperware Home Parties. Now she spends her time traveling with her husband and enjoying time with family and friends.

Jill Burns lives in the mountains of West Virginia with her wonderful family. She's a retired piano teacher and performer. She enjoys writing, music, gardening, nature, and spending time with her grandchildren.

Beajae Carman is a special education paraeducator in middle school. She lives in the Pacific Northwest with her dogs and a cat. She enjoys reading, writing children's stories, being outside in nature, and time with her family.

Barbara Carter-Donaldson has been an educator for over forty years. She based this story on events that happened while she was principal-teacher in a church school in Trenton, NJ. She has written about many of her experiences in a book entitled *Everyday Angels*. Barbara is married with two grown children. She lives in Maryland.

Debbie Centeno is an accountant with a passion for writing. She began writing as grief therapy after the loss of her son, which led to the creation of her blog, "Debbie's Reflection." Debbie enjoys gardening, yoga, and traveling. She wrote three books and another blog, "Traveler Wows," where she writes about her travel experience.

Mara Cobb is pursuing her master's in English from Indiana University

East. She works as an essay coach and enjoys writing novels and short stories. In her free time, Mara enjoys baking, playing piano, and hanging out with her family and the dogs, cats, goats, chickens, and horses who live on her family's farm.

Veronica I. Coldiron lives in Savannah and has been in Georgia most of her life. She's a mild-mannered accountant by day and by night she's an author, a singer/songwriter/musician, a mother, wife, sister, aunt, grandma, artist, and otherwise jack of all trades. Her writing is meant to inspire people and spread joy.

Gwen Cooper received her B.A. in English and Secondary Education in 2007 and completed the University of Denver Publishing Institute in 2009. In her free time she enjoys traveling, gardening, and exploring the outdoors with her husband and Bloodhounds. Follow her on Twitter @ Gwen_Cooper10.

Diane de Anda, Ph.D., a retired UCLA professor and third generation Latina, has published short stories, poetry, and essays in journals and magazines in the U.S. and Europe, sixteen children's books, and a collection of forty flash fiction stories, "L.A. Flash." Learn more at deandabookshop.com.

Sergio Del Bianco has a background in fine arts and psychology. He is an artist and writer, interested in the intersection of art, psychology, and the humanities. He resides in Europe with his spouse and growing family of rescue animals. E-mail him at sergiodelbianco@yahoo.com or through twitter @DelBianco97.

After living in metro Vancouver for sixteen years, **Kathy Dickie** and her husband recently moved back to Calgary to live closer to their family. In addition to having numerous adventures with her two granddaughters, Kathy also enjoys traveling with her husband, family festivities, quilting, ancestry research and writing.

Sharla Elton lives with her husband in Ohio, where she enjoys working at a school. She earned her MBA from the University of Akron and is a previous contributor to the *Chicken Soup for the Soul* series. Sharla enjoys her many nieces and nephews, pets, traveling, and spending time outdoors.

Melissa Face is the author of the award-winning collection *I Love You More Than Coffee: Essays on Parenthood*, published September 1, 2020. Her writing has appeared in numerous local and national publications. Read more at melissaface.com.

Marissa Fallon is a writer, story consultant and Pisces and Leo rising who lives in a coastal town with her husband, daughter and son. She adores nature, physical activity (though not running), and beautiful things. She believes women, empowered, can heal the earth.

Glenda Ferguson and her family kept the Christmas fund going for many years. She and her brother Mike still remember the bicycles gifted from Santa. Glenda lives in Indiana with her husband Tim. During the holidays, you can view their outdoor colorful light show. Glenda's other Christmas story appeared in *Chicken Soup for the Soul: Christmas Is in the Air*.

Jayne Jaudon Ferrer wrote her first story at the age of six, earned her first byline at nine, and has been writing ever since. A former advertising copywriter and freelance journalist, she is the author of seven books and the founder and host of www.YourDailyPoem.com. Jayne lives in Greenville, SC, where she enjoys gardening, hiking, and watching old movies.

Dalia Gesser, a theater arts/educator and writer, entertained audiences for twenty years with her delightfully original one-woman theater shows. Since 2000 she has been sharing her theater experience with children and adults through workshops and story sharing sessions. She lives in beautiful lake country north of Kingston, Ontario, Canada.

Holly Green has been a storyteller all her life, and her roles as mother and nurse have enabled her to hone that skill and accumulate enough material to last the rest of her life. She has also written four novels available on Amazon under her pen name, Anne Ashberg: *What Julia Wrote*, *Linger*, *Exactly Enough*, *Swan In Winter*.

Connie L. Gunkel received her criminal justice degree and Bachelor of Arts with honors, and dental assisting certificate in 1982. She raised three children and as an empty nester enjoys camping and playing keyboard in a band and at local retirement centers. She is learning Spanish and plans to finish her memoir this year.

Danielle Hack received her degree in education from West Chester University in 2006. She has been a Special Education teacher in New Jersey for the past sixteen years. She has been married to her husband for fourteen years and they share three children. Danielle enjoys reading, running, teaching, and being with her family.

Bonnie Compton Hanson is the author or co-author of sixty-nine books for adults and children, plus hundreds of articles, stories, and poems (including forty-three in the *Chicken Soup for the Soul* series). A former editor, she has also taught at several universities and writing conferences.

E-mail her at bonniehansen@earthlink.net.

Judith Hayes is a published freelance writer in Los Angeles, CA. She began writing at eight years old. It is her passion. She has been married for fifty-two years to her teenage love. She is the proud mother of two grown daughters and three adult grandchildren. She adores being a grandmother (a.k.a. Gamma).

Kayleen Kitty Holder is a journalist and author. Her children's book *Hello from the Great Blue Sea* was illustrated by an inspiring young man named Chad who battles a rare disease. All profits from their book on TheBookPatch.com go to the A-T Children's Project to help find a cure for her four-year-old niece and all A-T warriors!

Karen S. Hollowell enjoys spending time with her two amazing children, Belle and Noah, and her two furbabies, Ben and Arabella, in their home near Richmond, VA. Karen has a master's degree in reading and teaches school full time. In her free time, Karen enjoys movies, eating out, and spending time with family and friends.

Born and raised in California, **Miryam Howard-Meier** has lived in Alaska, Washington and currently Israel, where she is inspired to write about her many adventures.

Diane Hurles is originally from the Midwest but now lives with her husband and two cats in Lakeland, FL. A former newspaper lifestyle editor, she has been studying creative nonfiction for the past ten years with a writing group based in Chicago, IL. This is her third story to be published in the *Chicken Soup for the Soul* series.

Cyndy Irvine earned a B.A. in history from Texas Tech University and a B.S. in nursing from the University of Texas. She writes from her home in rural Wisconsin where she tends a large garden and a flock of chickens and counts down the days to the Birkebeiner cross-country ski race all year long.

Amita Jagannath is an engineer by profession, and a writer at heart. Her writing inspiration and contributions to the *Chicken Soup for the Soul* series emanate from being a keen observer of the vagaries of humanity, the miracles of nature and in finding the beatitude in the ordinary. She lives in Chicago, IL with her husband and daughter.

Gretchen A. Keefer earned a B.A. in English and German from the University of Michigan and an MSEDU from California State University East Bay. She taught English to non-native English–speaking adults for many years. Gretchen enjoys reading, writing and visiting grandchildren.

A few of her stories have been published locally.

Catherine Kenwell is an author and qualified mediator from Barrie, Canada. She is an avid gardener and community volunteer. Catherine lives with a brain injury and PTSD and is the co-author of *Not Cancelled: Canadian Kindness in the Face of COVID-19*. She lives with her biggest supporters: Kevin, Sunny, and Guinness.

Alice Klies is currently president of Northern Arizona Word Weavers. She is published in numerous anthologies and is a fourteen-time contributor to the *Chicken Soup for the Soul* series. Her latest novel, *Chased by the Hound of Heaven*, was released in July 2021. She hopes her stories bring a smile, a tear, or a belly laugh to her readers. Learn more at aliceklies.com.

A criminal court reporter by day, **Jody Lebel** writes romantic suspense novels and short stories which have sold to *Woman's World* and dozens of others. She was raised in charming New England, was an only child who had an only child (claiming she didn't breed well in captivity) and now lives with her two cats in South Florida.

Arlene Lassiter Ledbetter earned a Bachelor of Arts in English from Dalton College in Georgia. She has written adult Sunday school curriculum and been published in a number of magazines. Arlene's byline has appeared in seven previous titles in the *Chicken Soup for the Soul* series. She loves reading, sewing and her grandchildren.

Susan Lendroth has authored nine picture books for children, with *Piper and Purpa Forever!* being her latest. An earlier — and differently titled — version of her story about her mom, Carlyn Lendroth, was published in *Short Circuit #10, Short Editions* quarterly review.

Crescent LoMonaco is a frequent contributor to the *Chicken Soup for the Soul* series. She's an avid reader, writer, and artist. She used her experience as a previous salon owner to write the "Ask a Stylist" column for the *Santa Barbara Independent*. She lives on the California coast with her husband of twenty-five years and their son.

Singer, songwriter and worship leader **Allison Lynn** is drawn to the power of story to grow hearts and communities. Allison and her husband, Gerald Flemming, form the award-winning duo, Infinitely More. Their ninth album of original music will release in 2022. Learn more at www. InfinitelyMore.ca.

Melinda Richarz Lyons received her Bachelor of Arts in journalism from the University of North Texas. Her articles have appeared in many publications. She has authored four books and lives in Tyler, TX. Learn more at melindalyons.weebly.com.

Irene Maran is a freelance writer, retired and living at the Jersey shore with her four cats and turtles. She writes a bi-weekly newspaper column and runs a prompt writing group. Her humorous stories revolve around life, family and animals.

Karen Langley Martin lives and writes in Durham, NC. Learn more at karenthewriter.com.

David Martin's humor and political satire have appeared in many publications including *The New York Times*, *The Chicago Tribune* and *Smithsonian Magazine*. He has published several collections of his humor writing including *Dare to be Average* and *Screams and Whispers*, all of which are available on Amazon.com.

Jane McBride has loved to write ever since she was a small child when she entertained her friends with her stories. Writing for the *Chicken Soup for the Soul* series is a dream come true for her.

Melanie R. McBride is a freelance writer and editor with an M.A. in English Literature and Publishing from Rosemont College. A book lover and previous contributor to the *Chicken Soup for the Soul* series, she hopes to one day write a book of her own. Melanie currently lives in New Jersey.

Gill McCulloch has a B.Sc. (Honours) degree and runs a Red Cross first aid training agency with her husband in BC, Canada. She has a son and daughter and enjoys hiking and painting. Gill writes stories, articles and poetry and hopes her words help people with a snippet of knowledge or a good chuckle. E-mail her at gill@learnfirstaid.ca.

Brian Michael's English teacher once described him as the worst writer in his class. She claimed his writing style was silly and in no way based on reality. Brian responded to her, "So I'm no Ernest Hemingway; I just want to write stories that make the reader smile." For the past forty years, he has never changed that philosophy.

Jackie Minniti is a retired teacher and the award-winning author of three novels: *Project June Bug* (Women's Fiction), *Jacqueline*, and *One Small Spark* (MG Historical). She lives in Florida and has had several stories published in the *Chicken Soup for the Soul* series. Learn more at www.jackieminniti.com.

Marya Morin is a freelance writer. Her stories and poems have appeared in publications such as *Woman's World* and Hallmark. Marya also penned a weekly humorous column for an online newsletter and writes custom poetry on request. She lives in the country with her husband.

E-mail her at Akushla514@hotmail.com.

Sheree Negus is a late bloomer, receiving her B.A. in Education, with honors, in 2000. A single mom, she met the love of her life and is happily married to a funny and clever man and added another son to her world. Now retired, Sheree has time to attend classes in an MFA program for creative writing.

Jesse Neve lives in Minnetrista, MN with her husband, four children and their turtle. She loves to share her stories with others in hopes that they, too, can catch the little glimpses of joy that God sprinkles around in all our lives. E-mail her at Jessedavidneve@frontiernet.net.

TonyaAnn Pember is a retired teacher, former Girls Ministries Specialist, CASA and current volunteer at Forthechildren.org. An Oklahoma girl living in Colorado, she fills her time writing and loving her six grandchildren! *Inside Story, 52 Weeks in the Word* was published in August 2021. You, too, can offer joy for loss to a friend this Christmas; the complete message and suggested gift list are available at tonyaann.com.

Christina Peters lives in La Mirada, CA with her husband and two sons. She started her career as an elementary school teacher, then ran a home daycare for nine years. Now, she stays busy volunteering in her church and her community. She loves decorating cakes, woodburning, and all DIY projects!

Christy Piszkiewicz was born on Christmas Eve and always loved reading Christmas stories. This is her second Christmas story printed in the *Chicken Soup for the Soul* series. Finding joy in creating legacy stories, she writes about her serendipitous life. She and her husband live on a "hobby" farm in Ohio and are beekeepers.

K. R. Powers is, therefore she writes. Her goal is always to present truths in a way people can not only swallow but enjoy. She has a sweet husband, lots of sisters, and no cat, and often makes up for her lack of cat by being moody or cuddly herself. Learn more at www.krpowers.org.

Connie Kaseweter Pullen lives in rural Sandy, OR, near her five children and several grandchildren. She earned a B.A. degree, with honors, at the University of Portland in 2006, with a double major in psychology and sociology. Connie enjoys writing, photography and exploring nature. E-mail her at MyGrandmaPullen@aol.com.

Denise Fleissner Ralston is a life coach, Gracie Award-winning writer and producer, and the former Associate Producer for the television show, *The Golden Girls*. Denise lives thirty miles west of Washington, D.C.

where she enjoys coaching, writing, and inspiring people to clear out chaos and create simplicity in their lives.

Carol Randolph's first story appeared in *Chicken Soup for the Soul: Divorce & Recovery*. She is the founder of New Beginnings, a non-profit for people coping with separation/divorce since 1979 (www. newbeginningsusa.org). She believes that the quality of our relationships gives our lives meaning and is our greatest legacy.

Celia Reeves lives in Tucson, AZ. Affectionately known as the Medical Coding Mama, she shares stories of what goes on behind the scenes at the doctor's office and living life as a single parent. She can be reached by e-mail at reevescelia@gmail.com or on Twitter and Instagram and on her blog medicalcodingmama.wordpress.com.

Alarica Reichert is a freelance writer who lives in Ontario, Canada with her husband and young son. She has been a lover of words since she was a child and enjoys creating stories to inspire. She likes dancing, playing instruments, acting and spending quality time with her family.

Ana Reisens is a poetry farmer. You can find her poetry sprouting in the *Sunlight Press*, *The Belmont Story Review*, and the Fresher Press anthology *Winding Roads*, among other places. She loves spending time in nature and is always in search of her next meal.

Sue Rissman-Sussman writes books, plays, and movies. She won an EMMY for *There's No Such Thing as a Chanukah Bush, Sandy Goldstein*, her musical *Mario Lanza* recently ran in London, and her twenty-ninth book comes out next year. Sussman lives in Miami, FL with her husband of sixty years. They have three children and six grandchildren.

Jill Ann Robinson is an author, wife, and mother of two. She has been published in *Little Old Lady Comedy*, the *Chicken Soup for the Soul* series, *Her View from Home*, *Heartland Society of Women Writers*, and *The Order of Us*. She creates humorous writing memes for Moms Who Write. You can follow Jill on Instagram @firstdraftdotblog.

Sallie A. Rodman lives near the beach in Los Alamitos, CA with Mollie the Beagle and three bratty cats. Her work has appeared in numerous *Chicken Soup for the Soul* anthologies and magazines. She loves sharing the details of her life with others. Reach her at writergal222@gmail.com.

J. A. (Judith) Rost is an Indie author who writes cozy murder mysteries and romance with a Christian theme as well as other short stories. She's been battling cancer the last few years and has published her inspirational journey through cancer. She currently lives in the Hill

Country of Texas. E-mail her at booksbyjarost@outlook.com.

Ruth Rotkowitz is the author of two novels, *Escaping the Whale* and the prequel, *The Whale Surfaces*. She has published fiction, nonfiction, and poetry in literary journals. Ruth has taught English at both the college and high school levels. She is currently at work on a novel.

Michele Rule is a disabled poet and writer from Kelowna, BC. She is especially interested in the topics of chronic illness, relationships, and nature. Her first chapbook is titled *Around the World in Fifteen Haiku*. She lives with a sleepy dog, two cats and a fantastic partner.

Karen Ross Samford came to storytelling through the newspaper industry. The first *Chicken Soup for the Soul* book she read was a gift from her mother. Karen is a mother and grandmother who believes gardening is the best therapy and that every day is an opportunity to learn something new.

Karen Sargent is the award-winning author of *Waiting for Butterflies*. A retired English teacher, she writes for multiple *Guideposts* devotionals, leads book launches for authors, and enjoys teaching writing workshops. Learn more at KarenSargent.com.

Leslie C. Schneider was raised in Montana and currently resides with Bill, her husband of fifty-two years, in Colorado. Sons John and Bill live nearby with their wives and Leslie's five grandchildren. Leslie is a frequent contributor to the *Chicken Soup for the Soul* series. E-mail her at Leslie@airpost.net.

Christy L. Schwan is a native Hoosier author/poet living in Wisconsin. She's a rockhound, wild berry picker, wildflower seeker, astronomy studier, and quiet sports lover of kayaking, canoeing, snowshoeing and loon spotting. She's been published in *Ariel Anthology*, *8142 Review*, *Wisconsin Poet's Calendar*, and *Bramble Lit Mag*.

Claudia Irene Scott writes when the words will no longer stay in her heart but must be put to paper. A retired educator, she lives in Florida with her husband Barry. Art museums are her passion, and she has traveled extensively to fulfill that desire. She also confesses to being a jigsaw puzzle junkie. E-mail her at Cipscott@comcast.net.

Kayann Short, Ph.D., is the author of the Nautilus award-winning memoir *A Bushel's Worth: An Ecobiography* (Torrey House Press). Her work appears in *Mud Season Review*, *Burningword*, *Hawk & Handsaw*, *Midwest Review* and *The Hopper*, among others. Dr. Short organizes community writing events at Stonebridge Farm in Colorado.

Mary Shotwell is the author of small-town romances for every season. Her newest series, *Waverly Lake,* came out in 2022. She lives in Tennessee with her husband and three children and loves holidays, baking anything sweet, and hosting movie nights with her kids. Learn more at maryshotwell.com.

While writing Amish and women's fiction, **Laurie Stroup Smith** strives to inspire readers to serve others. This former certified athletic trainer is the author of *The Pocket Quilt* series. She lives with her husband and two daughters in Cincinnati, OH. Learn more at Lauriestroupsmith.com.

Diane Stark is a wife, mother, and freelance writer. She is a frequent contributor to the *Chicken Soup for the Soul* series. She loves to write about the important things in life: her family and her faith.

Eleanore R. Steinle has experienced being a caregiver and advocate for her daughter through cancer treatment and terminal lung disease. She shares her writings hoping to encourage and inspire others. She lives in New York with her husband, son, and their many pets. E-mail her at EleanoreRSteinle@gmail.com.

Michele Sprague wrote hundreds of stories for corporate magazines and newsletters during her writing career in communications departments. Since retiring, published pieces include a story in *Chicken Soup for the Soul: Running for Good*, womensrunning.com, *INSPIRED* senior living magazine, and her book *Single Again 101*.

Lindy Tedesco's experience comes from living and learning. She has three beautiful daughters, one beautiful stepdaughter, and married the love of her life after spending thirty years apart. With a passion for helping others enjoy life, she has the honor of serving her elders as activity director at a nursing facility.

Candy Thompson is a U.S. Army veteran. She is a member of Cheat River DAR and Pleasant Grove Baptist Church in Preston County, WV. She is happily married to her husband Larry and enjoys baking, her flower beds, photography, and writing.

John Torre worked in the building trades and as a freelance copy-writer. He has mentored at-risk adolescents, and enjoys playing guitar, traveling to Disney World, and spending time with his three daughters. He lost his wife Lynn in August of 2021 after a long battle with breast cancer. E-mail him at jt0229@mac.com.

Samantha Ducloux Waltz lives in Portland, OR where her family, pets, writing, and gardening keep her busy and happy. Her writings include anthologized and award-winning essays, her Seal Press anthology, *Blended:*

Writers on the Stepfamily Experience, and her novel, *The Choice of Men*.

Nina Ward is a published author and massage therapist. Her work has appeared in a variety of print and digital publications. Nina has written for local newspapers covering sports, news, and profiles. When she is not writing, you can find her kayaking along a lazy river or embracing a beach sunset.

David Warren resides with his wife Angela in Miami Township, OH. He is vice president of Lutz Blades and a part-time writer of inspirational stories and children's books. David has now appeared in twelve books in the *Chicken Soup for the Soul* series as well as multiple magazines. After surviving full cardiac arrest his motto is "You Only Live Twice."

Ray Weaver has been married for over sixty-three years and has resided in Florida for thirty-eight years. He has two children and six grandchildren. He has been writing for the last twenty years. His eleventh novel is due to be released in the fall of 2022.

Dorann Weber is a freelance photographer who has a love for writing — especially for the *Chicken Soup for the Soul* series. She is a contributor for Getty Images and worked as a photojournalist. Her photos and verses have appeared on Hallmark cards. She enjoys reading, hiking and spending time with her family.

Darci Werner resides in Iowa with her husband, ducks, and chickens. She has authored articles in *Mary Jane's Farm, Lyrical Iowa* and *The Dubuque Writers Guild*. Between gathering eggs and writing, she works with college students to meet their financial goals for a local community college.

Woody Woodburn is the author of the memoir *WOODEN & ME: Life Lessons from My Two-Decade Friendship with the Legendary Coach* and a Streaker who has run at least three miles every day for the past nineteen years (and counting), dating back to July 7, 2003. He lives, writes, and runs in Ventura, CA.

Amy Catlin Wozniak was raised in Nebraska — Go Huskers! — and now lives in Northeast Ohio. There she shares her life with her soul mate, four children, two grandsons, and a Great Pyrenees named Scarlett O'Hara, who has absolutely no problem living up to her namesake. You can find her on Instagram at amycatlinwozniak.writer.

Mary Jo Wyse is the iMOM Content Writer at iMOM.com. She has an MFA in creative writing and an M.A. in English. Besides writing and reading, she loves to be active outside, taking walks and working in her garden. She lives in Michigan with her husband, two kids, and their puppy.

Meet Amy Newmark

Amy Newmark is the bestselling author, editor-in-chief, and publisher of the *Chicken Soup for the Soul* book series. Since 2008, she has published 185 new books, most of them national bestsellers in the U.S. and Canada, more than doubling the number of Chicken Soup for the Soul titles in print today. She is also the author of *Simply Happy*, a crash course in Chicken Soup for the Soul advice and wisdom that is filled with easy-to-implement, practical tips for enjoying a better life.

Amy is credited with revitalizing the Chicken Soup for the Soul brand, which has been a publishing industry phenomenon since the first book came out in 1993. By compiling inspirational and aspirational true stories curated from ordinary people who have had extraordinary experiences, Amy has kept the twenty-nine-year-old Chicken Soup for the Soul brand fresh and relevant.

Amy graduated *magna cum laude* from Harvard University where she majored in Portuguese and minored in French. She then embarked on a three-decade career as a Wall Street analyst, a hedge fund manager, and a corporate executive in the technology field. She is a Chartered Financial Analyst.

Her return to literary pursuits was inevitable, as her honors thesis in college involved traveling throughout Brazil's impoverished northeast region, collecting stories from regular people. She is delighted to have come full circle in her writing career — from collecting stories "from the people" in Brazil as a twenty-year-old to, three decades later, collecting stories "from the people" for Chicken Soup for the Soul.

When Amy and her husband Bill, the CEO of Chicken Soup for the Soul, are not working, they are visiting their four grown children and their spouses, and their five grandchildren.

Follow Amy on Twitter @amynewmark. Listen to her free podcast — Chicken Soup for the Soul with Amy Newmark — on Apple, Google, or by using your favorite podcast app on your phone.

Thank You

We owe huge thanks to all our contributors and fans. We received thousands of submissions for this popular topic, and we spent months reading all of them. Laura Dean, Crescent LoMonaco, Barbara LoMonaco and Maureen Peltier read all of them and narrowed down the selection for Associate Publisher D'ette Corona and Publisher and Editor-in-Chief Amy Newmark. Susan Heim did the first round of editing, and then D'ette chose the perfect quotations to put at the beginning of each story, and Amy edited the stories and shaped the final manuscript.

As we finished our work, D'ette continued to be Amy's right-hand woman in working with all our wonderful writers. Barbara LoMonaco, Kristiana Pastir and Elaine Kimbler jumped in to proof, proof, proof. And yes, there will always be typos anyway, so please feel free to let us know about them at webmaster@chickensoupforthesoul.com, and we will correct them in future printings.

The whole publishing team deserves a hand, including our Vice President of Marketing Maureen Peltier, our Vice President of Production Victor Cataldo, Executive Assistant Mary Fisher, and our graphic designer Daniel Zaccari, who turned our manuscript into this beautiful, inspirational book.

About Toys for Tots

Your purchase of this *Chicken Soup for the Soul* book supports Toys for Tots and helps create Christmas miracles for children who might not receive gifts otherwise!

Toys for Tots, a 75-year national charitable program run by the U.S. Marine Corps Reserve, provides year-round joy, comfort, and hope to less fortunate children across the nation through the gift of a new toy or book. The gifts that are collected by  Marines and volunteers during the holiday season, and those that are distributed beyond Christmastime, offer disadvantaged children recognition, confidence, and a positive memory for a lifetime. It is such experiences that help children become responsible citizens and caring members of their community.

For over seven decades, the program has evolved and grown exponentially, having delivered hope and the magic of Christmas to over 281 million less fortunate children. Now, in its 75th year, the Marine Corps Reserve Toys for Tots Program also provides support year-round to families experiencing challenges and exceptional circumstances, thus fulfilling the hopes and dreams of millions of less fortunate children nationwide. The Marine Toys for Tots Foundation is a not-for-profit organization authorized by the U.S. Marine Corps and the Department of Defense to provide fundraising and other necessary support for the annual Marine Corps Reserve Toys for Tots Program.

You can learn more about Toys for Tots by visiting their website at https://www.toysfortots.org.

Changing your world one story at a time®
www.chickensoup.com